District Leadership for Racial Equity

T0397174

District Leadership for Racial Equity shows how transformative changes can occur across diverse districts when leaders take purposeful action in support of racial equity.

Developed as part of the Racial Equity Leadership Network initiative led by Southern Education Foundation, this collection provides an opportunity for leaders to learn from district reform efforts that have reduced disparities and improved outcomes for students of color across unique contexts. The cases presented acknowledge the challenges leaders face, but they also demonstrate that change is possible when leaders build will and capacity to support successful student outcomes. It examines the cases of racial equity leaders across four districts who have developed approaches that create new opportunities and outcomes for students who have been historically marginalized.

District Leadership for Racial Equity is an essential resource for emerging leaders, leader practitioners, and policymakers who are committed to reducing disparities and improving outcomes for all students, especially those who are marginalized and underserved in our schools and society.

Additional resources for download are found online here: www.routledge.com/9781032938882

Larkin Willis is a researcher and policy associate at the Learning Policy Institute, USA.

Desiree Carver-Thomas is a senior researcher and policy analyst at the Learning Policy Institute, USA.

Linda Darling-Hammond is Professor Emeritus at Stanford University and President and CEO at the Learning Policy Institute, USA.

"This powerful resource equips leaders with actionable strategies to dismantle systemic inequities in education. With inspiring case studies and insights that guide the creation of inclusive school environments where every student can thrive, *District Leadership for Racial Equity* is essential for anyone committed to transformative, lasting change in our education system."
— **Nancy Gutiérrez,** *The Leadership Academy*

"This book unpacks the hard work of school leaders in four districts committed to racial equity. It highlights the importance of visionary and collaborative leadership, and the power of systemic change. While there's no one-size-fits-all solution, this book expands our understanding of tried and true possibilities toward pursuing racial equity."
— **Will Jordan,** *The Wallace Foundation*

"For practicing professionals, this book offers guidance for what education leaders need to know and be able to do to close academic, social-emotional, and discipline gaps for students of color. And for policymakers, this book offers insights for creating productive policies grounded in educational practices that have been shown to advance racial equity."
— **Jabari Mahiri,** *Berkeley School of Education*

"One of the most challenging issues in public education is to confront long held beliefs of the intellectual capacity of students of color and their communities. The other is to break with the systems that uphold those beliefs by centering community, embracing local wisdoms, and acknowledging that we all have much to learn. The districts in this book show us that not only can it be done, but that the time for doing it is now!"
— **Mónica Byrne-Jimenez,** *University Council for Educational Administration, Executive Director, Michigan State University*

District Leadership for Racial Equity

Lessons from School Systems that are Closing the Gap

Larkin Willis, Desiree Carver-Thomas, and Linda Darling-Hammond

in collaboration with Maria E. Hyler, Marjorie Wechsler, Wesley Wei, and Peter W. Cookson, Jr.

Routledge
Taylor & Francis Group
NEW YORK AND LONDON

First published 2025
by Routledge
605 Third Avenue, New York, NY 10158

and by Routledge
4 Park Square, Milton Park, Abingdon, Oxon, OX14 4RN

Routledge is an imprint of the Taylor & Francis Group, an informa business

Library of Congress Cataloging-in-Publication Data
Names: Willis, Larkin, author. | Carver-Thomas, Desiree, author. |
Darling-Hammond, Linda, 1951– author.
Title: District leadership for racial equity: lessons from schools systems
that are closing the gap / Larkin Willis, Desiree Carver-Thomas,
Linda Darling-Hammond.
Description: New York, NY: Routledge, 2025. |
Includes bibliographical references and index. |
Identifiers: LCCN 2024062255 (print) | LCCN 2024062256 (ebook) |
ISBN 9781032938905 (hbk) | ISBN 9781032938882 (pbk) |
ISBN 9781003568087 (ebk)
Subjects: LCSH: Educational equalization—United States—Case studies. |
Educational change—United States—Case studies. |
Discrimination in education—United States—Case studies. |
Racism in education—United States—Case studies.
Classification: LCC LC213.2 .W586 2025 (print) |
LCC LC213.2 (ebook) | DDC 379.2/60973—dc23/eng/20250507
LC record available at https://lccn.loc.gov/2024062255
LC ebook record available at https://lccn.loc.gov/2024062256

ISBN: 9781032938905 (hbk)
ISBN: 9781032938882 (pbk)
ISBN: 9781003568087 (ebk)

DOI: 10.4324/9781003568087

Typeset in Galliard Pro
by codeMantra

Contents

Foreword

Despite decades of public education reforms, race remains one of the most reliable predictors of student success in school.[1] Although students of color experience these disparate opportunities across the United States, the straits are particularly dire in the American South, where more than half of all the students enrolled in public school are from low-income families, with a growing number of families living in extreme poverty. As the birthplace of anti-literacy laws and segregationist policies, the fraught legacy of racialized education translates into enduring barriers to educational resources and opportunities. This legacy is applicable to today's system of public education, as schools in the South educate more than half of America's Black children. Additionally, more than 55% of all students in southern public schools are students of color, rapidly changing the demographics of districts large and small. Yet, southern state leaders spend the least per pupil each year.[2] Even with historic steps to equalize the nation's public schools and subsequent education reform efforts, little has changed for students of color. Racially segregated schools persist. Over 334 school districts are under open desegregation orders from the federal government.[3] The resource chasm between majority White and majority minority schools continues to widen. Inherently racially biased and discriminatory education policies and practices still prevail, creating a two-tiered education system.[4]

The increasing diversity and inequities students and families confront create an imperative for us to reimagine how we create a system that increases access and opportunity for all children to learn, develop, and thrive. Exploration into the drivers that perpetuate these racial disparities, as well as into the pivotal levers for transformation, consistently points to the critical importance of district leadership. Superintendents wield tremendous influence and power to eradicate inherently racially biased and discriminatory education policies and practices in their districts. Yet, even when a superintendent demonstrates a willingness and commitment to using their role authority to effect change, they still often encounter several impediments to this work. The system we need now requires a bold and significant shift in educational leadership and practice. Leaders in every corner of our nation are being called to think, engage, and act differently in the face of the complex challenges they navigate. Strengthening the will, skill, and capacity of district leaders and their teams is an important lever for advancing authentic and enduring equity-centered system change.

In 2017, the Southern Education Foundation, in partnership with the Learning Policy Institute and the National Equity Project, answered this call by launching the *Racial Equity Leadership Network* (RELN) to support the capacity of district leaders to advance enduring equity-centered systems change as a solution to addressing racial, economic, and academic disparities in districts across the South. The Racial Equity Leadership Network is an 18-month fellowship program for executive leaders in districts who are committed to addressing racialized gaps in access, opportunities, and outcomes in their system and realizing a compelling vision of educational equity for every student. The RELN Fellowship supports participants as they prepare for more effective racial equity leadership, the skills district leaders draw upon to create the conditions for all children to succeed academically, develop their social-emotional skills, and prepare for work, life, and civic participation.[5]

More precisely, RELN helps school district leaders adopt *a racial equity posture* that challenges and equips them for racial equity leadership.[6] That is to say, RELN aims to cultivate the mindsets, knowledge, and dispositions needed to fundamentally shift the approach to district leadership to one that unapologetically centers race and race equity in decisions on how to best serve students.

Decades of "education reform," from the dawning of the standards movement to school accountability measures and required improvements in standardized testing—all of these eras only pointed to our challenges in education. These reforms have not led, however, to systemic improvements on the levels expected by the authors.

These persistent realities called for a more advanced approach to the preparation and continued professional development of school district leaders— empowering a bolder, more courageous and strategic brand of leaders willing to address issues of race, monetary wealth, and systemic failures that impact students' academic opportunities nearly as much as classroom instruction. For today's school district leaders, especially in the many racially, economically, and politically divided school districts across the country, adopting a racial equity posture and practicing racial equity leadership require school district leaders to center their work on race and equity. Using their expanded expertise, experience, and courage, school district leaders must also rally the educators and their communities to develop solutions that fully address inequities in students' opportunities and levels of success. In short, they make racial justice in education within the reach of schools, districts, and communities.

The broader purpose of the RELN Fellowship is to help fellows adopt a racial equity posture so they can practice racial equity leadership in a more conscious, deliberate, strategic way. The fellowship subscribes to a double-helix theory of change to cultivate a racial equity posture in leaders. This theory of change posits that two main areas of leadership must simultaneously grow and begin to thrive for district leaders to become the changemakers schools need at this moment in our society: *personal leadership abilities* and *knowledge of systems change*.

Personal Leadership Abilities

At its core, a racial equity posture means that leaders understand that their own leadership is the first critical lever for transformation and change in school systems.

To activate a racial equity posture, cultivating the three Cs for education leaders is key. These include:

- **Comprehension:** A clear and astute understanding that equity-focused leadership is required to change schools and students' experiences for the better—and it is their responsibility to push for equity and enact change in various ways. Many leaders see themselves only as instructional leaders. The RELN curriculum moves district leaders beyond the traditional view of being an instructional leader by recognizing that equity leadership is different, intentional, and necessary.
- **Commitment**: Beyond comprehension, leaders need a commitment to racial equity leadership. They possess and demonstrate an obligation and faithfulness to their responsibility to advance an equity agenda. This work comes with risks. It can be difficult and arduous, often requiring great patience and vision. Despite the potential risks to their careers, leaders challenge racial stereotypes and persevere through discomfort to ensure that meaningful conversations about race happen so that these discussions may lead to changes in behaviors.[7] Overall, RELN's approach also includes critical self-reflection, bias identification and confrontation, empathetic listening, and reimagined ways of identifying and tackling equity challenges by leveraging role authority to create desired changes in policy and practices.
- **Competency**: In addition to having the comprehension and commitment to ensuring that all children have access to a high-quality education, district leaders also need the knowledge and skills to do that effectively. Many competencies are required to build an equity posture. Leaders committed to racial equity seek out resources and opportunities to build their knowledge base and professional capacity to remedy racial imbalances in their districts.[8] These leaders ask which student populations are not being served and why. They use exemplars and best practices to better attend

to the needs of these students and their families.[9] They build teams and systems that can carry out their vision for racial equity.

Knowledge of Systems Change

A commitment to equity leadership also requires leaders to hone and further develop knowledge of systems change.

- **Systems analysis**: Racial equity leaders make connections between historical disparities and the present-day education policies and practices that continue to perpetuate racial disparities in student opportunity and outcomes. This requires a sharpened racial equity lens that provides greater understanding and knowledge of the role that implicit bias, privilege, history, and structural racism play in perpetuating present-day racial inequity in education.
- **Racial equity levers**: Leaders understand the nature and magnitude of racial disparities, the drivers or contributing factors to inequity, and those critical levers of transformation that can be pulled. They attend to the many interrelated aspects of a district system that impact student opportunities and outcomes, including access to resources, rigorous, culturally responsive curriculum and instruction, effective faculty and staff members, and whole child supports. This also requires a keen understanding and effective use of data to paint a compelling picture for change.
- **Continuous improvement**: Leaders strengthen their ability to diagnose—and ultimately create, prototype, or pilot innovative solutions to address and make progress on a specific racial equity challenge in a particular context/school system and improve the learning environments, experiences, and outcomes of Black, brown, and low-income students in a district.

To this end, the RELN Fellowship convenes cohorts of district leaders and offers a comprehensive menu of services and technical support, including on-site coaching and strategic consultation, to support them in building their racial equity posture and in the implementation of their strategies in their home districts. Over the span of four cohorts, the fellowship has reached 37 leaders from 43 school districts in 16 states, as of this writing. Overall, the designers of RELN feel tremendously proud of the accomplishments and success of the Racial Equity Leadership Network thus far. In just a few short years, RELN has grown from a notion or idea to a powerful model of leadership development and a thriving network of equity-oriented change agents working to transform schools.

Even beginning with the inaugural cohort of fellows, the Racial Equity Leadership Network has continually witnessed 'wins' within participating districts, including a number of formally adopted equity policies and the installation of critical new staff positions dedicated to equity. Each RELN fellow develops their own racial-equity challenge that requires them to put their expanded knowledge, skills, and new network of colleagues to use in the actual work of making schools more equitable. Fellows ideate about specific equity-related problems or areas of work facing their local system or community, then develop or adapt strategies to address the problem. Later, RELN fellows share the results with their colleagues, highlighting innovative solutions they discovered and developed as a result of their equity-focused leadership.

RELN fellows' lessons and experiences—and the racial equity-focused solutions they build, adapt, and discover—do not merely provide tips for school district leaders. Many RELN fellows share useful solutions for other school district leaders, even place-based solutions tailored to their specific communities' needs. Through education, these fellows have taken remarkable steps to address racial injustices that continue to plague many communities and introduce new and upgraded opportunities for students.

In the following accounts of RELN fellows in this book, read how these leaders have put their racial equity posture into action, bringing racial equity leadership to life in their school systems.

The research on the outcomes of RELN fellows' experience shows many specific outcomes for education leaders, including expanded racial equity leadership knowledge and aptitude that increases their capacity to improve learning opportunities and systems change; a new network of equity-focused practitioners in the South and beyond; the skills and knowledge to pinpoint and diagnose specific challenges and understand their connections to past racial injustices; and racial equity as a fundamental value that is clearly articulated and championed by all district community members, who work collaboratively to advance and sustain equitable opportunities and outcomes for students.

These accomplishments and the knowledge being built in research of the RELN program and similar fellowships are influencing the national discourse on education leadership and fostering a model with the potential to help transform many additional schools.

By launching the RELN, we have created opportunities to significantly contribute to national dialogue and literature around racial equity leadership. Additionally, the deep, sustained connections to executive school system leaders facilitated through RELN are an asset to the field in and of themselves. The expertise and knowledge of school systems leaders, honed by decades of service in the public education system, is often overlooked by academics, government officials, and even the nonprofit sector. RELN recognizes the intrinsic value of practitioner voices and values the opportunity to provide a platform to elevate the thoughts and concerns of leaders working within school systems. Lastly, the awareness of the Racial Equity Leadership Network model is steadily growing. Increasingly, organizations are reaching out to learn more about the model and trying to find ways they might be able to adapt aspects of the offerings or model for their own work.

Without vastly greater numbers of school district leaders dedicated and prepared to focus on racial equity in every part of their work, these destructive inequities among students of color may continue for generations to come. The failure to address racial inequities in students' educational opportunities will continue to diminish countless lives and devastate entire communities. Racial inequities also threaten our society by weighing down the economy, limiting the nation's labor force, leaving racial issues to fester, and countless other effects. Education leaders cannot solve many of those systemic issues alone, but research consistently points to the transformative role of education leaders in the life trajectories of children and their families.

by Kenita Williams,
Southern Education Foundation

Notes

1 Southern Education Foundation. (2020). https://www.southerneducation. org/
2 Southern Education Foundation. (2020). https://www.southerneducation. org/
3 Ujifusa, A., & Harwin, A. (2018). There are wild swings in school desegregation data. The feds can't explain why. *Education Week.* https://www.edweek.org/ ew/articles/2018/05/02/there-are-wild-swings-in-school-desegregation.html
4 Brown, K. M. (2010). Schools of excellence and equity? Using equity audits as a tool to expose a flawed system of recognition. *International Journal of Education Policy and Leadership, 5*(5), 1–12. www.ijepl.org
5 Hyler, M. E., Carver-Thomas, D., Wechsler, M., & Willis, L. (2020). *Districts Advancing Racial Equity (DARE) tool.* Palo Alto, CA: Learning Policy Institute; Smith, R. G., & Brazer, S. D. (2016). *Striving for equity: District leadership for narrowing opportunity and achievement gaps.* Cambridge, MA: Harvard Education Press.
6 Williams, K. (2021). Promoting racial equity to close student opportunity gaps in school systems across the South. [Doctoral dissertation, Johns Hopkins University]. http://jhir.library.jhu.edu/handle/1774.2/66826
7 Maxwell, G. M., Locke, L. A., & Scheurich, J. J. (2013). Case study of three rural Texas superintendents as equity oriented change agents. *The Qualitative Report, 18*(11), 1–23. http://nsuworks.nova.edu/tqr/vol18/iss11/2
8 Brown, K. M. (2010). Schools of excellence and equity? Using equity audits as a tool to expose a flawed system of recognition. *International Journal of Education Policy and Leadership, 5*(5), 1–12. www.ijepl.org; Larson, R., Galloway, M., Ishimaru, A., Lenssen, J., & Carr, C. (2013). *Leadership for equity assessment & development tool.* http://leadtool.educationnorthwest.org
9 Brown, K. M. (2010). Schools of excellence and equity? Using equity audits as a tool to expose a flawed system of recognition. *International Journal of Education Policy and Leadership, 5*(5), 1–12. www.ijepl.org; Maxwell, G. M., Locke, L. A., & Scheurich, J. J. (2013). Case study of three rural Texas superintendents as equity oriented change agents. *The Qualitative Report, 18*(11), 1–23. http:// nsuworks.nova.edu/tqr/vol18/iss11/2

Foreword

This instructive, engaging volume reveals how school leaders across a range of educational contexts were able to advance racial equity in their districts by initiating and sustaining strategic equity planning, the development of adult commitment and accountability, effective uses of data to track progress toward racial equity, and equitable acquisition and allocation of resources.

Together, the four districts described here reflect significant variation in size; they are urban, rural, and suburban; and they are in three Southern states. Revealing the complexities of leadership focused on pursuing racial equity across these different sites is one of the key strengths of this book. The researchers see racial equity leadership as specific leadership skills that are continually developing and purposefully used to create the conditions for all children to succeed academically, develop social-emotionally, and be prepared for work, life, and civic participation. They recognize that no district has fully achieved these goals. Yet, findings from their work "toward" racial equity provide comprehensive insights and guidance to leaders in school districts across the United States who understand the need to take strategic, systems approaches to increasing racial equity in schools and, ultimately, in society.

It's important that this collaborative research project directly targeted the pervasive issues and obstacles to equity that are tied to historic and contemporary inequities of race and class. Essentially, each district addressed critical questions like: what root causes may be producing and perpetuating racial inequities associated with an issue, and how do policy/practice initiatives either improve them or even deepen inequities? The final chapter synthesized the leadership strategies that were engaged across the four cases in addressing these and other site-specific research questions and brought these strategies into dialogue with what is known in existing research on these issues.

This book comes at a critical time when institutional and structural elements within U.S. and global politics, culture, and media work to re-entrench and normalize racist perspectives, practices, and policies that sustain inequities. In sites across the country, these issues and obstacles present themselves differently. So, a foundational insight from these studies is that to be effective, district leaders must identify or design strategies to reduce barriers and ameliorate problematic issues that are specific to their unique educational contexts and systems. However, the studies also revealed commonalities in approaches that resulted in or contributed to transformational perspectives, practices, and policies across each district.

One example was the role of distributive leadership. As part of their racial equity focus, superintendents guided and supported the work overall, but multiple teams of district leaders and stakeholders shared responsibility and accountability for developing district-wide strategic plans, generating and analyzing data to document progress, and directing the allocation and utilization of resources to move their districts toward racial equity. Another was the necessity and process of sustaining racial equity-focused leadership over time and across administrations. This institutionalization of racial equity priorities ensures that systems change has long-range impacts that are not constrained by the goals or tenure of a given leader or the shelf life of a given reform.

In the educational leadership programs at Berkeley where I teach, we frame learning objectives for emerging school leaders with the idea that being able to see the system in all its complexity and nuance is requisite to first understanding and then changing the results it produces. The systems we see—with their epistemologies, ideologies, and subsequent practices and polices—historically have been structured to perpetuate and exacerbate racial caste and class-based inequities. Consequently, challenges to effect racially equitable change must be strategically intentional and go beyond good intentions. This is why I feel the lessons, models, and stories from school systems that are closing the gap in *District Leadership for Racial Equity* are so important for leadership preparation programs, for practicing professionals, and for education policymakers across the country.

For leadership preparation programs, the lessons in this book are texts for learning how documented approaches to racially equitable change can be differentially applied across a variety of district-level educational contexts. These case studies (including the sophisticated methodology) offer models and scenarios for use in the academic training of emerging leaders to design and implement research/practice partnerships that result in productive impacts in the field beyond merely satisfying thesis, dissertation, or publication requirements. For practicing professionals, this book offers clear guidance and content for leadership development through leadership coaching and induction programs, and with communities of practice and racial affinity groups. These kinds of activities that directly focus on what education leaders need to know and be able to do to close academic, social-emotional development and inequitable discipline and special education gaps for students of color can be effectively guided by this work. And for policymakers, this book offers insights for creating productive policies that are grounded in real educational practices that have been shown to advance racial equity.

by Jabari Mahiri,
Berkeley School of Education

Preface

The set of district case studies in this volume seeks to deepen the field's knowledge of equity-oriented leadership and strengthen the capacity of district leaders to advance racial equity in their school systems. Racial equity leadership refers to the leadership skills that district leaders use to create the conditions for all children to succeed academically, develop social-emotional skills, and be prepared for work, life, and civic participation.[1] The study was written to inform the Racial Equity Leadership Network (RELN), a fellowship for superintendents and other district leaders in school districts across the South sponsored by the Southern Education Foundation, in partnership with the Learning Policy Institute and the National Equity Project. RELN is guided by the imperative to enable district leaders to advance racial equity so that race and class are no longer the most reliable predictors of student success. RELN fellows convene as a professional learning community to discuss their challenges, learn strategies, and receive coaching and technical assistance as they address racial disparities within their school systems.

Some of the case studies in this volume feature RELN leaders; others are intended to inform such equity-minded leaders wherever they are practicing across the country. The goal of the studies is to elevate and amplify the lessons learned by individual districts that have taken on an intentional equity strategy with some measure of demonstrated success for a broader audience interested in these same goals. The case studies are not exhaustive, one-size-fits-all manuals for advancing racial equity in school districts. Rather, they are intended to illustrate ways district leaders can interrogate their systems, set equity-oriented goals, and track progress over time. They offer grassroots examples of what some school districts are doing to advance racial equity by making strategic investments, supporting data-informed decision-making, and continually iterating toward equity.

The cases draw on thematic analysis of interviews with district administrators, campus staff, and community partners; observations of school-based activities, administrative meetings, and professional development sessions; and documents including district policies, evaluations and assessment results, media reports, board meeting transcriptions, and website postings.

This study demonstrates what is possible when school district leaders develop the collective vision, agency, and action necessary to pursue systemic change, passing the mantle of equity leadership across administrations to realize long-ranging impact over the course of decades. Indeed, effective racial equity leadership requires reciprocal relationships and collaboration throughout school districts and their communities to harness momentum, weather political storms, and gather key feedback to ensure each and every learner has the supports they need to thrive.

The findings of this research offer instructive lessons for emerging leaders, leader practitioners, and policymakers who are committed to meeting the challenges of reducing disparities and improving outcomes for all students, especially those who are underserved in our schools and society. The vision and implementation strategies to advance racial equity hold relevance for:

- **Leadership preparation and professional development programs** focused on leading for equity for emerging district and school leaders in academic and district-led programs supporting leadership credentials, master's degrees, and doctoral degrees.
- **Leadership induction programs** for new district and school leaders in the early years of practice.
- **Leadership coaching programs**, including the continuing development of coaches themselves.
- **Leadership communities of practice** comprised of role-alike and/or affinity group peers seeking to explore and apply examples of contexts, equity challenges, and implementation strategies into their leadership practice.
- **Policymakers** interested in insights and guidance for developing equity-centered leadership at site, district, state, and national levels.

While no district has 'achieved' racial equity as it is defined in this study, the profiled districts offer examples of many districts working actively to develop policy and practices to advance more racially equitable opportunities and outcomes. This volume presents their work in progress.

Note

1 Hyler, M. E., Carver-Thomas, D., Wechsler, M., & Willis, L. (2020). *Districts Advancing Racial Equity (DARE) tool*. Palo Alto, CA: Learning Policy Institute; Smith, R. G., & Brazer, S. D. (2016). *Striving for equity: District leadership for narrowing opportunity and achievement gaps.* Cambridge, MA: Harvard Education Press.

Acknowledgments

The authors thank our partners for their thought, practice, and feedback that shaped this study: Kenita Williams at the Southern Education Foundation; Victor Carey, Lashawn Route Chatmon, Lisa Laskey, Rodney Thomas, and Asali Waters at the National Equity Project; and the Racial Equity Leadership Network Fellows. We also thank our Learning Policy Institute (LPI) colleagues Ketrina Childs, Medora Jones, Maeve Skelly, Darion Wallace, and Kayla Williamson, and the LPI Communications team for their insights on its development. Without their generosity of time and spirit, this work would not have been possible.

This research was supported by the Southern Education Foundation. Core operating support for LPI is provided by the Heising-Simons Foundation, William and Flora Hewlett Foundation, Raikes Foundation, Sandler Foundation, and MacKenzie Scott. We are grateful to them for their generous support. The ideas voiced here are those of the authors and not those of our funders.

External Reviewers

This report benefited from the insights and expertise of two external reviewers: Will J. Jordan, lecturer at the University of Pennsylvania Graduate School of Education, and Jabari Mahiri, Professor of Education and the William and Mary Jane Brinton Family Chair in Urban Teaching at the University of California, Berkeley. We thank them for the care and attention they gave the study.

1 Introduction

Larkin Willis, Desiree Carver-Thomas, and Linda Darling-Hammond

Introduction

In March 2019, a dozen superintendents and cabinet-level district leaders in the Racial Equity Leadership Network (RELN) gathered to share strategies for addressing persistent racial inequities in public school systems across the Southern United States. Framing the conversation, Dr. Erica Taylor, Chief of Staff in Charleston County School District, vividly described the enduring legacy of racial oppression in her context:

> About 60% of enslaved Africans were paraded into America off the boat at the Port of Charleston, in the same space that our district office stands. There was a Law of 1835, [which] said that if a White person was found to teach a Black person to read or write, they would be punished by jail or death. This law was designed by people who lived in Charleston, and it was on the books for a long time. The history of not being fair to Black children, based in slavery, was enforced by law. Black children are not performing across the nation…but in Charleston, the racial disparities are huge. I don't know that closing those gaps will be achieved in my children's tenure in school.

Taylor emphasized that it was a huge undertaking to write racial oppression into Charleston law, which means that undoing the legacy of that oppression also requires a huge effort. Nonetheless, her leadership team believes that while racial disparities are entrenched, they are not inevitable: all children can learn. Their commitment to transformation draws from a deep understanding of Charleston and its community assets. Taylor held up a palmetto rose as she explained:

> I brought these palmetto roses. They were created by a 9-year-old who attends school in Charleston. They are made from sweetgrass, which is a plant. Weaving sweetgrass is a practice the slaves brought from Africa.

DOI: 10.4324/9781003568087-1

In Charleston, sweetgrass is still used to make decorative baskets. It takes a long time to grow sweetgrass, and then it has to sit in water to become malleable.

Earlier that spring, Charleston County School District community members engaged in a visioning project comparing various scenarios of what the future of the district might look like.[1] In the "1835" scenario, district leaders do nothing, and students continue to struggle against the legacy of the 1835 law. The "Sweetgrass Basket" scenario envisions an "intensive process like that of making a basket." Guided by stakeholders, the district implements a holistic set of evidence-based strategies—culturally responsive practices, competitive teacher compensation and professional development, and support services for students—in order to create a welcoming environment with improved outcomes for students of color. Other scenarios propose a top-down approach to quickly implement many new equity policies or adopt new technologies to personalize learning. Taylor reported that her community rallied in favor of the "Sweetgrass Basket" approach. As with the stiff harvest, the community believed in their ability to harness their collective wisdom to transform persistent patterns of racial inequity that appear unyielding. Further, they recognized that transforming these entrenched inequities would require more than a superhero leader proclaiming a slew of reforms or one cure-all strategy. Rather, like weaving a sweetgrass basket, it would take a methodical and holistic approach, sustained over time. Taylor expressed her optimism in charting a path forward and, at the same time, named her impatience with incremental progress given the urgent need for lasting change on behalf of Charleston and its children.

These sentiments were shared among the district leaders engaged in the discussion as they named their challenges and frustrations while building strategies that could move their districts forward with more effective steps toward equity. Their shared learning was a source of both ideas and hope as they undertook equity-focused cycles of inquiry aimed at disrupting centuries-old disparities and neglect. They needed to balance ambitious actions with efforts to bring along multiple publics holding different ideas and representing different constituencies. They needed to take into account the unique histories of their communities while not consigning those communities to live in the past. They needed to unify people and programs that may have been divided in order to build consensus around a more equitable future. In the course of this work, they sought exemplars to study and provided their own examples of powerful progress.

Purpose of the Study

The set of case studies in this volume seeks to respond to conversations like the one we describe above and to deepen the field's knowledge of equity-oriented leadership while strengthening the capacity of district leaders to advance racial equity in school systems. Racial equity leadership refers to the leadership skills that district leaders use to create the conditions for all children—including students of color—to succeed academically, develop social-emotional skills, and be prepared for work, life, and civic participation. Racial equity leaders seek to upend, rather than continue, longstanding patterns of inequity and to do so in a way that refocuses their communities on newly shared goals.

This volume profiles racial equity leaders in four districts who have put a stake in the ground by developing new approaches that create new opportunities and outcomes for students who have been historically marginalized. Our goal is to offer practitioners who are interested in advancing racial equity an opportunity to learn from district reform efforts that have reduced disparities and improved outcomes for students of color. Each district profiled in this study is situated in its own unique context, including district size, organizational culture, and funding structures; community characteristics such as racial and ethnic demographics, historical inequalities, and economic development; and overarching state and local policy landscapes. What they share is a demonstrated effort to name, understand, and reverse the conditions that make student race a predictor of student success. While all are in the South, they have tackled issues that are found across every region of the country.

Racial Inequity in US Public Schools

Despite decades of public education reforms, race and socioeconomic status remain among the most reliable predictors of student success in schools across the United States.[2] Socioeconomic status alone does not fully explain persistent racial disparities in education. Research tells us that racial inequality has a measurable effect on student learning and well-being above and beyond family income.[3] While highly correlated, educational outcomes for students of color are not a *function* of race; rather, they are a function of unequal access to key educational resources, including skilled teachers, quality curriculum, and adequate school funding.[4] As Prudence Carter and Kevin Welner detail in *Closing the Opportunity Gap:*

> Like a gardener trying to increase her fruits' growth merely by weighing them anew each day, we have measured and documented multiple test-score gaps, but we have never mounted a sustained effort to attend to the gaps in sustenance—in opportunities—that must be addressed before we can expect to see meaningful progress.[5]

As the COVID-19 pandemic highlighted and deepened barriers to educational access,[6] a nationwide racial reckoning emphasized that this reality is no accident; it is the direct result of housing, employment, environmental, and education laws that were explicitly designed to deny access to quality education for students of color.[7] Indeed, today's disparities in educational resources and opportunities reflect the anti-literacy laws and segregationist policies of the 19th and 20th centuries.[8]

It is evident that more attention and resources are needed to support sustained change that can eradicate entrenched racial opportunity and achievement gaps. This is certainly true in the South, where the districts highlighted in this volume are located. However, it is also true in every region of the country. In fact, some of the most segregated states with the largest achievement gaps are in the North and West. Across the United States,

- Black, indigenous, and Latino/a children are overrepresented among those living in poverty;[9]
- These students and others from low-income families experience consistent achievement gaps on standardized assessments of student progress, which have grown since the pandemic;[10]
- Black students face exclusionary discipline at higher rates than any of their peers;[11] and
- School segregation has been increasing for students of color over the last 35 years, and highly segregated schools are increasingly high-poverty schools that are significantly more likely to be served by inexperienced and uncertified teachers and to offer fewer college preparatory courses.[12]

While these conditions are widespread in the South,[13] the South is also home to large and resilient communities of color, an epicenter for racial equity activism, and the site of enduring legacies of what is possible when racial injustice is named, faced, and fought. Taken together, the persistent racial disparities and continuous work to advance more effective and equitable public education position the school districts we studied as compelling sites to explore and understand the dispositions, skills, and actions required for racial equity leadership.

The Role of District Leaders

District leaders have an integral role to play in driving racial equity efforts. Research on district-level leaders finds that sound leadership at the district level matters. A growing body of descriptive research indicates that successful and effective district leadership teams establish educational goals and priorities, direct resources toward those aims, and monitor systems data to track progress and determine effectiveness.[14] Effective superintendents coordinate these functions through instructional leadership that sets non-negotiable goals for student achievement and instruction, political leadership in the form of collaborative goal-setting aligning board support, and managerial leadership through continuous progress monitoring, autonomy for principals, and effectively utilizing resources.[15] An emerging body of research links effective and stable district leadership—including superintendents, district office staff, and school board members—to positive impacts on student achievement.[16]

While school districts may share similar aims and challenges, a growing body of research also demonstrates that district leadership is embedded within and influenced by context.[17] Superintendents express their leadership in different styles and approaches appropriate to the district characteristics, community characteristics, and overarching state and local policy landscapes. Indeed, these findings indicate that there is no one-size-fits-all playbook for effective district leadership, and part of effective leadership is responsiveness to variations in educational context. For example, a study of rural superintendents found high alignment with effective leadership practices, with differences in the use of direct, personal conversations over formal bottom-up approaches to goal setting due to the proximity and accessibility of rural superintendents to the communities and staff they serve.[18] More research is needed to understand district-level leadership skills and dispositions, especially among leaders pushing to transform their systems to advance educational equity.

Given the country's history, the political aspects of racial equity leadership are particularly fraught. Superintendents experience threats and contention related to managing divisive conversations and intensifying "culture wars" in education. [19] This challenging aspect of the role further exacerbates leadership instability that impedes meaningful change. Between 2019–20 and 2023–24, half of school districts experienced one or more superintendent departures, and districts serving higher proportions of Black students were significantly more likely to experience superintendent departures.[20] Pursuing educational equity requires district leaders who are equipped with the knowledge, skills, and dispositions to respond to complex challenges in new ways.[21] To advance racial equity, educational reform requires a research-based set of coordinated policies and practices that are measurably effective in removing barriers to learning and increasing opportunity for students of color. In other words, necessary change requires district leaders to operationalize educational equity—the conviction that every student should get what they need to succeed academically, socially, emotionally, and physically. Research suggests that acknowledging racial differences and the impacts of racism while finding ways to unite their communities around common goals are key skills for educators and educational leaders to advance more equitable learning opportunities and outcomes.[22]

District leaders can advance racial equity across several domains of educational policy and practice, including a clear vision for racial equity; deeper learning and culturally responsive instructional practices; safe, healthy, and inclusive school environments; resources that are equitably distributed;

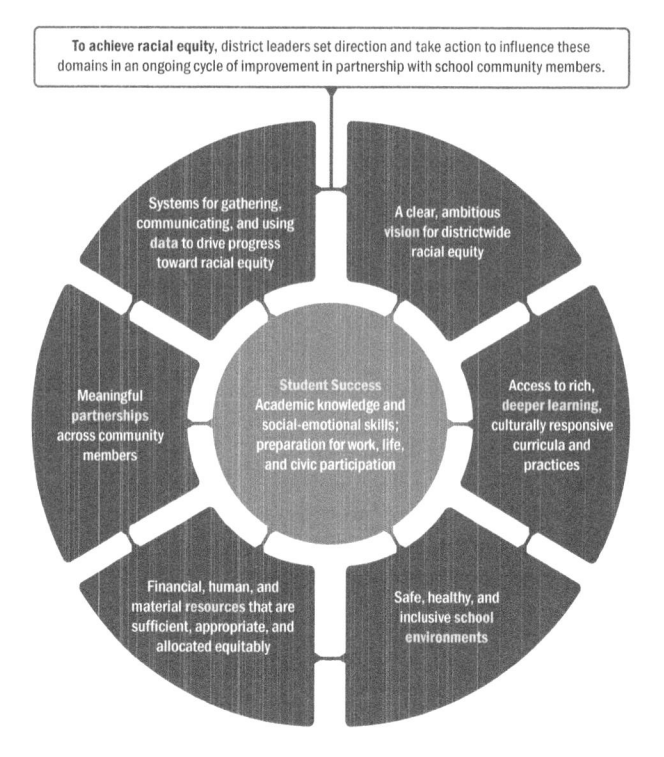

Figure 1.1 District Domains for Advancing Racial Equity.

Source: Hyler, M. E., Carver-Thomas, D., Wechsler, M., & Willis, L. (2020). *Districts Advancing Racial Equity (DARE) tool.* Palo Alto, CA: Learning Policy Institute.

meaningful partnerships with students and families; and data systems that drive progress toward racial equity (Figure 1.1). By examining the role of superintendents and their cabinet-level leadership teams in driving district reform, this volume adds new insight to the complex problem of racial equity leadership in U.S. school districts.

Volume Roadmap

In what follows, we provide in-depth case studies of the roles that leaders have played in advancing racial equity in four Southern school districts: (1) Edgecombe County Public Schools (ECPS), NC; (2) Hoke County Schools, NC; (3) Jefferson County Public Schools (JCPS), KY; and (4) Pflugerville Independent School District (Pflugerville ISD), TX. The school districts profiled in this volume vary considerably in size, student demographics, and context (Table 1.1). Yet we found some striking similarities in the ways leaders were able to make racial equity advances across these distinctive contexts.

Table 1.1 Districts At-A-Glance, 2022–23 School Year Data

Characteristic	Edgecombe County Public Schools	Hoke County Schools	Jefferson County Public Schools	Pflugerville Independent School District
State	NC	NC	KY	TX
Locale	Small rural county	Suburban/rural county near Fayetteville, hosting a military base	Large urban, suburban, and rural county	Medium urban/suburban district overlapping Austin
Number of schools	14	14	168	33
Total revenue	$66,965,000	$87,356,000	$1,491,611,000	$350,283,000
Revenue amount per pupil	$11,600	$9,652	$14,864	$13,268
Student Enrollment and Demographics				
Total Enrollment	5,279	8,674	103,432	25,445
American Indian/ Alaska Native	0.1%	7.6%	0.1%	0.3%
Asian American	0.1%	0.8%	4.8%	9.0%
Black	59.2%	34.3%	36.4%	15.4%
Latino/a	12.6%	25.5%	16.0%	48.3%
Multiracial	4.2%	9.4%	5.8%	4.7%
Native Hawaiian/ Pacific Islander	0.0%	0.4%	0.1%	0.2%
White (non-Latino/a)	23.7%	21.9%	36.7%	22.1%

Sources (accessed 6/24): NCES, https://nces.ed.gov/ccd/districtsearch/index.asp; Kentucky Department of Education, School Report Cards, https://reportcard.kyschools.us/; North Carolina Department of Public Instruction, Public Schools Statistical Profile, https://www.dpi.nc.gov/districts-schools/district-operations/financial-and-business-services/statistical-profile; Texas Education Agency, Public Education Information Management System, https://tea.texas.gov/reports-and-data/student-data/standard-reports/peims-standard-reports.

The first chapter profiles ECPS, a sparsely populated rural district in northeastern North Carolina that serves a predominantly Black student body. It includes the town of Princeville, the first town in the United States founded by formerly enslaved freed people after the end of the Civil War. The town was founded on the only land available to Black residents at the time, a swampy area on the Tar River, which has been a frequent site of devastating flooding since at least the 1800s. As the legacy of environmental racism continues to reverberate in the district, it is also one of the counties in North Carolina in most need of resource investments to support health, education, and economic development. When Dr. Valerie Bridges was promoted in 2017 from Assistant Superintendent to Superintendent of ECPS, the district had been identified by the state as low performing. Under the high stakes of state scrutiny, she has led the district in correcting resource disparities and launching innovations that have retained and retrained staff while dramatically improving opportunities and outcomes for students. Her strategy was one of acceleration rather than remediation, as she introduced project-based learning, along with social and emotional learning and restorative practices, a Spanish immersion program, and an Early College High School, among other reforms normally targeted to more advantaged students. Within two years under Bridges's leadership, the district saw substantial progress, as 12 of 14 schools met or exceeded their growth goals in 2019, with reading and math test scores gaining at twice the state rate of growth. Suspensions were sharply reduced, and graduation rates climbed. District leaders planted transformative program changes in the schools serving the highest-need students. By 2022–23, ECPS exited its low-performing district status and was known as a hub for innovation that drew creative educators who wanted to contribute to the emerging possibilities for transforming practice.

The second chapter profiles Hoke County Schools, also a largely rural county in North Carolina serving predominantly students of color (Black, Latino/a, and American Indian). The district was a candidate for state takeover when Dr. Freddie Williamson became the county's first Black Superintendent of Schools in 2006. According to an ongoing school finance lawsuit in which Hoke County was a plaintiff, generations of students had been deprived of their right to a sound basic education, and access to learning opportunities that would allow them to fully participate in the economy and society was limited. By 2020, when Dr. Williamson passed the mantle of leadership to his associate superintendent, academic achievement had measurably improved to levels approaching or meeting state averages for a more advantaged population of students, with the steepest gains for American Indian and Black students, and graduation rates had climbed to reach the state average. New programs and partnerships were offering students a cohesive suite of learning opportunities, including a burgeoning and more equitable Advanced Placement program, and the groundwork had been established to ensure that progress would continue. "The Hoke County Way," established by Dr. Williamson, was grounded in a conviction that "all means all:" all students deserve high-quality and relevant learning experiences that empower them to be lifelong learners and active citizens. He and his staff worked to transform Hoke County Schools into a "world class learning center" by using data, equalizing access to resources, strengthening relationships with students and families, building knowledge about effective 21st-century learning and teaching strategies, and growing shared commitment to meet the needs of each child.

The third chapter profiles JCPS, a large school district encompassing Louisville, Kentucky, and the surrounding county. JCPS serves a demographically diverse population of predominately Black, White, and Latino/a students. Building on a legacy of reform beginning with desegregation in the 1970s, JCPS has struggled toward racial equity with resilience and tenacity. A 2017 state audit found widespread racial disparities that demanded a corrective action plan, putting the district at risk of a state takeover. Superintendent Dr. Donna Hargens pushed forward and accelerated their efforts to put an impactful racial equity plan into effect, which her predecessors, most recently Superintendent Marty Pollio, have continued. As a result of its persistent efforts, JCPS is making strides in providing students of color equitable opportunities to learn: the district increased its rates of postsecondary readiness for every group, nearly doubling for Black graduates. JCPS also measurably increased access to advanced academics and decreased the number of disciplinary actions, with the greatest improvements for Black and Latino/a students. By 2020, JCPS was released from the state's corrective action plan. JCPS leaders built an infrastructure to advance its vision of racial equity: a well-staffed and well-funded Diversity, Equity, and Poverty division coordinates a growing suite of policies that persist through leadership changes. Led by Chief Equity Officer John Marshall, the Diversity, Equity, and Poverty division drives changes to practice by requiring every division to set and pursue racial equity goals. Recognizing that these increased expectations require supports, leaders invested in building human capacity to operationalize the equity vision, anchored in robust analyses of racially disaggregated data. The racial equity leadership strategy in JCPS has advanced a whole child approach to expanding academic opportunity, including rigorous and culturally responsive deeper learning and transformative school models.

The fourth chapter profiles Pflugerville ISD, a rapidly growing suburban district fueled by development and displacement in neighboring Austin, Texas. As Austin residents—many from the predominately Black and Latino/a community of East Austin—relocated to the City of Pflugerville, the district transitioned from serving majority-White students to majority students of color. With continuous support from the Board of Trustees and central office staff, leaders in Pflugerville ISD have rallied the community behind a sense of pride in cultural diversity. Entering the superintendent's office in July 2017 after many individual initiatives had been launched, Dr. Douglas Killian systematized the district's equity orientation by establishing its first-ever strategic plan, bringing a cohesive approach to change management, and allocating resources deliberately to enact its goals. He leveraged a shared commitment to "passionately serving the best interests of students" to drive educational reforms, programs, and investments aimed at advancing more equitable teaching and learning. Moreover, Killian developed a learning culture and practice of disaggregated data analysis that enabled staff to address educational inequities. Through creative planning, district leaders secured necessary funding and support to shift from pockets of excellence toward providing each and every student the right learning environments for long-term success. Three years into the strategic plan, the district saw promising improvements in educational outcomes, including decreased suspensions and increased rates of students graduating college- and career-ready, with the largest improvements among Black, Latino/a, and emergent bilingual students. The equity leadership strategy in Pflugerville ISD has expanded access to inspiring, engaging, and relevant educational experiences.

The final chapter, Conclusion: What Leading for Racial Equity Takes, synthesizes common themes across the four districts, considerations on contextual differences, common leadership strategies to advance racial equity, and a discussion on how these lessons build on prior research. The lessons learned across these cases can help current and prospective leaders ask and answer the critical question, "what will it take to disrupt the patterns in my system that continue to fail students of color year after year?" The four cases in this volume offer four approaches to what it looks like when leaders dare to answer that question with their actions.

Notes

1 Charleston County School District. (January 2019). Charleston shared future. https://web.archive.org/web/20190818230548/http://ccsdschools.com/about_us/shared_future_project

2 Golash-Boza, T. (2016). A critical and comprehensive sociological theory of race and racism. *Sociology of Race and Ethnicity*, 2(2), 129–41. https://doi.org/10.1177/2332649216632242.

3 Clotfelter, C. T., Ladd, H. F., & Vigdor, J. L. (2009). The academic achievement gap in grades 3 to 8. *The Review of Economics and Statistics*, 91(2), 398–419; Reardon, S. F., Robinson-Cimpian, J. P., & Weathers, E. S. (2015). Patterns and trends in racial/ethnic and socioeconomic academic achievement gaps. In H. F. Ladd & M. E. Goertz (Eds.), *Handbook of Research in Education Finance and Policy* (pp. 499–518). New York: Routledge; U.S. Department

of Treasury. (2023, June 9). Racial differences in educational experiences and attainment [blog]. https://home.treasury.gov/news/featured-stories/post-5-racial-differences-in-educational-experiences-and-attainment#_ftn19

4 Darling-Hammond, L. (1998). Unequal opportunity: Race and education. *The Brookings Review*, *16*(2), 28; Darling-Hammond, L. (2010). *The flat world and education: How America's commitment to equity will determine our future*. New York: Teachers College Press.

5 Carter, P. L., & Welner, K. G. (Eds.). (2013). *Closing the opportunity gap: What America must do to give every child an even chance*. Oxford: Oxford University Press.

6 Darling-Hammond, L., Schachner, A., & Edgerton, A. K. (with Badrinarayan, A., Cardichon, J., Cookson, P. W., Jr., Griffith, M., Klevan, S., Maier, A., Martinez, M., Melnick, H., Truong, N., & Wojcikiewicz, S.). (2020). *Restarting and reinventing school: Learning in the time of COVID and beyond*. Palo Alto, CA: Learning Policy Institute.

7 Cheatham, J. P., Baker-Jones, T., & Jordan-Thomas, E. (2020). Note on racial equity in school systems. *The Joint Initiative of the Harvard Graduate School of Education and Harvard Business School*. PEL-096 (pp. 1–21). Boston, MA: Harvard Business Publishing; Darling-Hammond, K., & Darling-Hammond, L. (2023). *The civil rights road to deeper learning*. New York: Teachers College Press. Ladson-Billings, G. (2006). From the achievement gap to the education debt: Understanding achievement in US schools. *Educational Researcher*, *35*(7), 3–12.

8 Crowe, M. (2022). *Economic vitality and education in the south*. Southern Education Foundation; Harris, F. R., & Curtis, A. (Eds.). (2018). *Healing our divided society: Investing in America fifty years after the Kerner report*. Philadelphia, PA: Temple University Press.

9 Federal Interagency Forum on Child and Family Statistics. (2023). *America's children: Key national indicators of well-being, 2023. U.S. Government Printing Office*. https://www.childstats.gov/pdf/ac2023/ac_23.pdf; The Annie E. Casey Foundation Kids Count Data Center. (September 2023). *Children in poverty by race and ethnicity in the United States*. https://datacenter.kidscount.org/data/tables/.

10 Brangham, W., & Hastings, D. (2022, October 24). "Nation's Report Card" shows test scores at lowest level in decades. PBS NewsHour. https://www.pbs.org/newshour/ show/nations-report-card-shows-test-scores-at-lowest-level-in-decades

11 Losen, D. J., & Martinez, P. (2020). *Lost opportunities: How disparate school discipline continues to drive differences in the opportunity to learn*. Learning Policy Institute; Center for Civil Rights Remedies at the Civil Rights Project, UCLA.

12 Darling-Hammond, K., & Darling-Hammond, L. (2023). *The civil rights road to deeper learning*. New York: Teachers College Press.

13 Crowe, M. (2022). *Economic vitality and education in the south*. Atlanta, GA: Southern Education Foundation; Harris, F. R., & Curtis, A. (Eds.). (2018). *Healing our divided society: Investing in America Fifty years after the Kerner report*. Philadelphia, PA: Temple University Press.

14 Annenberg Institute. (2023). *Studying the superintendency: A call for research*. https://annenberg.brown.edu/publications/studying-superintendency-call-research; Rorrer, A. K., Skrla, L., & Scheurich, J. J. (2008). Districts as institutional actors in educational reform. *Educational Administration Quarterly*, *44*(3), 307–57.

15 Goodman, R. H., & Zimmerman Jr, W. G. (2000). *Thinking differently: Recommendations for 21st century school board/superintendent leadership, governance, and teamwork for high student achievement.* Arlington, VA: Educational Research Service; Johnson, S. M. (1996). *Leading to change: The challenge of the new superintendency.* San Francisco, CA: Jossey-Bass; Waters, T. J., & Marzano, R. J. (2006). School district leadership that works: The effect of superintendent leadership on student achievement [Working paper]. Aurora, CO: Mid-Continent Research for Education and Learning. https://eric.ed.gov/

16 Marzano, R. J., & Waters, T. (2009). *District leadership that works: Striking the right balance.* Bloomington, IN: Solution Tree Press.

17 Bredeson, P. V., Klar, H. W., & Johansson, O. (2011). Context-responsive leadership: Examining superintendent leadership in context. Education Policy *Analysis Archives, 19*(18), 28. https://eric.ed.gov/

18 Forner, M., Bierlein-Palmer, L., & Reeves, P. (2012). Leadership practices of effective rural superintendents: Connections to Waters and Marzano's leadership correlates. *Journal of Research in Rural Education, 27*(8), 1–13.

19 Court, B., Rubenstein, G., & Schiemer, J. (2023). 2023 Voice of the superintendent: Key survey findings and crucial conversations for the year ahead. (Survey Brief.) EAB; White, R. S., Evans, M. P., & Malin, J. R. (2023). Superintendents experiencing threats and contention. (Policy Brief.) Center for Evaluation and Education Policy.

20 White, R. (December 2023). *U.S. superintendent attrition.* The Superintendent Lab, University of Tennessee. https://infograph.venngage.com/pl/CDsuXnzV9ek

21 Cheatham, J. P., Baker-Jones, T., & Jordan-Thomas, E. (2020). Note on racial equity in school systems. *The Joint Initiative of the Harvard Graduate School of Education and Harvard Business School,* PEL-096 (pp. 1–21). Boston, MA: Harvard Business Publishing; Leithwood, K. (2010). Characteristics of school districts that are exceptionally effective in closing the achievement gap. *Leadership & Policy in Schools, 9*(3), 245–91; Smith, R. G., & Brazer, S. D. (2016). *Striving for equity: District leadership for narrowing opportunity and achievement gaps.* Cambridge, MA: Harvard Education Press.

22 Apfelbaum, E. P., Norton M. I., & Sommers, S. R. (2012). Racial color blindness: Emergence, practice, and implications. *Current Directions in Psychological Science, 21*(3), 205–09. https://doi.org/10.1177/0963721411434980; Pollock, M. (2009). *Colormute: Race talk dilemmas in an American school.* Princeton, NJ: Princeton University Press.

2 Pursuing "Possible Futures"

Innovating toward Equity in Edgecombe County Public Schools

Desiree Carver-Thomas and Larkin Willis

Introduction

Over the course of a decade, leaders in Edgecombe County Public Schools (ECPS) positioned the district to pursue educational equity, upending expectations about what is possible in a rural, historically under-resourced, majority-Black district. Valerie H. Bridges was promoted from Assistant Superintendent to Superintendent of ECPS in 2017 and served as the first African American and woman to fill the role. As she took office, the district was designated among the lowest performing in the state based on an accountability model focused on standardized test scores.[1] Under the high stakes of state scrutiny, Dr. Bridges built the district's reputation for being innovative, which earned the district regional recognition, attracted staff talent, and ultimately improved learning conditions for students. The continuity of Dr. Bridges' leadership in the district beginning in 2012 enabled the racial equity efforts to continue to gain traction and realize results. Dr. Bridges was recognized as the 2022 North Carolina Superintendent of the Year,[2] the first Black woman to earn that honor, and ECPS exited its low-performing status in Fall 2023 under her leadership.[3]

Organization of the Case

In this case study, we examine the leadership strategies that enable ECPS leaders to successfully drive forward efforts to advance racial equity. The analysis is organized into five sections. "Setting a Foundation for Racial Equity" describes how district leaders have thoughtfully engaged a wide swath of community members to articulate a vision and strategic plan for the future of the district. At the heart of the district's approach is a commitment to innovation that guides the implementation of the district's racial equity vision. "Creating Equitable Access to Whole Child Education" describes how ECPS leaders developed a Framework for Learning that commits district-wide instruction to providing all students access to engaging and challenging coursework.

DOI: 10.4324/9781003568087-2

At the same time, ECPS has invested in whole child approaches, such as project-based learning, language immersion, accelerated learning, and social-emotional learning, to support and scale student success. "Developing Staff Capacity" discusses the district's concerted effort to attract, develop, and retain the staff needed to improve teaching and learning, spearhead innovation, and carry out the district's racial equity efforts. By building meaningful opportunities for leadership, the district has attracted a contingent of dedicated school and teacher leaders, who in turn support the growth and capacity of staff throughout the system. "Investing in North Edgecombe" describes how ECPS leaders have purposefully rolled out key initiatives in the district's most under-resourced schools. Rebranding North Edgecombe schools as the Innovation Zone, ECPS has attracted the resources needed to invest in North Edgecombe students. Further, the district targeted those resources to improve staff capacity and student access to rigorous, culturally relevant, project-based learning that supports students' social and emotional development and academic achievement. ECPS demonstrates that beginning racial equity efforts in the areas of greatest need can create momentum for expanding successful strategies to more students. Finally, this case study concludes with lessons learned, which include observations about what other districts, leaders, and educators can apply to their own contexts.

About Edgecombe County Public Schools

ECPS is one of several rural districts in northeastern North Carolina; however, the leadership's commitment to equity and willingness to transform what school can look like to support student learning make the district stand out. In 2022–23, ECPS served a student body that was roughly 60% Black, 25% White, 10% Latino/a, and 5% American Indian/Alaska Native, Asian American, Multiracial, or Pacific Islander (Table 2.1).

Table 2.1 Edgecombe County Public Schools Student Racial/Ethnic Demographics, 2022–23

Racial/Ethnic Demographic	Percentage
Black	59
White	24
Latino/a	13
Multiracial	4
American Indian/Alaska Native	0.1
Asian American	0.1
Native Hawaiian/Pacific Islander	0.03

Source: North Carolina Department of Public Instruction, Public School Statistical Profile, Pupils in Membership by Race and Sex, https://www.dpi.nc.gov/districts-schools/district-operations/financial-and-business-services/statistical-profile

Edgecombe County has the notable history of being home to the town of Princeville, the first town in the United States founded by formerly enslaved freed people after the end of the Civil War.[4] The town was founded on the only land available to Black residents at the time, a swampy area on the Tar River unwanted by White residents. While representing the community's commitment to self-sufficiency and self-determination, the town has also been a frequent site of devastating flooding since at least the 1800s. Most recently, Princeville endured back-to-back hurricanes in 1999.[5] Then, in 2016, the town was hit by Hurricane Matthew. The flooding was so severe that then-Superintendent Farrelly surveyed the damage by boat with the National Guard.[6] The disruption to students and families in the district was immense as schools closed, and Princeville residents, many descended from the town's founders, relocated to shelters and hotels. Thus, the legacy of environmental racism continues to reverberate in the district.

In addition to the environmental conditions in the county, Edgecombe County experiences economic and health disparities that can also impact student access to opportunities.[7] The North Carolina Public School Forum annually releases a statistical portrait called *The Roadmap of Need*, which compares districts across indicators ranging from health, youth behavior and safety, education, and economic development. In 2019, then Director of Accountability, Janet Morris, reported that:

> Edgecombe County has either been first, second or third on the low end in that report for the last three years. And this last year, we were [ranked last], which is certainly not where you want to be. So, when students come to school with us, there's a lot that we have to overcome. We, the team, not only school system personnel, but families.

Today, ECPS consists of 14 schools serving over 5,000 students. Schools are organized into one of three feeder patterns that staff refer to as north end schools, south end schools, or in-town schools located in the county seat of Tarboro. The district was formed in 1993 through a merger of the former Tarboro City Schools district and Edgecombe County Schools district.[8] As ECPS board member Ann Kent tells it, there were wide disparities between schools on different ends of the district at the time of the merger. North end schools served primarily Black students and, due to being under-resourced, "those schools looked like they were from the sixties," while the south end schools offered more educational opportunities and looked like "Jetson's schools" in comparison. The in-town Tarboro schools fell somewhere in between. According to Kent, early efforts to equalize conditions across schools after the merger were ineffective. Instead, she attributed the district's progress to a strategic focus on equity.

The equity leadership strategy in ECPS involved bringing the community together around a common cause and steadily building the capacity to deliver on a bold vision, particularly where the need has been greatest in the district. Indeed, ECPS demonstrates how much progress can be made when district leaders pursue educational excellence while focusing attention on the schools and students facing the greatest disparities in opportunities.

As a result of the equity efforts, the district has improved opportunities and outcomes for students, even in the face of the COVID-19 pandemic. Within two years under Bridges' leadership, the district saw stunning growth as almost every school (12 out of 14) met or exceeded its growth goals in 2018–19 compared to just 6 schools in 2016–17.[9] By school year 2022–23, ECPS exited its low-performing district status with Bridges at the helm.[10] As will be described in more detail in this case:

- between 2013 and 2019, the percent change in ECPS students testing "proficient" on regular state end-of-grade math tests was 88% compared to 40% statewide, and in reading, 73% compared to 30% statewide. During this period, Black students' math proficiency rates more than doubled (from 13% to 30%), and reading proficiency rates nearly doubled (from 13% to 23%)[11];
- between 2014 and 2015 and 2019 and 2020, the total number of short-term suspensions decreased by nearly 50%[12];
- in 2021–22, 88% of ECPS teachers received a rating of "effective" or "highly effective."[13] In 2021–22, 70% of principals in ECPS had served in their role for more than three years, compared to 7% of principals in 2015–16[14];

These outcomes suggest that, while there is more work to be done, ECPS is on the right track to providing more equitable opportunities to students.

Setting a Foundation for Racial Equity

In a district once characterized by high leadership turnover and wide disparities in opportunities between schools, the 2012 arrival of a new leadership team marked a pivot in the district's approach to supporting student growth and learning. First as Assistant Superintendent working with then Superintendent John Farrelly, then as Superintendent, Dr. Bridges launched a series of efforts and saw them through over the course of her time in ECPS. These efforts began with internal work to define: what is educational equity? ECPS Board Member Kent recalled a visual that illustrated the difference between equality and equity (Figure 2.1):

> I love [the] poster of the children watching the game of equality and equity. When I saw it for the first time, it made me understand the big

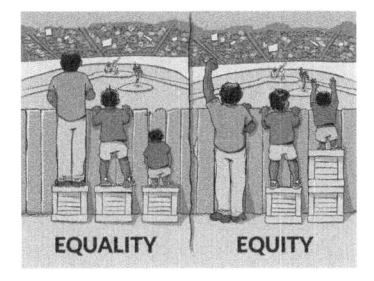

Figure 2.1 Equality vs. Equity.

Source: Interaction Institute for Social Change, Artist Angus Maguire.

difference in the two. Seeing that visual, it's like, "Oh yeah, if you're short, you really still can't see over the fence." We started going into our schools, looking for specific needs, and realized that, if we have equity in our schools, then they don't all look the same. What we need to do is look for the specific needs in our schools and move towards those. We have found that what works in the north end may not work in the south end, or in town.

Kent reported that this insight was foundational to "a whole different technique to approaching the problem" of meeting the needs of each and every learner in the district. First, the ECPS leadership team established a Blue-Ribbon Commission (BRC) to work hand in hand with families and community partners to develop a bold and tailored vision for teaching and learning in ECPS. Bridges then led a robust strategic planning process to ensure district capacity and resources were marshalled to achieve it. Along the way, the district has become a learning organization that seeks insight and support on how to innovate in the interest of students.

A Community Vision: The Blue-Ribbon Commission on Educational Equity

ECPS leaders launched the BRC on Educational Equity in the spring of 2017. At the time, then Superintendent Farrelly explained that the effort was designed to "define the future we imagine for our students and learn about opportunities and challenges we face in pursuit of that vision, specifically in the areas of equity; educating the whole child; and attracting, retaining, and developing human capital."[15] Within three months of launching the BRC, the district hosted community forums in each region of the county, seeking input from hundreds of stakeholders, including students, family members, business leaders, elected officials, non-profit partners, and district staff members.[16]

By using a range of listening strategies, the BRC operated in a fundamentally different way than the district had done before. According to Assistant Superintendent of Innovation and Strategic Planning Erin Swanson:

> Before convening the BRC, we weren't listening enough to the community. We had not created enough forums or spaces for people from across the community to come together and talk about what is it that we really want for kids.

Through the BRC, the district hosted "town hall meetings, we did focus groups, we did student interviews, we did school visits… At the end of every meeting…we asked this question: 'What is it you want for kids?'" There was a learning curve to taking this approach, which district leaders referred to as empathy work. Assistant Superintendent Swanson noted:

> The one thing I will say about empathy work, is that it's incredibly important but incredibly time consuming… It's just not the way we educators typically do business. We don't ask people what they need or what they want. We know or we read something…or somebody sends us an email and we're like, "that sounds like a good program, let's do that." Shifting the mindset away from that to a place where we're really thinking about how [to] merge learning science, research, and best practice with what the specific needs of a community are. [It] is a very different way of thinking, but it's one we're really trying to help people wrap their heads around.

According to BRC participants, what began as a district-led effort has become a widespread commitment to improving life in Edgecombe County. For example, Vichi Jagannathan, co-founder of the ECPS partner organization Rural Opportunity Institute, noted that the BRC has evolved to become "less about partnering with the district to do something in particular, but… more about the district being one of a number of different organizations and entities coming together around a future for children."

This holistic approach to goal setting has empowered the district to set a vision outside of the typical preschool-to-grade-12 framework. According to Assistant Superintendent Swanson, Superintendent Bridges pushed the committee to ask stakeholders, "What is it that you want for our students or our graduates by the time they're 25 years old?" The idea behind that target was that the:

> 25-year mark is a place where kids have graduated from college if they've gone to college. They've had a few years of work underneath them if they've decided to go right to work. They've started making a life for themselves.

District leaders recognize that in a community with historically limited resources, young people can benefit from having ongoing support even after high school graduation. As Superintendent Bridges put it:

> We are holding onto our kids until they're 25. We've made [an] effort to say, "Whether you're going to college, the military, or working in town, we want to stay connected to you [and] we want to still help you." Some of our kids [are the first in their families to] go off to college. Do they know what [classes] to take? If [they go to the military [or work] in town, how do we help them move along? What can we do in our community? If we take our hands off of them, what's likely to happen [is] what's always happened.

With the help of graduate student researchers at North Carolina State University, district leaders distilled community input into a set of five graduate aims. As stated in the district strategic plan,[17] by the time they are 25 years old, all ECPS graduates will be able to say:

* I know my purpose and passion, and I am living this out;
* I possess global awareness and agency;
* I can contribute positively to my community;
* I have opportunities to return or stay in Edgecombe County; and
* I am resilient in the face of challenges.

District leaders reported that the graduate aims have served as a beacon for the community at large. In the words of Daniel Riley, a BRC Commissioner and spouse to Swanson:

> In order for our entire community to meet the challenges of the 21st century, we needed to come together and define who we are and what we care about. Our graduate aims are not just a vision for students or schools, but for all of Edgecombe County.

ECPS leaders noted that, while they were able to synthesize these graduate aims from input across the county, they also recognized that they heard distinctive priorities across communities. Assistant Superintendent Swanson, for example, noted:

> Part of what is true in Edgecombe is that we're one county, but each section of our county has a different identity. I think there are different needs, and the community wants different things. Something that Dr. Bridges and myself and our team really feel is important is that as we think about school design that we're doing a lot of empathy work first

and really listening to the people in each community and saying, "what are your needs? What do you want?" Maybe these are the graduate aims that we're all going for, but you might actually feel like we need to get there differently.

A Strategic Plan for Racial Equity: Futures Reimagined

In addition to developing the five graduate aims, Superintendent Bridges supported her leadership team to use their community empathy work to design the district's 2019–24 strategic plan, *Futures Reimagined* (full text available in the Online Materials Package). This document puts forth a bold plan for how the district will ensure more equitable opportunities and outcomes for students. The strategic plan begins with an equity vision that "ECPS will be a place where opportunities are no longer predicted by social, cultural, or economic factors."

According to Superintendent Bridges, not everyone on staff believed that an equity vision was necessary in the district, despite data showing disparities in student opportunities and outcomes across race and other factors. Although the equity vision was ultimately approved by the board, she reported that implementing the vision required hard conversations about resource reallocation. She explained that board members:

> believe this is the right thing to do. But do we really want it? Because wanting it on paper is one thing. Wanting it in reality is another... It usually means shifting resources because there's not a lot of new money. And that's where they don't want to do it.

Leaders in Edgecombe developed a strategy to prioritize resources in the lowest-performing schools before scaling reforms district wide, detailed in a later section.

Another contentious component of *Futures Reimagined* was the overall district goal of "College acceptance for ALL." As Superintendent Bridges explained, this goal does not mean that every student will choose to attend college. Rather, "college acceptance means you are eligible to go to college. This means you have options, exposure, determination, and opportunity." She explained that setting this goal was challenging because it required community stakeholders to confront long-held low expectations for some of the district's students:

> Some of the pushback was, "all kids are not college material." But the person who's saying that, are they talking about their child? No, they're talking about yours, or somebody else's... It's a different mindset and a different way of thinking, but we have to keep pushing.

Futures Reimagined details five overarching priorities: (1) Academic Excellence, (2) Talent Recruitment and Development, (3) Equity in Action, (4) Purposeful Partnerships, and (5) Resilient Foundation. The "Equity in Action" priority includes seven actions to support learning environments that are "physically and emotionally safe, welcoming, inclusive, and responsive to the whole child." Among these, the district committed to conducting an equity audit using survey data and empathy interviews, supporting equity-focused leadership development, revising the code of conduct and launching student support teams to ensure restorative and trauma-informed practices, increasing students' college and career exposure and opportunities, and ensuring all Edgecombe County students have access to pre-kindergarten programs (Table 2.2).

In addition to the Equity in Action priority, ECPS leaders wove a focus on equity throughout the district's strategic plan. The plan includes measures of success that the district will track and disaggregate by student race and by school. These measures include graduation rates, postsecondary enrollment rates, student growth on standardized tests, chronic absenteeism, and discipline rates, among others. Additional priority areas in *Futures Reimagined* include actions related to increasing teacher diversity, employing an equity-based funding formula, and continuing purposeful countywide partnerships by developing a Family Resource Center as a hub to provide services to Edgecombe youth and their families from birth to age 25.

Embracing Innovation

One word came up consistently in interviews with district leaders, partners, and staff members about the hallmarks of ECPS: innovation. Although the word can sometimes ring hollow, in ECPS, it refers to an abiding commitment to doing things differently and challenging the expectations of what is possible in an under-resourced, rural, majority-Black district. This has not been by happenstance but has been part of a concerted effort by Bridges and her predecessor, Farrelly, to build up leadership capacity and district-wide systems to advance educational equity. Indeed, district leaders foster talent, pursue organizational learning, and engage in continuous improvement to implement and sustain innovation that advances equity.

Fostering Talent to Do Things Differently

Dr. Bridges' leadership in ECPS—first as Assistant Superintendent of Curriculum and Instruction, then as Superintendent—included a commitment to doing things differently, which attracted and sustained educational leaders willing to drive district-wide change. Dr. Bridges, along with her

Table 2.2 Edgecombe County Public Schools Strategic Plan Priority 3, Equity in Action

Action		Description
3.1	Equity audit	Create and implement a district- and school-wide equity audit process, leveraging data from the Panorama survey, standardized assessments, empathy interviews, and focus groups.
3.2	Equity-focused leadership development	Create space for district and school leaders to engage in conversations about race and privilege and explore their own biases and racial identity. Provide tools and professional development to support leaders in increasing equitable practices and consistently operating with an equity lens.
3.3	Trauma-informed practices	Develop and implement a trauma-informed school culture and classroom management approach which includes diversity, equity, and inclusion training for all staff.
3.4	Code of conduct	Revisit and revise the ECPS Code of Conduct and other school and district policies and procedures to ensure alignment with restorative, accountable, and trauma-informed practices.
3.5	Student support teams	Seek additional funding and reallocate existing funding to ensure each school has a student support team with the capacity necessary to effectively serve their students.
3.6	Closing the opportunity gap	Increase opportunities for students to find and live out their purpose and passion by providing them with more exposure to colleges, careers, and the community in elementary school; increasing course and extracurricular offerings, as well as college and career advising, in middle and high school; and redesigning the high school Graduation Project.
3.7	Pre-K for all	Ensure all students in Edgecombe County attend an ECPS Pre-Kindergarten program or another high-quality Pre-Kindergarten option in the community.

Source: Edgecombe County Public Schools (n.d.). *ECPS Strategic Plan: Futures Reimagined* (accessed 7/31/2023). https://www.ecps.us/apps/pages/index.jsp?uREC_ID=1689715&type=d&pREC_ID=1847182

predecessor, John Farrelly, hired staff who could advance racial equity in the district. Erin Swanson, a cabinet team member who first came to ECPS as an equity-minded school leader, described how the invitation to "do things differently" drew her into the district. She notes that when she was hired, Farrelly was forthright about the need to innovate to improve outcomes for students of color:

> [He was] very much up front in saying: 'We as a school system are not serving our kids the way we need to be. We serve primarily Black and Brown kids, and we are not closing achievement gaps. We're not graduating our kids ready for college. We're not sending enough kids to college.' He was very candid about that [and] clear that, if we were going to make a change, we couldn't just keep doing the same old things.

Swanson added, "that was compelling to me because I did not want to do the same old thing... to be at a school that was just trying to make tweaks on a model that was ineffective. That's why I came." With the support of district leadership, Swanson reported she "had the autonomy to take some risks and to really lead the way that I felt like our school community needed me to lead." The vision and leadership style were crucial to her choice to join ECPS and lead effectively as a school principal. Superintendent Bridges continued to support Swanson's leadership in two roles dedicated to scaling effective innovations as both Director of Innovation and then Assistant Superintendent of Innovation and Strategic Planning. By creating these roles and dedicating capacity to sustain innovation in a small, rural school district, Dr. Bridges makes a remarkable statement about the value of innovation in ECPS.

The later section on "Developing Staff Capacity" further details how ECPS leaders leverage the district's reputation for innovation in its hiring, recruitment, and retention strategies.

Leading a Learning Organization

Learning has been a key element empowering district leaders to take calculated risks in order to transform opportunities for district learners. When Dr. Bridges assumed the superintendency in 2017, she also joined two leadership cohorts that ultimately shaped her leadership approach and accelerated innovative, equity-focused reforms: the Racial Equity Leadership Network and the Transcend Model Sharing Community.

During her first year in the position, Superintendent Bridges joined the inaugural cohort of the Racial Equity Leadership Network. The Racial Equity Leadership Network is a fellowship for executive district leaders led by the Southern Education Foundation in partnership with the Learning

Policy Institute and the National Equity Project. Over the course of the 18-month fellowship, she learned alongside peers in Southern districts working to transform their systems to advance racial equity. Superintendent Bridges received coaching support to develop equity-oriented leadership, research on district policies and practices to advance racial equity,[18] and an approach to identifying and addressing equity challenges using a liberatory design process.[19]

Bridges reported that the concepts, skills, and relationships within the network provided invaluable insight on establishing and advancing racial equity initiatives. Coming into the program, she reported that her experiences as a Black woman informed her understanding of racial injustice. She explained, "As an African American female growing up in North Carolina, you really feel [that] of course you understand racial issues." However, she also understood that her own personal experience did not necessarily reflect those of all her students and families. She reflected, "I hadn't experienced this," referring to the depth of poverty many students face in ECPS.

Working in a cohort of district leaders with diverse identities, experiences, and organizational roles both expanded her racial consciousness and informed her approach to doing things differently. She compared her learning arc to a poem by Portia Nelson, "There's A Hole in My Sidewalk."[20] In the poem, the narrator continually falls into the hole, at first feeling "helpless," then in disbelief, until eventually the narrator learns to "walk down another street." In much the same way, Dr. Bridges explained that leaders continually fall into the trap of letting inequities slide by, feeling "helpless" in a situation that "isn't my fault." By failing to disrupt inequities that are apparent in district data, leaders reinforce those inequities and encounter the same problems again and again. The fellowship supported Bridges to deeply examine system inequities and develop leadership approaches to address them. Like choosing to walk a different path, she described returning from sessions on "full blast," energized to apply her learning to district initiatives. In her words:

> I started sharing with the leadership team in central office, strategically with people who I knew would help spread it. I shared with four people that were receptive, then they shared it with three more, and they share it with three more. Then we started to feel the machine [revving as we] processed [together].'

Bridges referred to a powerful visual (Figure 2.2) to explain her work advancing racial equity in ECPS. She first noticed how the status quo reproduced persistent racial and socioeconomic inequities in student proficiency data, then worked to sharply raise expectations and expand access to high-quality instruction district wide. In this way, she seeded district-wide

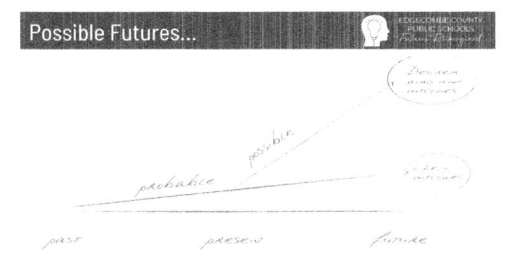

Figure 2.2 Possible vs. Probable Futures.

Source: Bridges, V. H. (2019, March 14). Edgecombe County Public Schools [Presentation to the Racial Equity Leadership Network]. Some of the material in this graphic is based on materials developed by Werner Erhard and Landmark Worldwide and is used with permission.

innovations that depart from the incremental progress of probable outcomes to pursue the steep change that's possible when leaders pursue more ambitious outcomes.

She reflected on the incredible effort this has required: "it sounds good and easy to say," but changing the status quo "is hard. It's easier to go along and get along, it really is." But Bridges didn't sign up for easy progress toward probable outcomes. She credited her participation in the Racial Equity Leadership Network (RELN) fellowship as a deep wellspring for both the inspiration and practical resources necessary to sustain her efforts. For example, Bridges and her leadership team drew from models in the RELN curriculum to develop an equity vision that commits the district to becoming "a place where opportunities are no longer predicted by social, cultural, or economic factors."

Superintendent Bridges remained active in the Racial Equity Leadership Network beyond her 18-month fellowship, stepping into a leadership role on the design team for the fellowship. In this capacity, she continued to develop her equity leadership by presenting on her work at conferences and building relationships with additional cohorts of fellows. In the spring of 2019, a group of RELN fellows took a site visit to ECPS to meet her leadership team and learn from their work to advance racial equity across the district (Box 2.1).

Another learning experience catalyzed Superintendent Bridges' equity reform work. The Model Sharing Community is a school redesign cohort led by Transcend, a nonprofit that offers professional learning and resources to support more equitable learning environments.[21] Superintendent Bridges assembled a team of ECPS leaders who visited innovative school sites across the country over a period of ten months. Together, they learned about how other school systems were closing educational opportunity and achievement gaps, then engaged in a human-centered design process to bring their learnings into

Box 2.1   The Racial Equity Leadership Network Visits Edgecombe County

On a clear morning in March 2019, ten cabinet-level district leaders disembarked from a tour bus in the parking lot of Edgecombe County Public Schools headquarters. Stretching their legs after the hourlong journey from Raleigh, North Carolina, they were greeted in a large conference room with fresh fruit, hot biscuits, strong coffee, and Superintendent Valerie Bridges.

Racial Equity Leadership Network facilitator Asali Waters set the stage by stating the learning goal for the site visit: to exchange ideas about how RELN fellows apply racial equity concepts and skills in the districts they lead. Her colleague, Rodney Thomas, then introduced their host:

> I get the honor of introducing our host today. She is the superintendent here, has been in the role for two years, and has risen in the ranks in the school district. She hails from neighboring counties, Wake County and Guilford County, [so she knows the geographical] history and context. I can tell you, just [from] being with Valerie in Cohort 1, my description of her is a "quiet storm:" she doesn't say a lot, but when she speaks, her words linger in the room. She's that type of leader. She's very thoughtful in her leadership moves, and it showed tremendously in her engagement in Cohort 1. She is one to be reckoned with and has a lot to give in [terms of] her leadership and her experience.

Bridges began her remarks by describing the challenge of a small, rural district striving to meet the needs of its community and prepare learners for ambitious futures. She explained that achieving this vision requires "exposure [and] surrounding students with opportunities [that] inform [their] choices and decisions." To see the leading edge of district innovation in action, the group then toured the Martin Millennium Global School and North Philips School of Innovation. The learning models at each school, detailed in later sections of this chapter, provide rigorous academic material while developing critical thinking, collaboration, and self-management skills. On a student panel at North Philips School of Innovation, fellows heard about the high level of trust students have in their teachers, who they said understand their experiences and pull them together like a family. Students also reported engaging in challenging material, with individualized goal setting and the ability to self-direct their learning by selecting topics and strategies for completing assignments.

After visiting schools, the group reconvened in the district headquarters. Superintendent Bridges introduced Lanetta M. Scott, Coordinator at the ECPS Family Resource Center, to share about community partnerships. Scott coordinates a robust series of district programs that provide year-round access to holistic educational, healthcare, and social services for students and families. When asked what makes her work possible, Scott reported close communication with a "wide array of people in our community [who], anytime I call them, or they call me, they know we're going to show up. We go where our families are [and] we band together to make a community team."

The group next heard from one such community partner. Reverend Richard Joyner, founder of Conetoe Family Life Gardens, spoke about a longstanding district partnership advancing nutritional equity. He began, "There is not another school administrator in the world like Dr. Bridges and her staff. She really gives our community the opportunity to participate in the educational development of opportunity for our youth." He described the prevalence of hunger in Edgecombe and lack of access to fresh, nutritious food. While district leaders secured a community eligibility provision to provide free school lunch, they also partnered with Conetoe Family Life Center Farm on a free summer program in which students engage in community-supported agribusiness to grow their own produce, turn a profit, and develop reading, math, science, and technology concepts. Joyner explained that subsistence gardening can seem unappealing to district students and their families. He himself grew up sharecropping and worked hard to get off the family farm. However, as a religious leader, he witnessed firsthand the effects of youth hunger, malnutrition, and disengagement. When asked what makes his partnership with ECPS effective, Reverend Joyner replied, "The biggest piece is trust." He encouraged fellows to "look at ways you don't take responsibility from the community," emphasizing that Superintendent Bridges and her staff support organizations like Conetoe Family Life Center Farm to manage their own resources and programs.

At the close of the day, fellows shared a word or phrase they took away from the visit. District leaders from around the country described the work in ECPS as inspiring, committed, relational, urgent, and strategic. Thomas reflected that Superintendent Bridges didn't do it alone; she both brings lots of people together to do the work on behalf of students and is intentional about crediting her collaborators within and outside of the district.

ECPS. One member of the site visit team, Assistant Superintendent Swanson, described being part of a national cohort as an "awesome opportunity for us that most rural school systems in Eastern North Carolina don't have." She continued, describing how model sharing galvanized ECPS leaders:

> That was just really illuminating for us. We had a chance to see what else is happening in education and how it's serving kids that look like ours and have some of the challenges that our kids have in a way that's really affirming of their identity [and] doesn't lower expectations for kids because they're coming in behind. We've really been thinking about how we create a school model that works for all kids. We still have a massively long way to go on that… but I think largely we've got a solid core group of school leaders that are really excited about that and are moving that forward.

Driving Continuous Improvement

As will be detailed in this study, Superintendent Bridges and her leadership team seized on their learnings and commitment to do things differently to enact a suite of equity-oriented innovations. Examples include launching the Innovation Zone on the north side of the county, growing their own teacher pipeline through the Scholar Teachers program, testing alternative ways of deploying staff, and rededicating learning time in creative ways to better meet student needs. Each of these initiatives involved a human-centered design process of testing, monitoring, and tweaking equity solutions. The North Philips School of Innovation, a groundbreaking school model that features design-for-change passion projects and personal identity development,[22] is a prime example of how ECPS leaders leveraged organizational learning in partnership with the Racial Equity Leadership Network and Transcend to test out bold approaches that push the needle on racial equity. The North Phillips School of Innovation is described in greater detail in the section on "Investing in North Edgecombe."

Creating Equitable Access to Whole Child Education

When Dr. Bridges entered ECPS in 2012, she saw a need to raise expectations and instructional rigor. She introduced a new vision for teaching and learning, which shifted from passive instruction toward engaging each and every learner in grade-level content that develops academic knowledge alongside co-cognitive skills like critical thinking. Former Assistant Superintendent of Curriculum and Instruction Dr. Abbey Futrell explained the challenge of disrupting the status quo that had become "steeped" in tradition:

> As in many districts, [we had to get] away from worksheets. I learned early on: you teach like you're taught. So, a hard move is to get teachers

away from teaching the way they were taught, or the way they were taught to teach. As I've learned more about theory and pedagogy, I've [realized that] we can't do school this way. This doesn't work, it's not effective. So, I think it's getting teachers out of that routine and that mindset that that's what school is. Change is hard, but it's [even] harder in a hometown district where those traditions are steeped and passed down. You know, [we] don't have new people coming in a lot, so it's hard to change the mindset. But kids just deserve so much more.

District leaders recognized the need to expand access to quality instruction. In 2018, Superintendent Bridges systematized emerging school-based practices in a holistic Instructional Framework for Learning (available in the Online Materials Package), described next. By implementing the Framework, Bridges (1) introduced a district-wide definition of cognitive rigor to evaluate the quality of learning experiences across district campuses and (2) established a process for instructional leaders to assess and scale high-impact instructional practices. While specific instructional practices differ across campuses, the Framework helps leaders ensure that all instruction aligns to the district-wide, equity-oriented vision for teaching and learning. In addition to developing the framework, Superintendent Bridges and her leadership team also supported the ongoing implementation of high-quality approaches, including project-based learning, Spanish language immersion, accelerated learning, and social-emotional learning.

   This approach appears to have accelerated academic growth for learners in ECPS. While reading and math proficiency trends indicate the district scores lower than the state averages, ECPS students have improved at a faster rate (Table 2.3). Composite grade level proficiency rates refer to the

Table 2.3 Comparison of Edgecombe County Public Schools and North Carolina Students Percentage Testing "Proficient" on Regular State End-of-Grade Math and Reading Tests (Grades 3–8), 2012–13 to 2022–23

Assessment		2012–13	2013–14	2014–15	2015–16	2016–17	2017–18	2018–19	2020–21	2021–22	2022–23
Math	ECPS	21.1	26.2	29.8	35.7	31.1	33.4	39.6	19.0	28.2	32.8
	NC	42.3	52.4	52.0	55.0	55.0	56.0	59.0	40.0	50.0	53.0
Reading	ECPS	20.6	31.8	31.3	33.6	29.9	33.6	35.7	25.4	29.2	30.3
	NC	43.9	58.0	56.0	57.0	58.0	57.0	57.0	46.0	48.0	50.0

Source: North Carolina Department of Public Instruction. North Carolina School Report Cards. https://www.dpi.nc.gov/data-reports/school-report-cards.

Note: Proficiency defined as students testing level 3 or above on regular state end of grade mathematics and reading tests. Assessments were canceled in 2019–2020 due to COVID-19.

percentage of students in grades 3 through 8 earning a score of 3 or above (out of 5) on a criterion-referenced math or reading exam. Statewide math and reading proficiency rates were especially low following the implementation of new state tests aligned to more rigorous standards in 2011–12. Since that time, proficiency rates have rebounded across the state and within the district.

Between 2013 and 2019, the percent of ECPS students testing "proficient" on regular state end-of-grade math tests increased in both math (from 21% to 40%) and reading (from 21% to 36%). These gains demonstrated an accelerated rate of growth relative to statewide growth: the percent change in math proficiency rates for ECPS students was 88% compared to 40% statewide, and in reading, 73% compared to 30% statewide. Although ECPS proficiency rates continued to fall below state proficiency rates in 2019, this accelerated pace of improvement helped narrow the gap in student outcomes between ECPS and the state.

As in other districts, the impact of the COVID pandemic caused a drop in achievement in spring 2020–21, but in ECPS, gains in both math and reading achievement by 2022–23 show that a turnaround was occurring that outpaced the rate of improvement in the state. Disaggregated reading and math proficiency trends show large and persistent racial/ethnic gaps within the district (Tables 2.4 and 2.5). However, academic gains were especially large for Black students, whose math proficiency rates more than doubled between 2013 and 2019 (from 13% to 30%) and reading proficiency rates nearly doubled (from 13% to 23%).

Table 2.4 Edgecombe County Public Schools Percentage of Students Testing "Proficient" on Regular State End-of-Grade Math Tests (Grades 3–8), 2012–13 to 2022–23, by Racial/Ethnic Group

Race/ethnicity	2012–13	2013–14	2014–15	2015–16	2016–17	2017–18	2018–19	2020–21	2021–22	2022–23
Black	12.8	17.5	20.1	26.0	22.2	25.3	30.3	10.3	19.0	23.9
Latino/a	28.6	27.2	36.4	43.1	40.2	43.4	50.7	32.0	42.1	48.6
Multiracial	25.0	35.6	38.2	41.1	38.7	36.6	39.3	16.1	29.9	35.0
White	34.0	42.7	44.8	50.4	43.8	44.8	54.0	33.0	43.6	47.8

Source: North Carolina Department of Public Instruction. Reports of Disaggregated State, School System (LEA) and School Performance Data, http://accrpt.tops.ncsu.edu/docs/disag_datasets/

Note: Proficiency defined as students testing level 3 or above on regular state end-of-grade mathematics and reading tests. Disaggregated data for American Indian and Asian students is not available due to small sample sizes. Assessments were canceled in 2019–2020 due to COVID-19.

Table 2.5 Edgecombe County Public Schools Percentage of Students Testing "Proficient" on Regular State End of Grade Reading Tests (Grades 3–8), 2012–13 to 2022–23, by Racial/Ethnic Group

Race/ethnicity	2012–13	2013–14	2014–15	2015–16	2016–17	2017–18	2018–19	2020–21	2021–22	2022–23
Black	13.2	23.0	22.0	24.7	21.1	24.3	26.2	17.9	20.9	23.1
Latino/a	23.4	29.0	31.1	35.6	33.3	37.0	40.7	28.3	31.4	36.1
Multiracial	14.3	44.4	43.6	46.4	30.6	35.2	42.4	33.0	41.4	34.2
White	33.9	49.5	47.7	47.9	44.5	49.7	52.5	39.6	45.6	46.4

Source: North Carolina Department of Public Instruction. Reports of Disaggregated State, School System (LEA) and School Performance Data, http://accrpt.tops.ncsu.edu/docs/disag_datasets/

Note: Proficiency defined as students testing level 3 or above on regular state end-of-grade mathematics and reading tests. Disaggregated data for American Indian and Asian students is not available due to small sample sizes. Assessments were canceled in 2019–2020 due to COVID-19.

Setting a Framework for Learning

Before Superintendent Bridges assumed leadership in the district, there was considerable variation in teaching practices across school sites, with some campuses spearheading whole child approaches not available district wide. The North Carolina Department of Public Instruction noted inconsistent instructional practices in a district needs assessment. To define expectations for instruction and systematize improvement, district leaders established Academic Excellence as the first priority in the ECPS strategic plan, *Futures Reimagined*. In this priority, the district committed to providing every student "access to rigorous, grade level content, such that they gain a deep level of understanding across a wide variety of content areas, while also learning to think critically and creatively." Actions aligned to this priority detail the strategic leadership approach to district-wide instructional change: first, define what constitutes meaningful, high-quality instruction in an Instructional Framework for Learning; next, train teachers to understand and enact the Framework; and, finally, use the Framework to develop and scale aligned learning experiences for each and every child in the district.

In 2018, then-Assistant Superintendent of Curriculum and Instruction Dr. Abbey Futrell led the district's Curriculum and Instruction Team to develop a first iteration of the Framework. This draft was presented to principals for feedback on the elements of effective instructional practices across campuses. Next, they brought the second iteration to then-Director of Innovation Erin Swanson and a small group of teachers. This group helped the Curriculum and Instruction Team to incorporate features of design thinking into the Framework, including the iterative cycle: design, facilitate, reflect, adjust (Online Materials Package).[23]

The resulting Instructional Framework for Learning defines not only district-wide expectations for what constitutes effective, high-impact instructional practice but also how these practices are developed, assessed, and scaled across district classrooms. This includes supporting teachers to recognize and pursue cognitive rigor, defined both in terms of the depth and extent that students are engaged and challenged to demonstrate their learning. When facilitating lessons, teachers are expected to include the ECPS Everyday Essentials, a comprehensive set of learning modalities that includes reading, reciprocal questioning, writing, speaking, communicating, collaborating, and developing student agency. Incorporating this wide range of learning modalities is foundational to providing a rich learning experience for students.

Teachers, students, and additional stakeholders, including administrators and family members, have responsibilities at each of the four stages of the framework. For example, in the design phase, teachers are responsible for designing "student learning experiences marked with cognitive rigor," while students "set and achieve goals for learning" and stakeholders "provide support for educational experiences." The cyclical nature of the instructional framework allows for rapid design cycles to develop high-impact, innovative teaching and learning. In this way, instruction is not identical across district campuses, but it is aligned to a district-wide and equity-oriented vision for teaching and learning. As noted by then-principal of Phillips Middle School, Jenny O'Meara, when it comes to teaching and learning, "innovation is not a laptop in every hand. It is thoughtful design work to create equity."

The Curriculum and Instruction team was charged with supporting educators at every level to learn and effectively teach using new pedagogies. Futrell reported that integrating the framework into daily instructional practice was key to getting ideas off the page and into action: "We wanted to make it a collaborative effort instead of this pretty framework that doesn't work. We wanted to take teachers through a process that they basically are in continually." In the 2019–20 school year, the Curriculum and Instruction team spearheaded an implementation strategy that enabled district coaches to provide instructors with continuous feedback aligned to professional development pathways. They developed, adopted, and iterated an aligned walkthrough rubric (available in the Online Materials Package), separate from the teacher evaluative instrument, for routine "growth walks." Futrell described the rationale for the growth walks to reframe the work of district coaches so that teachers "can honestly see us as the support system we are trying to be," using walkthroughs as an opportunity to see and support the nuances of instruction beyond flat evaluative scores. The new rubric guides district coaches in formative observations focused on identifying and developing instructors' strengths by assessing teaching skills like higher-order questioning. The Curriculum and Instruction Team reviews growth walk data each month to design and support teachers through personalized professional development pathways, described further in the next section of this report.

As district and campus leaders collaborated to design and implement the Instructional Framework for Learning, they engaged in continuous improvement that turned the pre-existing patchwork of campus-based learning initiatives into a cohesive toolkit of high-impact instructional practices. Campus leaders reported that these practices, described next, each meet shared expectations for cognitive rigor while supporting the specific mission and needs of a given school community.

Developing and Scaling Meaningful Learning Experiences

Starting in the 2013–14 school year, ECPS leaders launched a series of programs and initiatives to transform teaching and learning across the district. Project-based learning, Spanish language immersion, accelerated learning, and social-emotional learning represent the leading edge of educational practice in ECPS, anchored in the district's number 1 strategic priority to provide every student "access to rigorous, grade-level content, such that they gain a deep level of understanding across a wide variety of content areas, while also learning to think critically and creatively." In the words of Superintendent Bridges:

> We are continuing to push the lever and move. Lots of people don't want us to do the bells and whistles. They tell us, "Just teach." I don't think you can wait. We didn't get in low performance overnight, and we're not going to get out overnight.

Based on the district's equity orientation, ECPS leaders reported that there is no one-size-fits-all approach to teaching and learning. District leaders support campus teams to innovate in ways that best meet the needs of their learners and community, and they use the Instructional Framework for Learning to monitor, share, and scale effective practices over time. Former Assistant Superintendent of Curriculum and Instruction Dr. Abbey Futrell reported that district leadership is focused on creating opportunities to advance racial equity:

> When we talk about equity, it's about opportunities. One thing I like about Dr. Bridges' vision is she makes sure that there are a variety of opportunities. [We're] not trying to herd students in one direction. It's okay to have options, and it's okay for those options to be different. And the places that those opportunities can take you! Even in our traditional

schools there's some non-conventional routes you can take. You can attend the [school of innovation], you can attend the early college…there are opportunities and options here, and I think that's where it starts: when you start offering opportunities that aren't usually there.

The following subsections describe how district and campus leaders have brought the framework to life by developing and sharing high-impact instructional practices. Principal of Edgecombe Early College Matthew Bristow-Smith reported, "The Framework for Learning reflects what we do, and I think what we do reflects the framework. It works both ways."

Project-Based Learning in Edgecombe Early College

In 2013–14, Superintendent Farrelly promoted longtime district educator Matthew Bristow-Smith to serve as Principal of Edgecombe Early College High School. To advance the campus mission to support students who would be the first generation in their families to attend college, Bristow-Smith increased the cognitive rigor of coursework by introducing curriculum-embedded project-based learning schoolwide. Following the design thinking process described in the Instructional Framework for Learning, Bristow-Smith invested resources, trained instructional staff, and leveraged community partnerships to enhance meaningful learning experiences for Edgecombe Early College students. By 2018–19, Bristow-Smith was named Wells Fargo North Carolina Principal of the Year in recognition of Edgecombe Early College earning an "A" performance grade from the North Carolina Department of Public Instruction and exceeding its growth targets in each of the five years of Bristow-Smith's tenure.[24]

Edgecombe Early College was established in 2004 to expand educational opportunity by accelerating postsecondary pathways through a five-year program, beginning in 9th grade, which transitions seamlessly from high school to postsecondary learning that enables students to graduate with an associate degree.[25] The program is among over 100 Cooperative Innovation High Schools in North Carolina, which partner with local community colleges and receive supplemental funding from the state. Edgecombe Early College draws applicants from across the county. Whereas other early colleges in the state allocate opportunity through a blind lottery system, faculty at Edgecombe Early College use what they call a "compatibility model" to advance the school's equity mission by serving students who would be the first generation in their families to attend college. Bristow-Smith explained how faculty review comprehensive applications that include behavioral and academic profiles from middle school, student and parent interviews, and recommendations by core subject teachers:

It's an excruciating process to try and identify which kids come because you might be…a child that had a couple fights in middle school, might have straight B's or C's, and you might be more qualified to come than the child of somebody who's been raised in privilege. It does require professional judgment on our part. There are other early colleges that use a lottery system that is completely impersonal. [If] we're intentional about everything else that we do in education, why not be intentional about the kids that we select for this process, being true to our mission? That is a tough pill for some people to swallow: sometimes, the kids that are more appropriate for coming to our particular early college may be kids that need a restart. … [W]e try to grab them and put them in an environment where, every single day, they get validated as individuals, so they're not lost.

At Edgecombe Early College, more than 80% of students have parents who did not attend college.[26] The program serves roughly 30% Black, 25% Latino/a, and 45% White students.[27] Because students come in with varied academic backgrounds and learning needs, Bristow-Smith and his team developed project-based learning experiences to harness students' learning assets and accelerate their growth.

Bristow-Smith described project-based learning practices as emerging, yet piecemeal, when he entered as principal in 2013–14; a junior internship and senior project were "wedged in one semester," and students completed one-off projects in 9th and 10th grade. He strengthened project-based learning as the core instructional model by engaging staff, students, and community partners in the design process laid out in the Instructional Framework for Learning.

The grade-level instructional teams at Edgecombe Early College designed project-based learning experiences with clear and high expectations. When asked about what made the project-based instructional model possible at Edgecombe Early College, Principal Bristow-Smith responded, "It doesn't just happen. You have to build in structures behind the scenes for staff to collaborate." He used a combination of professional development from the Buck Institute and in-house continuous improvement focused on weaving project-based learning standards throughout the curricular map. Faculty at the Edgecombe Early College engage in extensive behind-the-scenes planning to develop project-based learning experiences like the Fall semester Science, Technology, Engineering, and Math (STEM) Challenge (see "STEM Challenge at Edgecombe Early College High School" at the end of this section). Bristow-Smith compensates cross-disciplinary instructional teams comprised of math, English, history, and science teachers to convene over the summer to design and budget for the next year's projects. He reported that budgeting appropriate time and resources is, "the key ingredient.

If you're going to do [project-based learning], have your teachers design it and find ways to fund it up front so that you can provide compensation to do that planning." He explained that, just like students, educators "need time to collaborate and communicate in an environment where they can be creative." He described his strategy to "invest in people first:"

> I budgeted $4,500 last summer to pay for staff to get together and to work. They needed summer employment. I could have spent that $4,500 a lot of different ways, but I do think investing in people really pays off. If I have a choice…I always invest in the people first. The truth is, if you really want to design [projects] at a high level, you need folks to have a chance to breathe a little bit. They got together over the summer, worked collaboratively, had a great time, and also built staff relationships.

Under the new model, student learning progresses along curriculum-embedded performance tasks that culminate in semester-long capstone projects in 9th and 10th grades and yearlong capstone projects in 11th and 12th grades. By the time they enter their fifth year of the program, "Super Seniors" have developed the academic knowledge and co-cognitive skills to hit the ground running at the community college. Bristow-Smith reported:

> By the time they get to their senior year, they have had a direct line of preparation—not multiple-choice assessments, not on a transcript, not on a test score of any kind—that helps to prepare them for real-world learning. When we think about equity…if we can prepare kids for what comes next after high school, if we can do that for all kids in an organized, systematic way, if we can provide support, if we can make it personal and relevant for them, and if we can individualize the experience, then we graduate kids that are ready for whatever they want to do. And that's what we've tried to do.

Bristow-Smith reported that his faculty engage students as co-designers through opportunities to (1) exercise their "voice and choice" on personalized topics and (2) differentiate instruction that is tailored to meet students' interests, strengths, and learning needs. Faculty have also created purposeful partnerships with community stakeholders to apply student learning in contexts that have relevance and value. For example, one classroom partnered with the City of Tarboro to conduct water quality analyses for each school in the county, another collaborated with an elementary school and hospital maternity ward to develop and distribute early literacy resources, and yet another installed a prototype bee garden on the community college campus.

While these projects vary in subject and scope, they are each anchored in rigorous district-wide standards and essential skills that advance the strategic priority of academic excellence. Bristow-Smith reported that project-based learning "helps to promote rigor and also equity because [we set] expectations at every step of the way, [which] apply to all kids." He continued, "Everything has to be a learning stretch, so we don't do easy projects." Teachers and students engage in iterative, structured cycles of feedback and revision, which are aligned to the "Reflect" and "Adjust" stages of the Instructional Framework for Learning. He reported that teachers use feedback to support students to embrace and learn through their revisions. For example, faculty introduced a new step in project development where students present their proposals to a panel of staff and community members in 2019. Bristow-Smith reported that "in about half of these cases, we rejected their topics because they weren't rigorous enough." He wasn't daunted—in fact, reviewing the proposal standards and revising topics for resubmission was a valuable and supportive part of students' learning process (Box 2.2).

These efforts are paying off for the students in Edgecombe Early College. In 2019, Bristow-Smith reported that 100% of students graduated the

---

Box 2.2   STEM Challenge at Edgecombe Early College High School

Walking into any classroom at the Edgecombe Early College High School, one of the first things you'll notice is tables arranged for groups of students to face each other. According to Principal Matt Bristow-Smith, "Seating arrangements matter. How we learn is as important as what we learn, and we learn by doing." Grouped tables help facilitate collaborative dialogue and problem-solving, which are essential skills on display during the Fall semester STEM Challenge.

At the start of the 2018–19 school year, a box of supplies awaited students at each table. Teachers introduced an engineering design process, then posed a problem: *We want you to build a desktop catapult. We're not going to tell you how…you and your team try to figure that out.* Bristow-Smith explained that, in a field where student creativity is often undervalued, students readily accept a challenge that requires different approaches to problem-solving. The six-week STEM challenge supported teams of students to communicate, collaborate, and think critically. Teams prepared their designs for the desktop catapult Olympics. Some projectiles flew across the room; others littered the ground beneath the launch site. All tests—successful or not—were recorded with detailed diagrams, measurements, and mathematical equations to demonstrate the underlying physics.

Next, classes analyzed the results from desktop trials to design a full-sized catapult. Students integrated successful features of desktop

> designs and then drafted them at scale on graph paper. Based on these plans, classes generated a materials list and calculated a budget, which they put to the test on a field trip to Lowe's. Supplies in hand, students worked with a guest carpenter and the engineering crew from a local automotive company, Keihin Corporation, to bring their designs to life. These expert community partners guided learning by helping students think through modifications to their designs, check angles, and use power tools safely. All the while, teachers monitored to ensure teams of students stayed focused, resolved conflicts, and worked collaboratively toward their outcomes. On catapult launch day, the joy was palpable as models were put to the final test.

five-year program with a high school diploma. Over 90% also graduated the program with an associate degree in arts or sciences (compared to roughly half of Cooperative Innovation High Schools students across the state),[28] and the remaining (8%) graduated with an industry-relevant certification.

Based on these successes, Bristow-Smith has consulted with additional district leadership teams to expand project-based learning to additional campuses, including efforts in the North Edgecombe Innovation Zone described later in the report.

Spanish Language Immersion Programs

Launched to transform a chronically underperforming middle school into a K-8 global school in 2014–15, the Spanish language immersion program is another example of district leaders introducing an innovative learning model to expand educational opportunity and accelerate academic improvement. Superintendent Farrelly strategically staffed Martin Millennium Academy with ambitious, equity-driven leaders who engaged in a design process to realize the district's vision of providing a global education to students and families in a small, rural community.

Superintendent Farrelly opened the first language immersion program in 2014–15 as a turnaround strategy, with the goal of transforming a middle school in crisis into a global learning center. Jennifer Craddock, Global Coordinator and founding staff member of Martin Millennium Academy, recalled that Superintendent Farrelly "knew that he needed to make a change. This was a failing middle school. A charter school had opened in our district, and we were losing a lot of scholars," roughly 700 in the past 3 years.[29] Farrelly's first challenge was to build a team up for the task: he promoted Craddock—a successful English language arts teacher with 18 years in the district under her belt—to Global Coordinator. He recruited outside the district to hire a school leader with a proven track record of success to serve as founding principal of the new K-8 global learning center. He hired Erin Swanson, who now coaches school leaders across the district as Assistant Superintendent of Innovation and Strategic Planning.

This new team followed a design thinking process to establish the instructional aims and community support for the new academy. Craddock reported that, together, campus staff and district administrators visited schools with established Spanish language immersion programs in neighboring districts to "see global schools in action, the success of the immersion program, and the benefits of the bilingual brain." Moreover, they brought along parents, teachers, and staff, who campaigned to establish a Spanish language immersion program in ECPS to revitalize the district's academic standing. Craddock said that the intensive redesign paid off:

> We shut down the former school and transformed it into the new K-8 Martin Millennium Academy. That was a huge overhaul. It was a successful one, but I mean, it was huge, literally changing the whole look of this school.

The Spanish Dual Language Immersion instructional model, which begins in kindergarten, establishes the foundations for bilingualism by age eight. Instruction focuses on fostering interpersonal, intercultural, and linguistic skills, in addition to growth mindsets in and beyond school. Global themes and project-based inquiry are integrated across subjects.[30] Principal Kelly Anne Mudd reported that K-5 homerooms are assigned a regional focus: for example, third-grade students explore Africa through a curriculum focused on literature by African authors and math or science activities anchored in the culture and histories of African peoples. Through a partnership with Participate Learning, school leaders recruit and hire international ambassador teachers at each grade level on three-year contracts from countries including Chile, Columbia, Costa Rica, Ecuador, Honduras, and Jamaica. Instructional teams form "global committees" that meet monthly to lesson plan, with support from campus leaders and an online resource bank also managed by district partner, Participate Learning.

As of 2023, Martin Millennium Academy remains the only K-8 global school in North Carolina. Principal Mudd reported, "We don't screen students. There are no qualifications other than that you live in Edgecombe County and you have a desire to be at MMA." Admission is open to all children in ECPS, including those with special behavioral and academic needs, on a first-come basis. The district provides transportation for all students who attend. Martin Millennium serves approximately 700 students. The school serves 69% Black students, 24% White students, 7% Latino/a students, and 70% students from low-income households.[31] From its launch in

2014–15 to 2018–2019, Martin Millennium Academy improved its North Carolina performance rating from an F to a C.[32]

Accelerated Learning

In response to widespread educational disruption, W. A. Pattillo Middle School Principal Lauren Lampron spearheaded a strategy to accelerate learning by expanding access to grade-level content and robust enrichment, rather than restricting the instructional focus on remediation. Through creative adjustments to the master schedule, Lampron and her faculty created routine student-directed flexible blocks for extended learning and extracurricular activities. Popular with both students and faculty, the model became a mainstay of the learning environment at W. A. Pattillo Middle School and has also expanded to additional ECPS campuses.

When the 2016–17 flood displaced over 90 of the 270 students enrolled at W. A. Pattillo Middle School, Principal Lauren Lampron and her staff recognized a need to accelerate student learning to recover lost instructional time. They launched a strategy called POWER blocks, an acronym for Plan, Organize, Work, Eat, and Relax. POWER blocks are periods of student-directed flexible time for extended learning and enrichment. During this time, students choose an activity from a fixed menu of clubs, tutoring opportunities, and content-focused study halls. Lampron reported that POWER blocks "make [school] more of a college atmosphere" where students are empowered to "go where you need assistance." She continued, "[We're] trying to make kids see that they're in charge of their own learning and they can take ownership for that."

Walking the halls during a POWER block, you might see a handful of students in one classroom walking through their problem-solving strategies for a mathematics standard, a larger group gathered at lunch tables to share and revise draft papers for an English language arts assignment, and yet another group practicing meditation on a sunny landing. Lampron reported that, in addition to extended focus on grade-level content, "kids are doing everything from mindfulness and Yoga to learning Japanese to going to Stocks Elementary to read to the elementary school students."

When asked what made POWER blocks possible at W. A. Pattillo Middle School, Lampron reported that the first hurdle was finding the time: she poured over the master schedule, ultimately deciding that a longer, more directed lunch period would provide greater access to accelerated learning than after-school programming. Principal Bristow-Smith, who adopted POWER blocks three days a week at Edgecombe Early College, explained the significance of this equity play for his students:

> Two years ago, a light bulb went off for me where we were clearly not being equitable in what we did, and we changed it. We had all our clubs

and enrichment after school. [The] 40% of our students who ride a bus weren't able to engage in after-school extracurricular activities, which meant that they missed that opportunity while everybody else stayed after and did clubs. So, we pivoted, and we built in a [POWER block] schedule every other week on Wednesday, Thursday, Friday. That has been a game changer for us in terms of inclusion, belonging, self-efficacy and student agency.

The second design hurdle was staffing the flexible learning time—unlike more passive traditional lunch duty, staffing POWER blocks involves active engagement with groups of self-directed students. Lampron and her team designed a rotation of teachers and instructional leaders on faculty to support POWER blocks based, in part, on routine analysis of formative instructional data by teachers and students. While students can be assigned to a particular POWER activity by their teachers, all students are encouraged to set and achieve goals for the accelerated learning time. School leaders collect and review student interest through biweekly surveys. For example, Principal Bristow-Smith sends a survey for Edgecombe Early College students to select their focus every two weeks, which he then breaks down into rosters for lead teachers. He acknowledged that it is "a ton of work," but that embedding this student-directed time during the school day has "been a game-changer for us" that expands educational opportunity. Former Principal of North Edgecombe High Donnell Cannon reported that he engaged in a similar process each week. He pointed to everyday requests from students owning their learning process as a clear marker of success:

It's super cool. I actually just got an email at like 8:30 that says, "Good Morning Mr. Cannon, I was emailing you about my POWER schedule for this week. We have robotics for POWER every day this week and I can't keep up every day knowing I have regular classwork to catch up on either end." So basically, she's requesting that instead of having so many days committed to robotics if she could scale back on robotics so she could push back into more standards labs on her schedule for her core courses.

A district educator explained that POWER blocks are an equity strategy that expands educational opportunity:

One of the premises that we operate on is the idea that it's not the achievement gap, it's the opportunity gap. So, everything that we do, every lens that we look through is: "What opportunity can we provide our kids so that they have the same accesses as students in other communities have?" We talk about, "how do we use POWER [blocks] to build up their passions and give them opportunity to explore different passions that they may not otherwise be able to explore?"

Social and Emotional Learning

Motivated by a desire to meaningfully engage students and disrupt cycles of exclusionary discipline, ECPS leaders and community members committed the district to "Revisit and revise the ECPS Code of Conduct and other school and district policies and procedures to ensure alignment with restorative, accountable, and trauma-informed practices" in the *Futures Reimagined* strategic plan. Beginning in 2017, Superintendent Bridges began a design cycle focused on supporting social-emotional learning in district schools and classrooms. Teams of district and school leaders have pursued funding and partnerships to implement trauma-informed and restorative practices, which are changing classroom experiences.

Rural Opportunity Institute co-founder Vichi Jagannathan, a district partner and member of the BRC, described the problem leaders set out to address: "Black children getting wrapped up in repetitive, drawn-out, punitive experiences from a very young age. It's an incredibly large pain point." She reported that the underlying causes are "not that simple. [It] has to do with policies, tradition…so many layers and people touching the process, it might not even be up to any one person. Disentangling all of that is a massive challenge," which she characterized as "the beast of making any systemic shift." Assistant Superintendent of Innovation and Strategic Planning Erin Swanson reported that the district strategy to support trauma-informed and restorative practices starts with the adults. She explained, "The idea is: this is about you and your reaction to the kids…this isn't actually about the kids. We need to train the grownups."

Then Director of Student Support Services Dr. Charlene Pittman reported that restorative mindsets "existed in pockets," and the first implementation challenge facing district leaders was to "make it a systemic conversation." Pittman explained the need to bring in expertise, which can stretch the budget of a small, rural district: "for us, [it's] the financial aspect: how do we, as a small LEA, connect with an organization who can help us with the heavy lift so that the work is done very effectively to help us navigate those conversations?" ECPS leaders partnered synergistically with the Public School Forum of North Carolina, Central Carolina Regional Education Service Alliance, and Rural Opportunity Institute to provide data analyses and professional development to deepen restorative and trauma-informed teaching practices.

Under Bridges' leadership in August 2017, ECPS joined seven other districts in a pilot hosted by the Public School Forum of North Carolina. The North Carolina Resilience & Learning Project focused on expanding educational opportunity by increasing educator awareness of the impact of adverse childhood experiences on student learning, improving trauma-sensitive learning environments and approaches to student discipline, and coordinating services among schools and social services.[33] Through this partnership, Public Schools Forum provided ongoing technical assistance at W. A. Pattillo Middle School and Stocks Elementary School to form multifunctional Resilience Teams comprised of principals, student services staff, and classroom teachers. With support, these Resilience Teams reviewed school-based data and developed action plans for integrating trauma-sensitive strategies across their campus. Leaders and staff received in-depth professional development and a project coach to support implementation through observation, problem-solving emergent challenges, and connecting with other participating schools. Over the course of two years, the Resilience Teams enacted trauma-sensitive strategies including restorative discipline practices, mindfulness breaks, self-care initiatives for staff, and school-wide self-regulation messaging for students.

Joint analysis of district-wide disciplinary data from 2014–15 to 2017–18 conducted by the Rural Opportunity Institute and Stanford Center for Education Policy Analysis found that just 30 students per school accounted for 58% of elementary referrals (of about 500 total students), and 30 students (of about 400 total students) per school accounted for 64% of middle school referrals.[34] Referrals were highest among males and in 6th and 9th grade transition years, when students move to a new school. In 2018, 50 ECPS educators attended a 2-day resilience training hosted by the Rural Opportunity Institute and funded by the North Carolina Department of Public Instruction. Jagannathan reported that the training supported educators to recognize how children express stress and change responses "from being punitive, isolating, or judgmental to one that's more validating" through a process that "recognizes your own biases as an adult and seeks to respond to it in a more equitable way" (Box 2.3).

Box 2.3   Restorative Practices in Action at W. A. Pattillo Middle School

Through a schoolwide initiative to implement restorative practices, W. A. Pattillo Middle School Principal Lauren Lampron sees learning opportunities in every interaction. "We're looking at behaviors and what we're realizing, as a staff, is that kids just don't have the skills [to resolve conflict]." So, what do educators do? "We're modeling that as adults."

Lampron recalled an incident in the hallway where a student, overcome by emotion, hurled her Gatorade bottle against a wall. The explosion turned heads. She reflected on how she might have responded in the old way of doing business, "as a principal, I would have had to come up with some severe consequence because all of these people saw that incident in a public space." Instead, she held a restorative conversation with the child who threw the bottle, two additional kids who witnessed it, custodial staff, the classroom teacher, and another responding administrator. She ushered this group through a structured series of questions, including: What are the facts? What do you think of what happened? How are we going to fix the harm that was caused? Lampron reported that the power of the process is its ability to surface solutions. The student reflected on her own feeling of overwhelm, noting, "I just feel like I need additional support while I'm going there. Once I'm there, I can't get back down. I think it would be best if you guys could figure out how to help me before I get there." They decided on using a code word derived from her least favorite flavor: "Cucumber Gatorade," or CG for short.

A short time later, Lampron observed the same student leave a mess behind in her classroom. She recognized it as an opportunity to exercise greater self-awareness. Walking over, she said, "I'm coming to CG." The student paused, then responded, "Okay, I'm prepared. What is it?" With just a gentle reminder, the student returned and cleaned the space, saying cheerfully, "I'm trying to keep it together!" These small moments of de-escalation, built on authentic and supportive relationships, are the proof points for restorative practices in W. A. Pattillo Middle School.

The emergent work to implement restorative practices had promising pre-pandemic results. Between 2014 and 2015 and 2019 and 2020, the total number of short-term suspensions decreased by nearly 50%, from 2,534 to 1,307 (Table 2.6). After the pandemic year (2020–21), when school closures depressed suspension rates, the trajectory increased higher than the rates in 2019–20. The vast majority of suspensions were issued to Black students, who comprise roughly 60% of the population.

District leaders continue to monitor these data and efforts to spread, scale, and systematize restorative practices into district policy and procedures. In 2018, then Director of Student Support Services Pittman traveled with a team of district administrators and school-based leaders to a two-day development session on revising district discipline codes to reduce recidivism and improve learning cultures and climates, organized by the Central Carolina Regional Education Service Alliance and facilitated by Carol Lieber.[35] Upon return, she replicated activities from the trainings in monthly district leadership team meetings. After returning from pandemic closures, Student Support Services Director Dr. Chanda Battle launched a yearlong process of working with parents, students, and community

Table 2.6 Edgecombe County Public Schools Short-term Suspension Actions (Count), 2014–15 to 2021–22, by Racial/Ethnic Group

Race/ethnicity	2014–15	2015–16	2016–17	2017–18	2018–19	2019–20	2020–21	2021–22
American Indian/ Alaska Native	0	0	0	0	0	0	1	0
Black	2,001	1,736	1,363	1,208	1,187	1,051	51	1,384
Latino/a	65	92	56	73	64	49	1	62
Multiracial	68	50	62	66	38	33	3	63
White	388	347	297	266	243	174	16	286
Total	2,534	2,227	1,779	1,614	1,533	1,307	72	1,800

Source: North Carolina Department of Public Instruction. Discipline, ALP, and Dropout Annual Reports. (accessed 7/2023) https://www.dpi.nc.gov/data-reports/dropout-and-discipline-data/discipline-alp-and-dropout-annual-reports#2020-21-4402

members to redevelop the district Code of Conduct. This process involved unpacking exclusionary data and empathy listening sessions to understand patterns of exclusion and alternative responses to disengagement. In 2021, the Board of Education adopted a new Code of Character, Conduct, and Support (available in the Online Materials Package). Swanson reported that "having a better policy in place is a step in the right direction." District leaders are now building the capacity of their educators to effectively implement the new code by developing training and support for teachers, administrators, and counselors to intervene in other ways.

Developing Staff Capacity

While ECPS is a major employer in the area, the district had a 20% rate of teacher turnover from 2006 to 2018.[36] When she first came to ECPS as an assistant superintendent, Bridges described feeling shocked by how the staffing needs differed from those encountered during her prior experience in a better-resourced school district near the state capital:

> Coming to Edgecombe, I had the feeling of, "Oh my god!" I mean, I hadn't experienced this. I knew poverty. Poverty in Wake County is not poverty in Eastern North Carolina. That's not the same kind of poverty. The things that would be appalling to me: I raised two children in Wake County public schools, and there was never a day when we had back-to-school teacher [meetings] where my children did not have the teacher in the classroom. Here, that happens. There's a long-term sub. I've had kids who, for two years in a row, have not

had a certified teacher because we couldn't find one. That was unheard of in Wake County.

Then Superintendent Farrelly harnessed staff turnover as part of his turnaround plan by hiring leaders and teachers invested in the strategic vision of more equitable opportunities and outcomes for ECPS students. Dr. Valerie Bridges was among those hires and continued to develop staff capacity in her role as superintendent. One challenge is the lack of competitive compensation: in the State of North Carolina, all teachers receive the same base pay with a local supplement based on the tax base of their school districts.[37] Under Dr. Bridges' leadership, former Director of Innovation Erin Swanson reported that ECPS leaders continued to leverage the district's commitment to innovation—anchored in the shared equity values of *Futures Reimagined*—to both attract educators and to design more personalized professional development that "breaks barriers" to serving the best interest of students:

> For us, it has historically been very challenging to recruit and retain great educators. As you can see, we're not situated in a major metropolitan area. It's an hour, hour-and-a-half drive to the triangle [of Raleigh, Durham, and Chapel Hill]. What we can afford to pay teachers is definitely not on par with some of the wealthier areas here in our state. All those things are challenging. We've really had to work hard on recruitment and retention, and I think the connection in innovation is one of the reasons we've been able to recruit and retain some of the talent that we have. Like me, people want to work in a place where they can do things differently, where they can take risks, where they feel they're empowered. Again, this is a place where I think people generally feel that. I work to support our principals and our school leaders. I see my role as the barrier breaker: let me help ease the path for you to do what you feel like you need to do for kids. That's a top priority.

District leaders developed a strategy to tackle the challenge of attracting and retaining teachers and school leaders who improve academic achievement, social-emotional habits, and school culture. This strategy, outlined in Priority 2: Talent Recruitment and Development of the *Futures Reimagined* strategic plan, includes five actions (Table 2.7). [38]

Taken together, these components outline a theory of action district leaders are advancing to develop staff capacity in ECPS: first, recruit and hire educators committed to transforming educational opportunities for district learners, and second, retain effective educators through personalized professional development and high-impact teacher leadership positions.

Table 2.7 Edgecombe County Public Schools Strategic Plan Priority 2, Talent Recruitment and Development

2.1	Institutions of higher education partnerships	Establish and strengthen partnerships with local institutions of higher education to increase the number and diversity of teacher and school administrator interns and new hires. Place specific emphasis on recruiting males and educators of color.
2.2	Educator retention	Retain educators by evaluating and redesigning our incentive structures and retention strategies. Develop and implement specific strategies for retaining educators of color.
2.3	Growing Edgecombe's own	Using the Scholar Teachers program as a model, partner with career and technical education and Edgecombe Community College to develop a robust Teacher Cadet program at all ECPS high schools. Develop a similar program to recruit promising ECPS educators to become administrators.
2.4	Personalized professional development	Develop and implement personalized professional development pathways and job-embedded coaching for teachers, teacher leaders, administrators, and teacher assistants that address all key aspects of their roles.
2.5	Opportunity culture teacher leadership	Continue investing in Opportunity Culture roles—Multi-Classroom Leaders, Expanded Impact Teachers, and Reach Associates—to increase the number of students with access to an excellent teacher each year.

Source: Edgecombe County Public Schools (n.d.). *ECPS strategic plan: Futures reimagined.* https://www.ecps.us/apps/pages/index.jsp?uREC_ID=1689715&type=d&pREC_ID=1847182 (accessed 7/31/2023).

Recruitment and Hiring

Attracting talent is a major challenge for district leaders in a rural district with limited housing and long commutes. Former Assistant Superintendent of Curriculum and Instruction Abbey Futrell reported, "In Edgecombe, we don't have anything extra to draw people here. To let them fall in love with being here, we have to get them here first. That's been a struggle for us." To broaden the pipeline of teachers and leaders entering ECPS, district leaders have established and invested in purposeful partnerships with Edgecombe Community College, North Carolina State University, and Teach for America, described further in this section.

Through both initiatives, ECPS leaders aim to strengthen the pipeline of teachers and leaders from Edgecombe County and the surrounding region, who are knowledgeable about and invested in the district's equity vision, assets, and challenges. Former North Edgecombe High School Principal Donnell Cannon likened his hiring efforts to grassroots organizing:

> One thing I love, especially on the northside, is seeing talent recruitment as a form of grassroot organizing. We're bringing talented individuals who are willing to do something really big and broad for kids and harnessing our communal energy and talent in pursuit of that big goal.

When asked about their hiring priorities, district and school leaders reported that their primary focus is on equity mindsets. *Futures Reimagined* states, "To realize our vision, we must employ people in every position who possess the dispositions necessary to excel in their roles, who are deeply committed to our ideals, and who are lifelong learners." Superintendent Valerie Bridges explained that the district uses behavioral interview questions to screen for mindsets by asking candidates to describe their analysis of and approach to challenging situations in schools and classrooms. She reported that this helps ensure educators harness collective efficacy to drive improvement, rather than leading the charge alone:

> If you continue to hire people who don't have an equity mindset, you'll be pushing forever alone. As people transition or move, when I'm selecting, that's what I'm looking for. It doesn't mean you don't want to get [staff with] content knowledge or certain [skills], but I need you to have that equity mindset, because, if I'm the only person thinking about it, it's not going to be realized and it's exhausting.

Likewise, school leaders screen for equity mindsets in school-based hiring efforts. Edgecombe Early College Principal Matt Bristow-Smith reported, "I've hired half of our teaching staff over the last five years, [during which time] we've developed an institutional understanding of how we do things. I hire based on values." He continued, specifying that a belief in the capabilities of students in ECPS was paramount to specialized content knowledge, which he can support staff to develop over time: "We all believe the same thing here about kids. The particular teaching pedagogies or the professional development all folds in with what we all agree about kids."

Indeed, results from the 2022 North Carolina Teacher Working Conditions Survey indicate that ECPS educators share a common equity-oriented mission.[39] When asked if the district had a clearly defined mission and vision for all schools, 100% of ECPS respondents agreed. Over 90% agreed that teachers are held to high professional standards for delivering instruction, that teachers believe what is taught will make a difference in students' lives, and that their school emphasizes showing respect for all students' cultural beliefs and practices. In order to recruit and hire staff with these shared beliefs, ECPS leaders have led efforts to strengthen both their teacher and leader pipelines, described next.

Strengthening the Teacher Pipeline

In ECPS, the leadership approach to strengthening the teacher pipeline involved ushering long-term stability while also contingency planning for the district's high staff turnover. In the words of Superintendent Bridges:

> A lot of times, in school systems, we don't have a backup plan. If some-thing happens and that one irreplaceable teacher leaves, we don't know what to do… Instead, we have to figure out multiple ways forward, so that we have a backup plan. This is why we have Teach for America and Scholar teachers coming. Some would say, "Well, you're doing too much." But I'm like a mama. If I don't do enough, what happens then, right?

District and school leaders reported that the decades-long partnership be-tween ECPS and Teach For America, a lateral-entry fellowship program that enables the district to hire uncertified teachers who obtain professional licensure as they teach, has both helped to fill annual vacancies and also contributed to the high rate of teacher turnover. Principals recognized the short-term benefit of this program, placing passionate and dedicated teach-ers in vacant positions for two-year contracts. However, consistent with national research on teacher preparation and attrition,[40] principals also re-ported that fellows were more likely to leave at the end of their two-year contract than full-time teachers who received more comprehensive preser-vice preparation through a regular certification program. District leaders named both high rates of turnover and the presence of lateral entry teachers as rationale for major investments in long-term, high-retention strategies to attract teachers into the district. These include a grow-your-own Scholar Teachers program that covers college tuition for ECPS graduates to return to teach in the district, in addition to personalized professional development pathways and differentiated staffing models described later in this section.

Starting in 2015, district leaders engaged in a design cycle, grounded in the district's graduate aims, to build an internal pipeline of ECPS gradu-ates able to return to the district and teach. In the words of then Board of Education Chair Rev. Raymond Privott, the rationale for the program was to grow their own:

> These kids who grew up in the county know the county, know the school system, they benefited from it. If we can entice them, if we can grow our

own, and encourage them to come back by paying that tuition, then we have a direct pipeline of home-grown educators.[41]

The district formed a team, comprised of district cabinet members, Edgecombe Early College Principal Matthew Bristow-Smith, and National Board-Certified teacher and ECPS graduate Leigh Ann Webb, who was recruited to direct the program and honored in 2019 as ECPS Teacher of the Year. This leadership team studied the effective North Carolina Teaching Fellows program, which pays all college costs in return for several years of teaching,[42] as a blueprint for designing a district equivalent. They decided to house the Scholar Teachers program at Edgecombe Early College to leverage the existing partnership with Edgecombe Community College and enable participants to graduate with a two-year associate degree.

The Scholar Teacher program enables high school students interested in teaching to complete all prerequisite courses and requirements for entry into the College of Education at partnering state universities and provides a college scholarship if they commit to returning to ECPS to teach.[43] Students enter the program as rising high school juniors, build a portfolio of coursework and over 200 internship hours with a mentor teacher, and graduate with a high school diploma and two-year associate degree (Box 2.4). Webb designed the curriculum to introduce the basics of teaching through topics that include understanding the North Carolina standards, creating trust in your classroom, lesson plan design, student tracking and assessment, and differentiated instruction.[44] Bristow-Smith reported that the design of the program is meant to provide participants the opportunity to explore a career in teaching while also forming relationships with district students and faculty that may inspire them to return.

Box 2.4   Scholar Teachers Model

1. **Rigorous selection process.** Candidates complete a competitive application, personal interview, and academic testing process to gain admission to the Scholar Teachers Program, which is located at Edgecombe Early College High School.
2. **Challenging Pre-College Coursework.** Scholar Teachers complete four pre-service courses—Teacher Cadet 1, 2, 3, and 4—in addition to 25–50 hours of college credit.
3. **Site-Based Internships.** Each Scholar Teacher completes over 200 internship hours working with a cooperating mentor teacher at Martin Millennium Academy, Pattillo Middle School, or Princeville Elementary.

4. **College and Scholarship Support.** Scholar Teachers will receive personalized support through the college application and scholarship process from the Early College Staff. The classroom and field experiences as Scholar Teachers will make them highly competitive candidates.
5. **Student Teaching.** Scholar Teachers may complete their clinical teaching experiences in Edgecombe County Public Schools, thus positioning themselves for a seamless transition into their careers.
6. **Entering the Profession.** Scholar Teachers will be at the top of our hiring list in Edgecombe County, filling key vacancies and generating an immediate "return on investment."
7. **Beginning Teacher Support.** As new teachers in ECPS, Scholar Teachers will be supported through our Beginning Teacher Support Program and our Opportunity Culture System.
8. **Giving Back through Service.** Scholar Teachers return to Edgecombe County to work, live, and give back to the community. They make a lasting difference in the lives of thousands of students for years to come.

Source: Urquart, M. and McNeill, C. (March 23, 2022). *Education NC.* Edgecombe's Scholar Teachers program looks forward to first cohort of teachers coming home this fall. https://www.ednc.org/edgecombes-scholar-teachers-program-looks-forward-to-first-cohort-of-teachers-coming-home-this-fall/

Before the ambitious Scholar Teachers program could open its doors, the leadership team had to tackle the challenge of funding the new coursework and scholarships. ECPS leaders established a $501(c)(3)$ nonprofit foundation to process program donations, and Superintendent Bridges reported that the district plans to build a $2 million endowment to perpetually fund program scholarships. Leaders leveraged the board of education and partners in the BRC to garner community support and fundraise. The Barnhill Family Foundation, the first investors in the Scholar Teachers program, also provided funding for a full-time director to staff the ECPS Educational Foundation. The director, Arlane Gordon-Bray, is charged with raising funds for the Scholar Teachers program and other innovative programming for ECPS.

Quoted in an article for *Education NC*, Bristow-Smith reported,

We've gotten a tremendous amount of support from local businesses, from the corporate community, and from the philanthropic community.

We've also gotten a tremendous amount of support from our board of education and from individuals in the community who all share one common thread, and that is they care about the quality of education in our community.[45]

The same article quoted local donors and ECPS parents, Ricky and Kay Thompson, describing what investing in the Scholar Teachers program means to them:

"When you're part of a community, you want your school system to succeed," said Ricky. "This is just a great way to get kids we have here in town to stay here in town." "I have two of my children living here," Kay added. "One day, the very people who are going through this program may be standing up in the classroom with my little grandchildren sitting in the desk or on the carpet or in the circle."

In this way, the Scholar Teachers program instantiates district leaders' vision for enacting a widespread commitment to improving life in Edgecombe County that extends beyond a typical preschool-to-grade-12 framework. By leveraging the early college partnership with Edgecombe Community College, effective and experienced instructional leaders, and grassroots fundraising with a broad slate of community stakeholders, ECPS leaders created a supportive pathway for students to graduate, obtain a teaching credential, and return to teach in the district. Leaders at the Edgecombe Early College launched the inaugural cohort of the Scholars Teachers program in the school year 2015–16. The program has served roughly 12 students annually. ECPS welcomed its first program graduates back into the district in Fall 2022–23, and by January 2024 the district employed five program graduates, three of whom were Black and two White. By January 2024, the Scholar Teachers program supported a total of 19 aspiring teachers, a majority of whom were students of color (eight Black and six Latino/a).[46]

Strengthening the Leadership Pipeline

In the face of high leadership turnover rates, ECPS leaders invested to cultivate strong, committed school leaders who can provide stability and continuity to advance racial equity. Edgecombe Early College Principal Bristow-Smith, who has served in the district for more than two decades, credited the consistent leadership of long-term district employees with sustaining the equity efforts in ECPS, "We are a district that's seen a lot of transformation, and with that, you see the innovation occurring. […] Long-term change requires sustainability and people who are in positions to see their visions carry through." To strengthen the leadership pipeline, superintendents Farrelly and Bridges (1) partnered with Northeast Leadership Academy to equip and promote school leaders within the district and (2) leveraged the innovative, equity-oriented learning culture to recruit experienced and effective leaders into ECPS. These efforts appear to have paid off: in 2021–22, 70% of principals in ECPS served in their role for more than three years, compared to just 7% in 2015–16.[47]

Since 2010, ECPS has participated in the Northeast Leadership Academy, a program through North Carolina State University designed to develop highly skilled school leaders in a consortium of 13 rural, high-need school districts.[48] ECPS leaders support staff to apply, who then undergo a rigorous selection process. Participants receive a full scholarship, paid internships, and materials and technology expenses to earn a North Carolina school principal license and Master of School Administration degree. All program graduates make a commitment to lead in high-need schools in northeast North Carolina for a minimum of three years.

District staff reported that graduates from the Northeast Leadership Academy "saturate" ECPS leadership teams. Indeed, most schools have one or more leaders that have entered through this pipeline. Bristow-Smith, who graduated from the Northeast Leadership Academy in 2014, emphasized the importance of the program's equity focus on how leadership teams advance equity in ECPS:

> The truth is that the [Northeast Leadership Academy] has a real commitment to issues of equity. Part of our masters involves social justice and racial equity training. [It means] that we now have a large cadre of the administrators across our district that believe the same things about the roles of school, particularly in rural counties like ours.

Graduates of the Northeast Leadership Academy reported infusing their equity orientation, which is focused on learning conditions in the rural northeast, through ongoing work with their campus leadership teams. Principal Cannon reported, "I still talk about equity and implicit biases at a real level in my school. Having that training, I know how to facilitate similar conversations so that we're checking our blind spots collectively."

In addition to cultivating internal pathways to leadership, Farrelly and Bridges established and modeled a leadership culture that attracts experienced and effective leaders into the ECPS. Reflecting on her collaboration with North Edgecombe High School Principal Donnell Cannon in the Innovation Zone, former Phillips Middle School Principal Jenny O'Meara reported:

> I think it's worth noting that we were recruited to come here. I don't think either of us would have chosen to apply to come here if the previous

superintendent hadn't leveraged connections to reach out to us, and so I think there's also this level of feeling valued with knowing we recruited you because we want you and we value you as a whole human. I feel that.

District staff reported that trusting and affirming relationships are foundational to the leadership culture. Principal Cannon explained, "my colleagues, the people I work with every day, closely understand that identity is important to the work we're doing." He added that authenticity is modeled all the way from the district leadership team to his work with students:

> Farrelly was a pretty charismatic guy with wild hair. He was different from every other superintendent I'd met. He was himself, and I was like, "Yep, I'm coming. He's allowed to do that, so certainly no one's going to put a shield up against me." And then [Dr. Bridges] is the same way. She talks about things that matter to her. […] That saturates the culture. It helps satiate my own desire to run towards the things that matter to me. Seeing someone else do it gives me permission, and I'd hope the same thing for our building. That [I give] permission to my teachers to live in that way. […] From a racial equity perspective, I don't feel like I have to shed my identity [to be] the archetype principal. I don't feel crunched into whatever the fantasies are that other people have for me. I don't crush kids into the fantasy that we have for them.

In this way, equity mindsets in ECPS extend beyond a screener item on a hiring checklist; district and school leaders continuously model and develop identity-safe, trusting, and authentic relationships within and across campus teams. ECPS leaders recruit, promote, and support campus leaders to enact their vision of expanding educational opportunity and success in ECPS.

Retention and Professional Development

When Superintendent Bridges assumed the mantle of district leadership in 2017–2018, she saw a need to retain the effective educators that were essential to the district turnaround work that was underway. She said of the ambitious goals set in *Futures Reimagined*, "I can't do it without the teachers. I can't." Superintendent Bridges initiated a two-pronged strategy to develop and retain excellent educators, leading to major investments in (1) personalized professional learning pathways aligned to the Instructional Framework for Learning and (2) the implementation of new, high-impact teacher leadership positions.

Research has shown that access to professional development opportunities, especially teacher-led learning and coaching among colleagues, positively affects teacher retention.[49] Over time, these investments have fostered greater stability in district schools. For example, then Principal of West Edgecombe Middle School Claude Archer reported that he entered his role in 2014–15 with 60% teacher turnover on staff from the prior year.[50] By 2019, he retained roughly 90% of his staff from the prior year. Archer credited that change to increasing teacher leadership: "My teachers know that, when they enter this building, they are going to be put in a position to lead. There is no micromanagement." On the 2022 North Carolina Teacher Working Conditions Survey, 84% of district-wide respondents agreed that teachers are recognized as educational experts, 83% agreed that teachers are trusted to make sound professional decisions about instruction, and 91% agreed that teachers are encouraged to participate in school leadership roles. When asked about district strategies that have strengthened teacher leadership, district and school leaders reported rethinking their approaches to professional learning and school staffing.

Professional Development

As a district dedicated to embracing innovation as a learning organization, ECPS leaders allocate time and resources to improving classroom teachers' instructional practice. Cassandra Cherry, a former teacher leader at Phillips Middle, reported that district staff takes a proactive response to instructional knowledge gaps. Cherry coached members of her math and science team with a focus on developing effective and equitable instructional strategies: "We're going to figure out, for all our students, what strategies work for them and get them where they need to be."

As part of their work to design the Instructional Framework for Learning in 2017–18, the Curriculum and Instruction team developed a robust suite of aligned coaching and professional learning services.[51] Former Assistant Superintendent of Curriculum and Instruction Abbey Futrell reported that time constraints posed a challenge to teachers accessing professional learning:

> We're short on people. We're even shorter on time. If we were to rely on traditional face-to-face PD, teachers would be at school until 6:00 because you have to wait for every [school] to dismiss. So, what we're looking at now are those personalized pieces. You can't stick everybody on an online course. Some teachers don't do well with an independent micro-credentialing type. What we're looking at now is: how do we personalize and roll out a professional development so teachers can get what they need?

To address the time constraints, the Curriculum and Instruction team shifted from a traditional model of sit-and-get professional learning toward more personalized pathways. Each year, campus leaders support every teacher to develop a professional development plan, which identifies a focused set of instructional skills to advance throughout the year. Futrell explained that these plans, which are aligned to the Instructional Framework for Learning, serve as a "roadmap" for professional learning experiences that engage teachers in routine practitioner learning communities, after-school and early release development days, and online modules. Throughout the year, leaders on the Curriculum and Instruction team coach and support teachers' professional learning using the new walk-through rubric described earlier in this report. The full suite of professional learning experiences includes:[52]

- teacher talk sessions throughout the year with training specifically tailored for beginning teachers;
- one-on-one coaching, during which experienced educators help newer teachers hone their talent and build their careers;
- opportunities to work with school and district-based mentors in every ECPS school;
- support for teachers who want to pursue their National Board Certification; and
- district- and school-level professional development events focused on educator needs—from trauma-informed teaching to social-emotional learning.

Professional learning, like all priorities in *Futures Reimagined*, includes an explicit equity focus. Staff reported equity themes cut across the range of district-hosted professional learning sessions. For example, in 2017–18, teachers attended a training through the Sanders Institute focused on addressing opportunity gaps by engaging every student in grade-level instruction. In practitioner learning communities, K-8 mathematics teachers read about how implicit biases impact student learning and collaboratively planned equity-based interventions to ensure instruction develops student self-confidence and self-efficacy, and school counselors attended a SPARK training (Speaking to the Potential, Ability, & Resilience Inside Every Kid) on responding to adverse childhood experiences.

In addition to professional learning offerings, the Curriculum and Instruction team coordinates opportunities for campus leaders and staff to share and scale effective practices. In partnership with the Friday Institute, ECPS leaders host Amplify Day, a district-wide mini-conference that features campus teams presenting on practices related to personalized, trauma-informed, and project-based learning. School leaders reported that they exchange ideas and problem-solve continuously throughout the year. In the words of then Phillips Middle School Principal Jenny O'Meara:

It ends up being really powerful. There's a group of principals [who] all send out weekly newsletters every week, and we cc or forward our emails to each other, so I'm getting emails every week from Matt Smith at the Early College, Lauren Lampron at Pattillo, these people who do think really similarly and are doing really cool stuff at their school. I can be like, "Oh, that's really neat. I'm going to grab that."

Campus leaders reported that these peer-to-peer relationships fostered lateral learning and helped scale the whole child instructional practices described earlier in this report. Similarly, teachers described peer learning with teacher leaders, discussed next, to be a cornerstone of professional learning in ECPS.

Opportunity Culture

Another part of the strategy to retain effective educators in ECPS involved creating teacher leadership roles. In an interview with *Public Impact*,[53] Superintendent Bridges characterized the investments in teacher leadership as "common sense," explaining,

The last thing you want to do is [have] your star teacher feel like they have to become an administrator in order to move their career along. This is perfect: you can be a career teacher, make more money, have more impact with your staff and students, and still be able to stay in the classroom. That's what lots of people want to do, and that's what we want teachers to do.

In 2016, a leadership design team comprised of both school and district staff secured a grant from the North Carolina Department of Public Instruction to participate in the statewide Advanced Teaching Roles pilot.[54] Through this grant, ECPS joined five other North Carolina districts contracting with Public Impact to implement a multi-tiered staffing model called Opportunity Culture.[55] As district leaders developed a three-year rollout plan, they made an equity play by launching the new teacher leadership roles in the least-resourced schools on the north side of the district, as part of a newly designated "innovation zone" described further in the next section of the report.

Under the Opportunity Culture model, the design team developed new roles for the schools in North Edgecombe: Multi-Classroom Leaders receive higher pay to serve on the school's leadership team while co-planning, co-teaching, and coaching instructional teams of two to six teachers, while paraprofessional Reach Associates provide supervised instructional support and handle administrative classroom tasks.[56] Partners at Public Impact provide training to all Multi-Classroom Leaders, Reach Associates, and campus leadership teams on how to effectively coordinate and support instruction across multi-tiered roles. These trainings include leadership skills like cognitive coaching and managing team dynamics, in addition to developing data-driven instruction and corrective action plans in practitioner learning communities. School staff reported two major benefits of the new staffing model: highly effective teachers have greater impact, and less experienced teachers have more support.

The primary motivation for adopting the multi-tiered staffing model was to expand the impact of highly effective district teachers. Multi-Classroom Leaders serve as the teacher of record for all students across instructional teams. District leaders reported that this design feature fosters a sense of shared accountability for student outcomes. Superintendent Bridges explained,

> We're selecting teachers with a proven track record, we pay them a little extra, and they support other teachers in the school. They push in as needed to help those teachers get their instruction where it needs to be, and help students fill in [learning] gaps.

In this way, the teacher leader positions in Opportunity Culture opened a new avenue for career advancement in ECPS that focused on instructional skill. Superintendent Bridges reported that teacher leaders have shifted the leadership culture in district schools from an emphasis on behavioral interventions toward fostering classroom practices that engage students in meaningful instruction.

> A lot of times, principals don't know a particular subject area, so it's hard for them to speak to it. We focus on behavior that's not appropriate, rather than academics. You know, we can look at all those [behavioral outcomes], but how are you changing your classroom practices?

For example, Amy Pearce left an administrative role in the district to return to teaching as a Math Multi-Classroom Leader at Phillips Middle School. As she tells it:

> I was an administrator before I came into this role. I'd hit the point [where] I remember looking at Erin [Swanson] one day, and I was like, "Can I just help my teachers teach?" My frustration came because I was working in a school that didn't have a team of folks to help lead in specialty areas, and I couldn't be everything for everybody at one time. So, this [position] let me be that person... Not only does [Opportunity Culture] help retain teachers, but it helps retain leaders in schools,

which is critical because there was a lot of leadership change [in the North] side of the district.

Another motivation for adopting the new staffing model was supporting novice teachers to develop their instructional skills. Cassandra Cherry, a former Multi-Classroom Leader at Phillips Middle School, reported that the most impactful thing about the differentiated staffing model is the level of support available to instructional teams. She described what this increased level of support looked like in action:

> For example, I have a first-year teacher coming in having never taught this size group. Having someone there who's had experience, can help coach [her] in the right direction, and support [her] is probably going to be the most impactful thing to teachers in this profession. I think back to when I first started as a first-year teacher: there was no support, I was just kind of thrown in there, as a lateral entry teacher. Eventually, the support came along but…these roles allow us to support our teachers in a way, like, I've never seen in education.

In her third year teaching at North Edgecombe High School, Caroline Harris took on Biology as a new subject area. Harris reported that she was able to prioritize lesson planning because her direct supervisor, a Multi-Classroom Leader, spent time analyzing her student data into digestible and actionable reports. She explained:

> That was a huge relief off of my brain space. I can say very, very confidently: if I hadn't been in Edgecombe County and I'd just been a regular teacher, I for sure would have quit at the end of my third year just because I was so stressed out, like beyond stressed. [I might have felt] like I couldn't have any life, like I was working at a job where I was only failing because there were so many areas I was expected to succeed and so many hats I was expected to wear, but I couldn't wear them all. Just having that support, a teacher who had experience, who was there to coach me, who was there to help with some of that extra that I just didn't have the time for, that was huge.

Harris also credited the administrative support of a paraprofessional Reach Associate with further enabling her to focus on developing her instructional practice. She said,

> I was originally spending about two hours after school each Monday getting copies ready for the week, printing and stapling everything.

> Mrs. Williams does that for me now, and that's a huge relief. I just don't have that time, so that's huge.

District leaders first implemented Opportunity Culture through a three-year rollout in the North Edgecombe feeder pattern before expanding to additional schools in the district. Assistant Superintendent of Innovation and Strategic Planning Erin Swanson reported the importance of communicating the qualifications and responsibilities of Multi-Classroom Leaders to assuage staff concerns about differential pay:

> When we first implemented, there were a lot of questions around, "Well, why does this person now get this different job and this differential pay?" We were very intentional in the design process to communicate the purpose, expectations, and the qualifications for the Multi-Classroom Leader. And so, people understood why we are doing this, what this person has to do—this is actually a really big job—what they are responsible for, and how you can become qualified. You have to have data that show you move kids more than a year in a year, and [a behavioral interview that shows] you are ready to lead adults. Once people understood that, and we got through the first couple of years of implementation, we've had very little pushback. In fact, most of our teachers would say, "I don't know what I would do without my [Multi-Classroom Leader]."

Indeed, the model is working to retain high-quality educators in ECPS. Swanson reported that "retention of our multi-classroom leaders has been pretty incredible. Many of our multi-classroom leaders who started with us in the first three years of implementation are still with us, which is great." In 2021–22, 88% of ECPS teachers received a rating of "effective" or "highly effective" on the North Carolina Educator Evaluation System, based on measures of teacher leadership, respect for diverse populations of students, content knowledge, facilitation of learning, and reflection on their practice.[57] Superintendent Bridges reported that advanced teaching roles have been foundational to sustained academic growth in ECPS. In a 2021 interview with *Public Impact*,[58] she reported, "You don't exceed growth [targets] three years in a row by mistake." She characterized the extra effort as worthwhile: "Is it easy? No. Is it smart? We think so. Is it the right thing to do for our kids? When we look at our data, we know it is."

Based on the successes of the multi-tiered staffing model, district leaders scaled Opportunity Culture to 12 out of 15 district campuses by 2023–24. When asked about what makes the multi-tiered staffing model successful, Swanson reported the need to pair school-based agency with district-level support. In her words:

It's really critical that schools have the autonomy to design advanced teaching roles, approaches, or models that work best for their school. [And] you need leadership at the superintendent level that's supportive of the work, that understands the work, and is going to make sure that it's a priority in terms of funding and human capital.

In Fall of 2023, ECPS entered a redesign cohort with other North Carolina districts, led by the Innovation Project, to continuously improve their use of Opportunity Culture. One of their goals is to expand their model to remaining campuses, which are high schools that do not qualify for Title 1 funding that sustains advanced teacher leadership positions.

Investing in North Edgecombe

The reform efforts in the Innovation Zone demonstrate how district leaders harnessed a shared equity orientation, design thinking, and investments in educator capacity to transform teaching and learning for ECPS students. By rebranding North Edgecombe schools as the Innovation Zone, ECPS leaders secured the resources needed to invest in the district's most under-resourced schools by improving staff capacity and increasing student access to rigorous, culturally relevant, project-based learning that supports holistic academic development and achievement. One district leader described the transformation:

Three years ago, this was the lowest performing feeder pattern in our school district. This was the area where we had the most challenge recruiting teachers, retaining teachers, student performance was very low in many content areas and grade levels. And now, these three schools are three of our most successful schools in the school system which is really exciting. [....] That's really what the work of our past two years has been: how to change the narrative and the story that people around the community told about our kids, told about our school, and told about our community.

North Edgecombe is a predominately Black region that has endured a history of disinvestment visible in its three schools: Coker-Wimberly Elementary, Phillips Middle School, and North Edgecombe High School. ECPS graduate and parent Tarrell Perry described differences in the facilities and resources between regional high schools:

You could see differences in what the schools had. Everyone would say that if Edgecombe County got a bunch of money, most of the money would go to Southwest, [in-town] Tarboro High would get [some], and North Edgecombe, if there was some left over, we might possibly get that. That's how it seemed when I was in school.

District leaders described several factors contributing to these persistent racial inequities: the power differential of Whiter schools having more vocal school board representation and the relative ease of attracting and retaining staff in better-performing schools, compared to the cyclical vacancies on the North side. Then Director of Innovation Erin Swanson remarked:

> In many ways, our North side community felt kind of forgotten. There were classrooms in those schools that were vacant for years. There were kids who had not had a consistent math teacher for three years, only substitutes, which is really bad [and] not okay.

Swanson added, "It wasn't that there was this big or outward animosity [from the community], it was more of a hidden or quiet animosity, and rightfully so."

Made a strategic decision in 2016, carried forward by Superintendent Bridges, to focus resources to transform North Edgecombe schools. Then Director of Innovation Erin Swanson described the intentionality of this new approach:

> Our former superintendent, as he looked across the district, it was very clear that this feeder pattern was struggling the most, and that we, honestly, had just not poured the resources and the attention into this part of the district that [it] needed to have. You know, the majority of our kids in this part of the district are Black and Brown. Almost all of our kids qualify for free- and reduced-price lunch. […] I also think the families in this part of the district probably felt like they just didn't have a voice. After years and years of folks seeing their teachers leave, seeing the schools were not doing well… Some of them have said [to us], "We just didn't feel empowered, like anybody was going to listen to us." Obviously, that is not okay. We did start on this side of the district for that reason.

The Innovation Zone

In 2016, Farrelly petitioned the State Board of Education to secure Restart status for schools in the North Edgecombe feeder pattern. The state Restart program gives low-performing schools additional flexibility over the budgetary, curricular, hiring, and scheduling decisions to expand educational opportunities for students.[59] This new flexibility enabled innovative efforts to direct resources, develop instructional capacity, and transform learning experiences in the North feeder pattern schools. As she took the mantle of leadership in 2017–18, Bridges collaborated with campus leaders in the Innovation Zone to transform learning experiences through new staffing and learning models.

This school redesign work was supported through Superintendent Bridges' participation in equity-oriented leadership cohorts, Transcend and RELN. Both Transcend and RELN provided peer networks and coaching supports to guide a district leadership team through a design thinking process anchored in explicit equity values. Superintendent Bridges, together with the Innovation Zone leadership team consisting of then Director of Innovation Erin Swanson, Principal of North Edgecombe High School Donnell Cannon, and Principal of Phillips Middle School Jenny O'Meara, leveraged these partnerships to plan and implement the pilot "micro school" in 2017–18 and launched it in 2018–19.[60] These experiences provided structure and support for iterative development and evaluation. Moreover, the collaborative design work fostered a sense of collective efficacy and trust. O'Meara explained:

> When I talk to colleagues in other districts, there's a sense of fear to make decisions without getting prior approval, but I literally have never once worried about that. I genuinely believe that if I were to make a decision and mess something up—which has happened—[Dr. Bridges] is going to look at it as a learning opportunity and a growth moment for me, and not [think] it's time to get rid of this principal. She gives really authentic feedback. She gives tough feedback sometimes, but I know that she's not holding back. I really appreciate that.

The first few months of planning involved proactively convening students, families, and community members using empathetic listening strategies described earlier in this report. District leaders introduced their intention for investments in the Innovation Zone and gathered input, which reversed the pattern of "quiet animosity" in the region.[61] To paint a picture of the kind of learning transformation possible in North Edgecombe, district leaders shared the latest science on learning and development and gathered feedback on what students and families wanted from school.[62] District leaders reported that this approach created an important platform to surface and respond to important community concerns. For example, families in the Innovation Zone questioned whether experimental learning models might further disadvantage students. Swanson reported:

> There is some questioning, which I think is justified, about, "Why are we getting things now? Because this is an innovation zone, are you trying out stuff on our kids that may not work, and is that fair?" I don't think it's widespread, but that question has certainly come up and again, I think that's justified, too. We have tried the best as we can to say, "No, we do not seek to put your children at risk in any way." As we've tried things [that] have worked, we've really sought to share that as well to invest

people and to bring them along. The point of the empathy work is certainly to bring them along, but also to bring them into the conversation.

Swanson added that, while not every family member feels completely engaged, she believes the Innovation Zone leaders are making important progress in how community members are involved in the decisions shaping educational environments in North Edgecombe schools. On the other hand, leaders have used empathy listening sessions to field concerns from community members outside the Innovation Zone. Swanson reported, "The other implication is our south side folks now feel like, 'Hey now, you're giving all this attention to the north side, what about us?'" She described the real challenge of equitably allocating the district's limited resources and capacity "in a way that doesn't rob Peter to pay Paul." District leaders have responded to these concerns by presenting the equity gaps that motivated initial investments in the Innovation Zone and by pursuing initiatives in North Edgecombe as a pilot that can evaluate and spread effective models, like Opportunity Culture, into additional schools.

The North Phillips School of Innovation

At the end of the planning year, Innovation Zone leaders had developed a new learning model that would support students working in smaller learning communities on curriculum-embedded projects connected to state standards.[63] Based on a review of attendance and performance data, they decided to pilot this new model as a strategy to ease middle-to-high school transitions, where outcomes data showed a drop in engagement and outcomes.[64] North Edgecombe High Principal Donnell Cannon and Phillips Middle Principal Jenny O'Meara launched a pilot in Fall 2018 with 30 students in 8th and 9th grade. By fall of 2020, they expanded the pilot into North Phillips School of Innovation to encompass all 400 6th–12th grade students in the feeder pattern.

Staffing the North Phillips School of Innovation

Principals Cannon and O'Meara spent the spring and summer of 2018 recruiting staff to carry out their new vision for teaching and learning in the Innovation Zone. The north side of the county was historically very difficult to staff, but by the following spring, a district partner observed, "You can't get a job up there right now, in a lot of places, and I think two of the three schools are fully staffed and were all before the first day of school. That is like, unheard of."

They built a diverse instructional team of staff who represented the school's larger Black and Latino/a population, possessed deep knowledge of the community, and added fresh perspective from experiences outside the district. Principal Cannon reported that a non-negotiable requirement was for all Innovation Zone teachers to "elevate students' sense of palpable optimism in terms of what they understand and accomplish in life, or what they're able to do right now." He added, "We are very intentional about recruiting people who believe in exactly what we believe."

The Restart flexibility and Opportunity Culture enabled Cannon and O'Meara to leverage instructional teams, led by expert teachers, to deliver instruction in small cohorts of students. The differentiated staffing model created a structure for continuous collaboration and coaching to provide personalized supports for learners. O'Meara reported working with then Finance Director Laurie Leary to take "a hard look" at the "wildly complex" restart budgets to be able to create new positions for instructional leaders. In addition to a Multi-Classroom Leader, Cannon reported that they also harnessed restart flexibility to hire a school culture and climate specialist who could support the curricular model focused on personal identity exploration.

Learning in the North Phillips School of Innovation

The learning model in the North Phillips School of Innovation involves meaningful, curriculum-embedded project-based learning that is culturally responsive and supports students' social and emotional development. Director of Innovation Erin Swanson described how these components of the curriculum build content knowledge while advancing co-cognitive skills in one instructional unit:

> There are three bets that we're making in this block: one is that kids can really master their ELA and social studies content, another is that kids really can explore their own purpose and passions, and a third is that kids are going to develop critical thinking skills and agency by engaging in the human-centered design process.

Through district-supported professional learning and Opportunity Culture coaching, all teachers in the north feeder pattern receive training and continuous feedback to plan and facilitate project-based learning. A district leader described firsthand the change from passive instruction to engaged learning: "It has been so amazing to walk into a classroom and see kids grappling... They're learning so much more than if they just sat and got a lecture on it." Research has shown that, by building students' ability to apply knowledge to complex problems, curriculum-embedded performance tasks help students develop co-cognitive skills such as collaboration, grit, resilience, perseverance, and a growth mindset.[65]

The North Phillips School of Innovation shows promising gains across holistic measures of student success. ECPS leaders partnered with a 12-person team from IBM Service Corps to evaluate the success of the North Phillips School of Innovation.[66] Over the course of four weeks, the team integrated student-level data into a comprehensive dashboard displaying attendance, behavioral outcomes, academic growth and achievement, and student sense of belonging. In the 2018–19 school year, students in the North Phillips School of Innovation had higher attendance rates, lower rates of disciplinary infractions, and a higher sense of school safety and belonging than peers across the district. [67] The same year, students at the North Phillips School of Innovation also outperformed their peers on state reading and science assessments.[68] All three schools in North Edgecombe met or exceeded growth in 2021–22 and 2022–23. Based on these academic gains, the North Carolina Department of Public Instruction authorized ECPS to continue its Restart Model in the Innovation Zone for five additional years, beginning in 2024–25.

Arlane Gordon-Bray, former North Phillips Community Engagement Partner and current Director of the ECPS Educational Foundation, was quoted in a 2020 report on the Innovation Zone work in ECPS.[69] She said the district can serve as a model for engaging rural students of color in authentic learning that opens doors:

> We have answered the question of how to redesign a school system that was never designed for our students. We have become an example of what can come out of rural communities. Rural communities are often an afterthought. People ask, "What are you contributing?" Especially because the technology sector is centered around big cities. But we have assets. We have innovation. We are intergenerational. And we have human connectedness down pat. We also have the potential to create economic benefits for ourselves. We are seeing how our system has forced students to show up in certain ways by only focusing on certain skills. Society asks people to go to work and mimic White businessmen. Society does not focus on authenticity. That's why we ask students to do identity work to understand their history and what it means to them. That's why, as a school, we ask students to develop their own purpose and path so that they can form a new, collective vision and accomplish new things.

Lessons Learned

As detailed throughout this case study, Superintendent Valerie H. Bridges transformed the learning environment in a rural, historically under-resourced, majority-Black school district from one of passive learning and persistent underperformance to a learning organization committed to expanding educational opportunity and ambitious graduate aims. This was possible, in large part, due to strategic investments in recruiting and developing a cadre of educators who were prepared and supported to advance more holistic, student-centered approaches to teaching and learning. District leaders have ushered immediate improvements in the learning environments and educational opportunities in district schools and classrooms. They will continue to see the impact of these reforms on the learning outcomes for students of color and students from low-income families over time, though early decreases in rates of exclusionary discipline and increases in math and reading proficiency rates indicate that the equity-oriented reforms are beginning to take effect.

Dr. Bridges characterized these changes as necessary, but not easy. Over the course of ten years, leaders enacted strategic approaches to developing the will and skill to advance racial equity across the district. Key features of the leadership strategy in ECPS include:

Leaders in ECPS established a long-term, community-developed vision for educational equity that anchors and coordinates a dynamic suite of reform efforts. District leaders strategically and meaningfully engaged hundreds of stakeholders in discussions about how district schools can best serve each and every student. Starting with the launch of the BRC on Educational Equity, leaders have consulted students, family members, business leaders, elected officials, non-profit partners, and district staff members on the co-design of graduate aims, strategic planning, and new educational models aligned to the Instructional Framework for Learning. This holistic approach to goal setting has empowered the district community to think beyond a typical preschool-to-grade-12 framework, cultivating resources and partnerships that support ECPS learners into their postsecondary experiences and beyond. Over time and with consistent effort, leaders in ECPS shifted limiting narratives and gained a reputation as a collaborative and innovative community dedicated to removing barriers to student success.

District and school leaders pursued innovative, research-based instructional practices that expand opportunity for learners. United by a shared focus on cognitive rigor, campus instructional teams have developed high-impact instructional strategies including project-based learning, Spanish language immersion, accelerated learning, and social-emotional learning. District leaders systematized these practices through a holistic Instructional Framework for Learning, which both provided a common language to ensure high-quality learning experiences for every student in ECPS and established a process for leaders to assess and scale high-impact instructional practices to additional classrooms and campuses. The framework helps leaders ensure that all instruction aligns with the district-wide, equity-oriented vision for teaching and learning as campuses innovate to meet the specific needs of their student populations.

In the face of high turnover, ECPS leaders created innovative strategies for teacher development, retention, and leadership. District leaders pursued a strategy to attract and retain innovative educators who improve academic achievement, social-emotional habits, and school culture. Leaders aggressively recruited teachers and school leaders committed to transforming educational opportunities for learners in rural, high-poverty districts. They also worked to retain effective educators through personalized professional development and high-impact teacher leadership positions. As a result, many members of the district leadership team—including Superintendent Valerie Bridges—have developed as effective leaders along a trajectory of increasing roles and professional supports.

Through strategic investments in North Edgecombe, ECPS leaders demonstrated that beginning racial equity efforts in the areas of greatest need can accelerate transformation. District leaders intentionally leveraged state, federal, and philanthropic funding to launch innovative educational strategies in its most under-resourced schools serving a majority-Black and historically marginalized community. They recruited an energized and dedicated leadership team to implement project-based learning models and new teacher leadership. This strategy enabled district leaders to both address the system's largest equity gaps while creating momentum to scale successful programs into additional schools—expanding, rather than rationing, success.

This case study details how ECPS leaders pursued a vision for educational equity through innovations in district-wide staffing, instruction, and investment strategies. At the helm, Superintendent Bridges fostered leadership at the classroom, school, and district levels. This leadership provided the necessary coordination and continuity to realize a decade of improvements, which continue to fuel ongoing efforts.

Notes

1 Fofaria, R. (2022, September 2). Education NC. *Criticism of school accountability model grows as more schools are designated 'low performing.'* https://www.ednc.org/school-accountability-model-low-performing-performa/

2 Edgecombe County Public Schools (n.d.). *Bridges named North Carolina superintendent of the year.* https://www.ecps.us/apps/news/article/1528151

3 Edgecombe County Public Schools. (n.d.). *ECPS exits low performing district status.* https://www.ecps.us/apps/news/article/1813956

4 Roy, E., & Ford, J. (2019). *Deep rooted: A brief history of race and education in North Carolina.* Charlotte, NC: Center for Racial Equity in Education.

5 Mizelle Jr., R. M. (2016). Princeville and the environmental landscape of race. *Open Rivers, Issue 4: Fall 2016 Open Rivers: Rethinking the Mississippi*, 32. https://openrivers.lib.umn.edu/article/princeville-and-the-environmental-landscape-of-race-2/

 6 Bell, L. (2016, December 13). North Carolina center for public policy research. *Leading through the storm*. https://nccppr.org/leading-through-the-storm/
 7 Public School Forum of North Carolina (2020). *Roadmap of need, 2020.* Public School Forum of North Carolina. https://www.ncforum.org/wp-content/uploads/2023/02/2020_Roadmap-FINAL.pdf
 8 Mungo, S. D. (2011). An intergenerational oral history of African American students in Edgecombe County, North Carolina from 1930–1980. [Doctoral dissertation, University of North Carolina Charlotte]. ProQuest Dissertations & Theses Global.
 9 Mitchell, C. (2021, February 17). Nurturing talent at home to revive a struggling region. *EdWeek*. https://www.edweek.org/leaders/2021/nurturing-talent-at-home-to-revive-a-struggling-region
10 Edgecombe County Public Schools (n.d.). ECPS exits low performing district status. https://www.ecps.us/apps/news/article/1813956 (accessed 10/20/2023).
11 Proficiency defined as students testing level 3 or above on regular state end-of-grade mathematics and reading tests. North Carolina Department of Public Instruction: Reports of Disaggregated State, School System (LEA) and School Performance Data. http://accrpt.tops.ncsu.edu/docs/disag_datasets/
12 North Carolina Department of Public Instruction. Discipline, ALP, and Dropout Annual Reports. https://www.dpi.nc.gov/data-reports/dropout-and-discipline-data/discipline-alp-and-dropout-annual-reports#2020–21–4402 (accessed 7/2023).
13 North Carolina Department of Public Instruction. NC School Report Cards. https://www.dpi.nc.gov/data-reports/school-report-cards
14 The North Carolina Department of Public Instruction defines "inexperienced principals" as administrators who are in their first three years of serving as the administrative lead of a school. In contrast to beginning teachers, inexperienced principals might have served for many years in an assistant principal (or some other leadership) role. Inexperienced principals often require additional support from the central office or other, more experienced principals to support them in their new roles. North Carolina Department of Public Instruction. NC School Report Cards. https://www.dpi.nc.gov/data-reports/school-report-cards
15 Edgecombe County Public Schools (n.d.). *ECPS announces creation of Commission on Educational Equity*. https://www.ecps.us/apps/news/article/673729 (accessed 7/28/2023).
16 Edgecombe County Public Schools (n.d.). *ECPS strategic plan: Futures reimagined*. https://www.ecps.us/apps/pages/index.jsp?uREC_ID=1689715&type=d&pREC_ID=1847182 (accessed 7/31/2023).
17 Edgecombe County Public Schools (n.d.). *ECPS strategic plan: Futures reimagined*. https://www.ecps.us/apps/pages/index.jsp?uREC_ID=1689715&type=d&pREC_ID=1847182 (accessed 7/31/2023).
18 Hyler, M. E., Carver-Thomas, D., Wechsler, M., & Willis, L. (2020). *Districts Advancing Racial Equity (DARE) tool.* Palo Alto, CA: Learning Policy Institute; Smith, R. G., & Brazer, S. D. (2016). *Striving for equity: District leadership for narrowing opportunity and achievement gaps.* Cambridge, MA: Harvard Education Press.
19 National Equity Project (n.d.). *Introduction to liberatory design.* https://www.nationalequityproject.org/frameworks/liberatory-design
20 Nelson, P. (1977). *There's a hole in my sidewalk: The romance of self-discovery.* Los Angeles: Popular Library.

21 Transcend (n.d.). *Model sharing community.* https://transcendeducation.org/what-we-offer/model-sharing/

22 Haywoode, A. (2020). *A journey into educational innovation with Edgecombe County Public Schools and Transcend.* https://drive.google.com/file/d/1pI5M ECv2g7ayKpWN26UnPoWYiM2sB4W1/view (accessed 8/2/2023).

23 Edgecombe County Public Schools (2018). *ECPS framework for learning.* https://www.dropbox.com/s/l6jnq0zk9rnxc19/ECPS_Framework%20 for%20Learning.pdf?dl=0

24 Edgecombe County Public Schools (n.d.). *Matt Smith named 2019 North Carolina principal of the year.* https://www.ecps.us/apps/news/article/1041723#:~:text=Matthew%20Bristow%2DSmith%2C%20a%20past,awards%20 luncheon%20today%20in%20Cary

25 Bell, L. (2019, December 16). Here's how the Principal of the Year leads his early college in Edgecombe County. *EdNC.* https://www.ednc.org/principal-of-year-leads-early-college-high-school-in-edgecombe-county/

26 Bell, L. (2019, December 16). Here's how the Principal of the Year leads his early college in Edgecombe County. *EdNC.* https://www.ednc.org/principal-of-year-leads-early-college-high-school-in-edgecombe-county/

27 Data provided by Edgecombe Public Schools (2024, January 29).

28 Bell, L. (2019 December 16). Here's how the Principal of the Year leads his early college in Edgecombe County. *EdNC.* https://www.ednc.org/principal-of-year-leads-early-college-high-school-in-edgecombe-county/

29 Krais, R. (2014, September 2). Global school in rural Edgecombe is 'recipe for success.' *WRAL News.* https://www.wral.com/story/global-school-in-rural-edgecombe-is-recipe-for-success-/13966879/

30 Mangels, A. (2017, May 25), *Participate learning blog.* Global Education Case Study: Edgecombe County Schools. https://lessons.participatelearning.com/blog/global-education-case-study-edgecombe/

31 Edgecombe County Public Schools (n.d.). *Martin millennium academy. Who we are.* https://www.mmatrailblazers.com/apps/pages/index.jsp?uREC_ID=434570&type=d&pREC_ID=1105837

32 North Carolina Department of Public Instruction. NC School Report Cards. https://www.dpi.nc.gov/data-reports/school-report-cards

33 Public School Forum of North Carolina (2018). *NC resilience & learning project.* https://www.ncforum.org/wp-content/uploads/2018/10/Resilience-Learning-October-2018-Update.pdf

34 Stenhaug, B., & Saeugling, S. (2022). Discipline Data analysis for edgecombe county public schools from 2015–2018. Rural opportunity institute and Stanford Center for education policy analysis. https://www.ruralopportunity.org/discipline-data-analysis-for-edgecombe-county-schools/

35 Central Carolina Regional Service Alliance (2023). Event: District and schoolwide discipline and student support: Challenges and remedies. https://www.ccresa.net/meetings/district-and-schoolwide-discipline-and-student-support-challenges-and-remedies/

36 Edgecombe County Public Schools (n.d.). *ECPS educational foundation.* https://www.ecps.us/apps/pages/index.jsp?uREC_ID=2037968&type=d&pREC_ID=2112096

37 North Carolina Department of Public Instruction (n.d.). Educator compensation. https://www.dpi.nc.gov/educators/recruitment-support/educator-compensation

38 Edgecombe County Public Schools (n.d.). *ECPS strategic plan: Futures reimagined.* https://www.ecps.us/apps/pages/index.jsp?uREC_ID=1689715&type=d&pREC_ID=1847182 (accessed 7/31/2023).

39 North Carolina Department of Public Instruction 2 (2022). North Carolina Teacher Working Conditions Survey. https://nctwcs.org/

40 Carver-Thomas, D., & Darling-Hammond, L. (2017). *Teacher turnover: Why it matters and what we can do about it*. Palo Alto, CA: Learning Policy Institute; Darling-Hammond, L., Bastian, K. C., Berry, B., Carver-Thomas, D., Kini, T., Levin, S., & McDiarmid, G. W. (2022). *Educator supply, demand, and quality in North Carolina: Current status and recommendations*. Palo Alto, CA: Learning Policy Institute; Ingersoll, R., Merrill, L., & May, H. (2014). *What are the effects of teacher education and preparation on beginning teacher attrition?* Research Report (#RR-82). Philadelphia: Consortium for Policy Research in Education, University of Pennsylvania; Henke, R., Chen, X., & Geis, S. (2000). *Progress through the teacher pipeline: 1992–93 College graduates and elementary/secondary school teaching as of 1997*. Postsecondary Education Descriptive Analysis Report. U.S. Department of Education. Washington, DC: National Center for Education Statistics.

41 Urquart, M., & McNeill, C. (2022, March 23). Edgecombe's Scholar Teachers program looks forward to first cohort of teachers coming home this fall. *Education NC*. https://www.ednc.org/edgecombes-scholar-teachers-program-looks-forward-to-first-cohort-of-teachers-coming-home-this-fall/

42 The North Carolina Teaching Fellows program was launched in 1986 and continues to operate at a reduced level today. Evaluations have found that the program is a high-retention pathway, prepared some of the most effective teachers in the state, and expanded the teaching pool in North Carolina by increasing the number of males, minorities, and math and science teachers. Darling-Hammond, L., Bastian, K. C., Berry, B., Carver-Thomas, D., Kini, T., Levin, S., & McDiarmid, G. W. (2022). *Educator supply, demand, and quality in North Carolina: Current status and recommendations*. Palo Alto, CA: Learning Policy Institute; Henry, G. T., Bastian, K. C., & Smith, A. A. (2012). Scholarships to recruit the 'best and brightest' into teaching: Who is recruited, where do they teach, how effective are they, and how long do they stay? *Educational Researcher, 41*(3), 83–92; National Commission on Teaching and America's Future. (1996). *What matters most: Teaching for America's future*.

43 Edgecombe Early College High School. (n.d.). *Edgecombe early college high school scholar teachers program*. https://eechs.ecps.us/apps/pages/index.jsp?uREC_ID=1822558&type=d&pREC_ID=1982049; Osborne & Urquhart, M. (2020, September 23). Faced with 20% teacher turnover, this district decided to 'grow their own.' *Education NC*. https://www.ednc.org/faced-with-teacher-turnover-this-district-decided-to-grow-their-own-edgecombe-nc/

44 Osborne & Urquhart, M. (2020, September 23). Faced with 20% teacher turnover, this district decided to 'grow their own.' *Education NC*. https://www.ednc.org/faced-with-teacher-turnover-this-district-decided-to-grow-their-own-edgecombe-nc/

45 Urquart, M., & McNeill, C. (2022, March 23). Edgecombe's Scholar Teachers program looks forward to first cohort of teachers coming home this fall. *Education NC*. https://www.ednc.org/edgecombes-scholar-teachers-program-looks-forward-to-first-cohort-of-teachers-coming-home-this-fall/

46 Data provided by Edgecombe Public Schools (2024, January 29).

47 The North Carolina Department of Public Instruction defines "inexperienced principals" as administrators who are in their first three years of serving as the administrative lead of a school. In contrast to beginning teachers, inexperienced principals might have served for many years in an assistant principal (or some other leadership) role. Inexperienced principals often require additional support

from the central office or other, more experienced principals to support them in their new roles. North Carolina Department of Public Instruction. NC School Report Cards. https://www.dpi.nc.gov/data-reports/school-report-cards.

48 North Carolina State University. (2023). *Northeast Leadership Academy.* https://nela.ced.ncsu.edu/about-nela-2-0/; Edgecombe County Public Schools. (n.d.). *ECPS teachers selected for northeast leadership academy* https://www.ecps.us/apps/news/article/588173

49 Darling-Hammond, L., Bastian, K. C., Berry, B., Carver-Thomas, D., Kini, T., Levin, S., & McDiarmid, G. W. (2022). *Educator supply, demand, and quality in North Carolina: Current status and recommendations.* Palo Alto, CA: Learning Policy Institute.

50 Hinchcliffe, K. (2016, August 4). NC principal vows to 'break this cycle' after 60% of teachers leave in one year. *WRAL News.* https://www.wral.com/story/nc-principal-vows-to-break-this-cycle-after-60-of-teachers-leave-in-one-year/15903501/

51 Edgecombe County Public Schools. (n.d.). Join a phenomenal team of talented educators today. [Recruitment Brochure]. https://4.files.edl.io/89a5/02/01/21/163246-64c9eb0e-159e-4597-a152-cba5ad9f804f.pdf (accessed 11/8/2023).

52 Edgecombe County Public Schools. (n.d.) Join a Phenomenal Team of Talented Educators Today. [Recruitment Brochure]. https://4.files.edl.io/89a5/02/01/21/163246-64c9eb0e-159e-4597-a152-cba5ad9f804f.pdf (accessed 11/8/2023).

53 Public Impact (2012–23). *Edgecombe county public schools.* https://www.opportunityculture.org/edgecombe-county-public-schools/

54 Pittman, C., & Lewis, T. (2023). *Teacher leadership in practice: A program evaluation of opportunity culture in a small, rural North Carolina School District* [Doctoral dissertation, East Carolina University].

55 Public Impact (2012–23). *Edgecombe County Public Schools.* https://www.opportunityculture.org/edgecombe-county-public-schools/

56 Backes, B., & Hansen, M. (2018). *Reaching further and learning more? Evaluating public impact's opportunity culture initiative.* CALDER Working Paper No. 18, p. 5. https://caldercenter.org/publications/reaching-further-and-learning-more-evaluating-public-impacts-opportunity-culture; Public Impact. (n.d.). *Multi-classroom leadership.* https://www.opportunityculture.org/multi-classroom-leadership/

57 North Carolina is reporting on the effectiveness of teachers across the State, which is measured using the North Carolina Educator Evaluation System. Educators are assigned effectiveness ratings based on their overall performance on the five observational standards and the overall growth rating (where available). The classification process is the same for educators whether they are on a comprehensive, standard, or abbreviated evaluation process. See North Carolina Department of Public Instruction (n.d.). Educator effectiveness model. https://www.dpi.nc.gov/districts-schools/districts-schools-support/district-human-capital/educator-effectiveness-model; North Carolina Department of Public Instruction. NC School Report Cards. https://www.dpi.nc.gov/data-reports/school-report-cards

58 Public Impact (2012–23). *Edgecombe county public schools.* https://www.opportunityculture.org/edgecombe-county-public-schools/

59 Granados, A., & Hinchcliffe, K. (2018, March 19). Restart program gives some low-performing schools flexibility to help struggling students. *EdNC.* https://

www.ednc.org/restart-program-gives-some-low-performing-schools-flexibil-ity-to-help-struggling-students/

60 Edgecombe County Public Schools (n.d.). "Transcending" expectations in the I-Zone. https://www.ecps.us/apps/news/article/883664

61 Haywoode, A. (2020). *A journey into educational innovation with Edgecombe County Public Schools and Transcend.* https://drive.google.com/file/d/1pI5M ECv2g7ayKpWN26UnPoWYiM2sB4W1/view (accessed 8/2/2023).

62 Haywoode, A. (2020). *A journey into educational innovation with Edgecombe County Public Schools and Transcend.* https://drive.google.com/file/d/1pI5M ECv2g7ayKpWN26UnPoWYiM2sB4W1/view (accessed 8/2/2023).

63 Haywoode, A. (2020). *A journey into educational innovation with Edgecombe County Public Schools and Transcend.* https://drive.google.com/file/d/1pI5M ECv2g7ayKpWN26UnPoWYiM2sB4W1/view (accessed 8/2/2023).

64 Haywoode, A. (2020). *A journey into educational innovation with Edgecombe County Public Schools and Transcend.* https://drive.google.com/file/d/1pI5M ECv2g7ayKpWN26UnPoWYiM2sB4W1/view (accessed 8/2/2023).

65 Darling-Hammond, L., & Adamson, F. (2014). *Beyond the bubble test: How performance assessments support 21st century learning.* San Francisco, CA: Jossey-Bass.

66 Sorrells, A. (2019, November 26). What's the state of student data? We found out on the ground in Edgecombe County. *EdNC.* https://www. ednc.org/whats-the-state-of-student-data-we-found-out-on-the-ground-in-edgecombe-county/

67 Sorrells, A. (2019, November 26). What's the state of student data? We found out on the ground in Edgecombe County. *EdNC.* https://www. ednc.org/whats-the-state-of-student-data-we-found-out-on-the-ground-in-edgecombe-county/

68 Haywoode, A. (2020). *A journey into educational innovation with Edgecombe County Public Schools and Transcend.* https://drive.google.com/file/d/1pI5M ECv2g7ayKpWN26UnPoWYiM2sB4W1/view (accessed 8/2/2023).

69 Haywoode, A. (2020). *A journey into educational innovation with Edgecombe County Public Schools and Transcend.* https://drive.google.com/file/d/1pI5M ECv2g7ayKpWN26UnPoWYiM2sB4W1/view (accessed 8/2/2023).

3 "All Means All"

Creating an Equity Framework in Hoke County Schools

Maria E. Hyler, Linda Darling-Hammond, and Larkin Willis with Peter W. Cookson

Introduction

Hoke County Schools is a small, racially diverse, rural school district in North Carolina that serves a majority of students of color. When Dr. Freddie Williamson became the county's first Black Superintendent of Schools in 2006, the district was struggling and was a candidate for state takeover. At that time, the district's 14 campuses were poorly resourced, and measures of academic achievement indicated that many of its roughly 9,000 students, both students of color and White students, were falling behind their peers in the state. According to an ongoing school finance lawsuit in which Hoke County was a plaintiff, generations of students had been deprived of their right to a sound basic education, and access to learning opportunities that would allow them to fully participate in the economy and society was limited. Equally disturbing, there was not a plan to rectify these shortcomings and failures. The Hoke County School District was in crisis.

By 2020, when Dr. Williamson left Hoke County to become Superintendent of Schools in nearby Robeson County and passed the mantle of leadership to his Assistant Superintendent, Dr. Debra Dowless, the district had changed considerably. Academic achievement had measurably improved, new programs and partnerships were offering students a cohesive suite of learning opportunities, and the groundwork had been established to ensure that progress would continue.

During the 15 years of Dr. Williamson's leadership, student outcomes improved on multiple academic measures, and graduation rates climbed to reach the state average. As described in more detail in this case,

- Between 2012–13 and 2018–19, the percentage of grade 3–8 students meeting proficiency levels in math increased from 30% to 54% (an 80% increase, which was double the statewide rate of growth). Math proficiency rates increased for every group and approximately doubled for both American Indian/Alaska Native and Black students (Table 3.2).

DOI: 10.4324/9781003568087-3

- Between 2012–13 and 2018–19, the percentage of grade 3–8 students meeting proficiency levels in reading increased from 31% to 52% (an increase of more than two-thirds, more than doubling the rate of growth statewide). Reading proficiency rates increased for every group and approximately doubled for both American Indian/Alaska Native and Black students (Table 3.3).
- Between 2001–02 and 2019–20, Advanced Placement (AP) enrollments increased by more than sixfold. During this period, AP enrollments became more racially representative of district demographics for each group, with especially large gains for American Indian/Alaska Native and Black students (Table 3.4).
- Between 2014–15 and 2019–20, the percent of students meeting or exceeding the state benchmark on the ACT exam increased for every group, nearly reaching the state average (Table 3A.2).
- Between 2014–15 and 2019–20, the district's four-year cohort graduation rate rose 13 percentage points to 88% overall, reaching the state average. Disaggregated district graduation rates show gains of more than 10 percentage points for every racial group (Table 3A.3).

This record of improvement shows that the story of Hoke County Schools is one of continuous improvement for all students, especially students of color. How did this happen? How did Hoke County Schools shed failure and embrace success? How did a small, rural, racially diverse, inadequately funded school district in the upper South become a world-class learning organization that prepares students for success in a fast-moving, competitive global environment? How did the district implement reforms fully and equitably? What were the leadership moves that supported change, and how did the district's theory of action facilitate academic gains?

For the purposes of this study, in which we focus on racial equity leadership, additional questions are critical: what was the impact of the district's actions on racial equity in educational opportunity and outcomes? What evidence is there that the teaching and learning reforms the district put in place between 2006 and 2020 resulted in access to better learning opportunities for students of color? How intentional was the district in creating greater access, and in what ways did it do so?

The Hoke County Schools case study features a dynamic superintendent, Dr. Freddie Williamson, who mobilized his district through a theory of action that was cohesive, collaborative, and conceptually consistent. This case study draws on firsthand perspectives from Dr. Williamson and his colleagues, capturing how they co-created an equity strategy with the school board and the community. Their accounts depict the leadership moves Dr. Williamson made during his tenure and how the district's culture of improvement became a defining feature of "The Hoke County Way."

Organization of the Report

The first section of this case explores the "Hoke County Way," a term Dr. Williamson coined to describe the leadership moves, relationships, and strategic vision that have made progress possible. The next three sections detail areas of district work that have transformed the learning experiences of students, aligned to strategic priorities. The second section, "Empowering Learning Experiences," describes how educators in Hoke County Schools provide rigorous and relevant coursework from prekindergarten (pre-K) through college- and career-ready programs. These efforts, including visionary pre-pandemic investments in a Center for Digital Teaching that provides robust instructional leadership, seek to ensure every learner in the district receives a "world class education." The third section, "Safe and Productive Learning Environments," discusses how leaders in Hoke County Schools promote a whole-child vision featuring positive relationships between staff and students that support social and emotional development. This section details how district staff cultivate safety through coordinated student support services, culturally relevant programming, and a Multi-Tiered System of Supports (MTSS). The fourth section, "Pursuing Resource Equity," describes how leaders in the low-wealth district advance resource equity by capitalizing on the limited financial and material resources available and investing in excellent educators. This section presents strategies for resource allocation that staff report "level the playing field" for learners in the district. The case study concludes with observations about what educators can learn from the "Hoke County Way" and the implications of these findings for advancing racial equity.

A Profile of Hoke County Schools

In 2019–20, Hoke County Schools served a majority of students of color, including 33% who identify as Black, 24% Latino/a, 11% multiracial, and 8% American Indian/Alaska Native (Table 3.1). American Indian/Alaska Native students and families are most represented along Hoke County's southeast border with Robeson County, the political center of the Lumbee Tribe. Black students and families are most represented in the urban hubs of Raeford and Silver City. White students and families are most represented in suburban Rockfish and Five Points near the military base at Fort Liberty,[1] the largest army installation in the world and home to about 10% of the U.S. active armed forces.

Poverty and deep poverty are pervasive across communities in the district: children in Hoke County experience poverty at 1.4 times the North Carolina rate, with 26% living in poverty and over 10% in deep poverty.[2] In 2019–20, roughly two-thirds of students in Hoke County Schools were identified as "economically disadvantaged" (see Table 3.1), comprising

Table 3.1 Hoke County Schools Student Demographics, 2019–20

Demographic	2019–20
Black	33%
White	24%
Latino/a	23%
Multiracial	11%
American Indian/Alaska Native	8%
Asian American	<1%
Native Hawaiian/Pacific Islander	<1%
Economically Disadvantaged	76%
Total Student Population	8,790

Source: North Carolina Department of Public Instruction (n.d.). Public School Statistical Profile, Pupils in Membership by Race and Sex, https://www.dpi.nc.gov/districts-schools/district-operations/financial-and-business-services/statistical-profile.

campus enrollments ranging from roughly 40% at Rockfish Hoke Elementary to 80% at Hawk Eye Elementary.[3]

In this context, leaders in Hoke County Schools rally behind an equity orientation that is focused on eliminating barriers to learning associated with living in poverty. Dr. Donna Thomas, the district's Assistant Superintendent of Human Resources, described the lived experiences impacting academic success in Hoke County in vivid detail:

> We're a high poverty district. […] It's eye-opening when you see that a lot of your children are living in campers behind trailers and electricity is being run to those campers with a drop cord. You … realize that, maybe this child doesn't have the means to have a pencil at school that day.

The efforts to advance equity in Hoke County Schools are situated within a legacy of local advocacy for not only greater access to public schooling but also quality education that opens doors to greater political agency and economic independence. Families and educators in the region have persisted in their calls for equal educational opportunity against systemic inequities embedded in North Carolina's public schools.[4] Despite North Carolina being the first state to offer publicly funded universal education in 1825, the state school system offered unequal education based on race until North Carolina districts began desegregating in 1963.[5] Hoke County Schools maintained a "triple school system" with separate schools for Black, White, and Native students for another six years, until the district integrated in the fall of 1969.[6] The legacy of racial exclusion and discrimination has shaped educational policy, practice, and experiences in Hoke County Schools.

As a high-poverty district, the focus on eliminating barriers associated with poverty in Hoke County Schools is unifying. Hoke County Schools was the lead plaintiff in *Leandro vs. the State of North Carolina (1997)*, a watershed North Carolina Supreme Court case that takes the name of Robert A. Leandro, a White student in the district. In the *Leandro* case, Hoke County Schools and four other low-wealth districts argued that their lack of adequate funding violated North Carolina's constitutional obligation to provide a sound, basic education for their students.[7] In 1997, the North Carolina Supreme Court ruled that economically disadvantaged districts must receive supplemental funding to correct unconstitutional disparities in educational resources. The case was relitigated over subsequent years due to inadequate progress in correcting the inequalities. Two decades later, the court initiated a study, *Sound Basic Education for All: An Action Plan for North Carolina*, which delivered specific recommendations for providing public schools in the state with the resources necessary to ensure equal opportunity to a sound basic education.[8] The recommendations of this study have been partially adopted, but many of the most central are still unimplemented.

The fight for resource equity is far from over. Using the taxable resources that are available in a county per child for education as a measure of a district's wealth, a 2020 report found that Hoke County Schools was the fifth poorest school district out of 115 in the state.[9] Its local funding is less than half of that generally available in the state ($1,004 vs. $2,321 per pupil), and although it has more high-need students than the state average, its combined federal, state, and local funding continues to be less than the state average.[10] Underfunding puts pressure on high-poverty districts to balance students' significant needs for many services with educational needs as well. Confronting these challenges requires courageous leadership that inspires, mobilizes, and coordinates changes in policy and practice that bring about meaningful change.

The Hoke County Way

Dr. Freddie Williamson's vision for educational transformation, which came to be known as the "Hoke County Way," was born of experience. A North Carolina native and first-generation high school graduate, Dr. Williamson led the district from an intimate knowledge of the values, assets, and aspirations of the community it serves. Before coming to Hoke County, he served as a coach, teacher, assistant principal, program director, and associate superintendent in surrounding districts. This work, as well as his own educational journey, convinced him that equity is not one of many goals, it is the fundamental goal that organizes and aligns all district work. When asked to describe how his vision of education advances racial equity, he replied, "It forces one to think about the barriers that exist and the obstacles that may reinforce [inequity] unintentionally; it compels you to realize how social capital empowers some groups more than others and how it impacts accessibility." For him:

> All means all. If there are barriers or obstacles in the way of success for any student, then our policies or practices are not equitable. We may be providing opportunities, but are they truly accessible for all? Opportunity may not always equal accessibility.

To mobilize action for equity in the context of Hoke County, Williamson has characterized his leadership and his expectations of staff's behavior as "color-blind." This framing is not a sign of failure to recognize the disparities that have existed in the education system, but rather a means of establishing that all students are entitled to the same educational opportunities—and that any student not accessing those opportunities is every educator's responsibility. The heart of the "Hoke County Way" is a conviction that all students deserve high-quality and relevant learning experiences that empower them to be lifelong learners and active citizens. His paramount vision was to transform Hoke County Schools into a "world class learning center."

Dr. Williamson built the will and skill for the adults in the system to enact the "Hoke County Way" across all aspects of district work. Known among the district leadership team for his emphasis on "no random acts," Dr. Williamson built commitment and coherence by establishing a new leadership culture that replaced fear of failure with continuous improvement based on data and common purpose and by leading public strategic planning processes that engaged district stakeholders in setting key priorities.

Establishing a New Leadership Culture

In a district that had drifted for much of its history, Dr. Williamson recognized that the culture and mindsets in Hoke County Schools needed to change. He described the lack of leadership capacity when he began his superintendency:

> So let me take you back to 2006 when I started in this district. They didn't have the capacity, [and] they didn't know [that] they didn't have the capacity. I'll never forget my first summer. I walked over to the accountability office, and I got that deer-in-the-headlights look. I wanted to look at [the testing data], and they [didn't] have it. Why? No explanation.

The district needed leaders who were collaborative, reflective, and forward-thinking. This required shifting not just leadership roles, but also the expectations that were associated with those roles. He described the skills he needed in leaders: "first, passion and people skills, and second, content knowledge and skills." Dr. Williamson interviewed district leaders and campus principals, then replaced those that did not fit the description. This was politically risky in a small district with long-established relationships. Staff who had comfortably served the district over the years were suddenly vulnerable to losing their jobs. He knew the full support of his board was essential:

> I had that conversation with my board. I was honest with them. If you want change and improvement, I'll commit to stay to get that work done. I'll keep you informed. You won't be surprised. Let me do the day-to-day work, and you help me with the policies and procedures. Are you ready for the ride? I'm going to get rid of some of your cousins because they're not doing their jobs.

The threat of state takeover and the early, honest conversations with board members gave Dr. Williamson the board coverage to move forward with substantial staffing changes among site leaders that set the district on a new path. He replaced 14 of 15 principals in the district within his first month, looking largely to staff already in the district—particularly assistant principals—who were committed to change, had an instructional knowledge base, and who had and were willing to acquire additional knowledge and people skills.

Once he hired leaders with these skills and mindsets, Dr. Williamson placed his trust in them: "Let the talented people you have do the work. Education is too large, too dynamic, and too complex for one person to make all the decisions." In this way, Dr. Williamson established what he called a "structure for defined autonomy," or distributed leadership. The new leadership culture replaced fear of failure with willingness—and support—to drive change.

Overcoming the Fear of Failure

Dr. Williamson's bold staffing decisions were driven by a desire for leaders able to experiment and grow. He expressed his vision for improvement in near-poetic terms:

> We grow. We improve. I'm not moving the boundaries. [My staff] move them. So, [I] force folks to [act], and give them the freedom not to be afraid, to challenge, to try things. [I] give them the freedom to experiment.

Educators in Hoke County Schools have had not just the permission, but the expectation to improve. Each year, the full staff reads a book together, diving into titles like *Teaching with Poverty in Mind* and *Results*

Now.[11] This annual practice involves everyone—teachers, bus drivers, and district administrators—in an ongoing, research-based discussion about educational improvement and organizational change. District and campus leaders subscribe to a firm "no excuses" policy that applies strictly to adults, not children, in the district. Principal of Upchurch Elementary AJ Hammond characterized this as shorthand for an unwavering commitment to serving every student: "We don't accept excuses for where students come from and how they come. We just know when they come into our building, we have to make a difference." Attitudes about children and what they are capable of learning shape nearly every aspect of district work.

Using Data to Target Support

Establishing habits for data transparency was another key leadership strategy to drive the district toward more equitable learning experiences. Soon after Dr. Williamson's arrival, he supported principals in accessing data about their schools and sharing it regularly with other administrators and academic coaches through data discussions. One principal explained how data discussions work in the district:

> You start the discussion because you're supposed to own your data. Everybody in that room is listening to you: the principal, the assistant principal, and academic coach talk about your data. They talk about how they'll be able to help. I think that really encourages us because, you know [leadership] is working with you to help make sure you reach that end.

The purpose of these data discussions is for principals to understand the instructional outcomes of their schools and to request available support. In this way, underperformance is met with resources and growth, rather than blame or punishment. Routine data sharing has made instructional decisions more transparent. Then Assistant Superintendent of PreK-Elementary Curriculum and Instruction Dr. Debra Dowless explained that, through progress monitoring, "it's no longer okay just to say the problem is solved. Now we say, 'show us your data to show where it's improving.'" She added that progress monitoring has helped build instruction among educators: "It [data analysis] is making teachers work collaboratively as problem-solvers." When they experience a challenge with a student, "the first response is: let's sit as a team and see what we can do to collectively make things better."

In this way, Dr. Williamson shifted the leadership culture of a failing district by removing the fear and excuses that blocked necessary change.

Building Relationships

To pursue the vision of becoming a "world class learning organization," it was critical for Dr. Williamson to build relationships within the district and its community that were centered on transparent communication and trust. He welcomed and encouraged public discussion among a range of viewpoints to inform decisions by the school board, cabinet, and campus leadership teams.

It is common for teachers and leaders in Hoke County Schools to say, "Relationships matter." Building relationships is about creating community. Then Principal of Hawkeye Elementary School Hayden Simon described the district as "a very close-knit community," which fosters a level of trust that encourages leaders to seek advice and support from their colleagues. In Hoke County Schools, relationship-building does not stop at the schoolhouse door. It also means reaching out to family members, especially those who may not have felt safe or welcome in their own schooling experiences. In the words of Dr. Williamson:

> A lot of the parents had a bad experience in school. I work with principals and teams to understand that. I tell them, don't be upset. They're not mad at you. They're mad at something that happened in the past. That's why they don't trust us, and our job is build that trust. A lot of our parents never finished school. But that gets the child an opportunity to take the lead [and we can] engage the parents [in their child's schooling experience].

Building relationships is more than talk. Dr. Williamson introduced a strategy of home and community visits to build awareness of students' living circumstances. Educators in Hoke County Schools reported that this level of awareness was key to maintaining relationships with students and families. These relationships, detailed further in the Safe and Productive Classroom Environments section, provide a more holistic understanding of students' strengths and needs. In the words of one principal, "When you build relationships with children, it changes everything."

Creating a Strategic Roadmap to the Future

While establishing this new leadership culture, Dr. Williamson also led strategic planning to direct and coordinate improvement efforts. Over the course of nearly two decades in the district, Dr. Williamson gathered broad stakeholder input on the goals and priorities for three strategic plans. The introduction to the third of these—the 2016–21 strategic plan—emphasizes this collective effort:

Our strategic planning team—composed of administrators, teachers, staff members, students, parents, school board members, and community members—worked long hours discussing the district's strengths and areas of improvement in order to set goals for the future. This plan will provide us with guidance and benchmarks to ensure all internal and external stakeholders in the district have a clear vision of what we expect to achieve and how we plan to achieve our goals.[12]

Getting the district to think of itself as a united front, rather than schools with divergent interests and practices, was the first step. Dr. Williamson said that the first strategic plan in 2006 "allowed us to start viewing ourselves as a district. Processes and procedures became more systemic, and the school did not dictate a student's ability to learn." In this way, the first strategic plan established consistency that helped build credibility and buy-in from the school community. Concretizing Dr. Williamson's belief in "no random acts," every department had a set of ambitious priorities, and "the plan kept us aligned, with all the arrows heading in the same direction." A member of Dr. Williamson's team explained that, while a central office leader serves as a point for district initiatives, "it wasn't just us sitting in a room trying to generate ideas. We pulled in our school personnel and board members so there was a lot of conversation." Another leader explained:

> We know we have a proven leader. We have a vision. We've bought into that vision. Our parents, our business leaders, stakeholders have bought into that vision as well. Everything we do in Hoke County is geared towards that particular vision.

The second strategic plan, in 2010, focused on reaffirming those established processes and outcomes to support long-term change. Dr. Williamson said, "It was one thing to see growth in our district, but we wanted to see our district outperform districts similar to ours." To move that needle, district leaders analyzed data comparing Hoke County Schools against peers in the state and set a renewed focus on improving student literacy. Dr. Williamson framed his goal for literacy in this frequently asked question: "Can the students think, can they read, can they write?" He explained that "literacy became the focus. It became the lens through which everything was viewed. All teachers became teachers of reading." District teachers learned how to incorporate explicit literacy instruction across content areas.

The third strategic plan, titled *Transformation—Preparing Today's Students for Tomorrow's World*, established priorities, goals, and strategies for 2016–21 (full text available in the Online Materials Package). It maintained the focus on literacy goals while establishing even more ambitious goals to prepare Hoke students to "graduate college and career ready, globally competitive, and prepared for life in the 21st century." The plan outlined the following priorities for performance:

1. Every student will graduate from high school prepared for work, higher education, and citizenship.
2. Every student will have a personalized education.
3. Every student, every day, will have excellent educators.
4. Every school will have up-to-date technology systems to serve its students, parents, and educators.
5. Every student will be healthy, safe, and responsible.

In each of these initiatives, the district pursued district-wide change in a holistic rather than incremental fashion, addressing all schools and classrooms at once. Dr. Williamson explained that a whole district approach "has always been my practice: not piecemeal, but always the whole district, whole building approach." He argued that when initiatives are tackled piecemeal, "we're not having the same conversation. That is not a clear vision to identify what it is we're trying to achieve for this group of kids. That common language piece is really, really so important."

"The Hoke County Way" provides the framework for understanding the leadership culture and three strategic priorities that drove improvement in Hoke County Schools from 2006 to 2020. The next three sections of the report describe the responsible actors, goals, strategies, and evaluation measures that advanced racial equity alongside strategic priorities in Hoke County Schools: empowering learning experiences, safe school and classroom environments, and resource equity.

Empowering Learning Experiences

> The Hoke County School System is a world-class learning organization. We engage all members of our diverse student population in rigorous and relevant schoolwork that prepares them for life in the 21st century.
> – Hoke County Schools 2016–21 Strategic Plan[13]

This section examines some of the major teaching and learning reforms that Dr. Williamson established in the period between 2006 and 2020. At the heart of these reforms was the spirit of his leadership culture: don't let fear of failure stop you from thinking boldly, act on the understanding that all students can learn, and use data for continuous improvement that holds the adults accountable for student success. Dr. Williamson and his leadership team set a vision for empowering learning experiences that starts with pre-K programs and continues through high school and early college graduation. Eventually digital literacy became an important element of this focus.

The work to establish empowering learning experiences has coincided with increases in the academic outcomes in the district. North Carolina

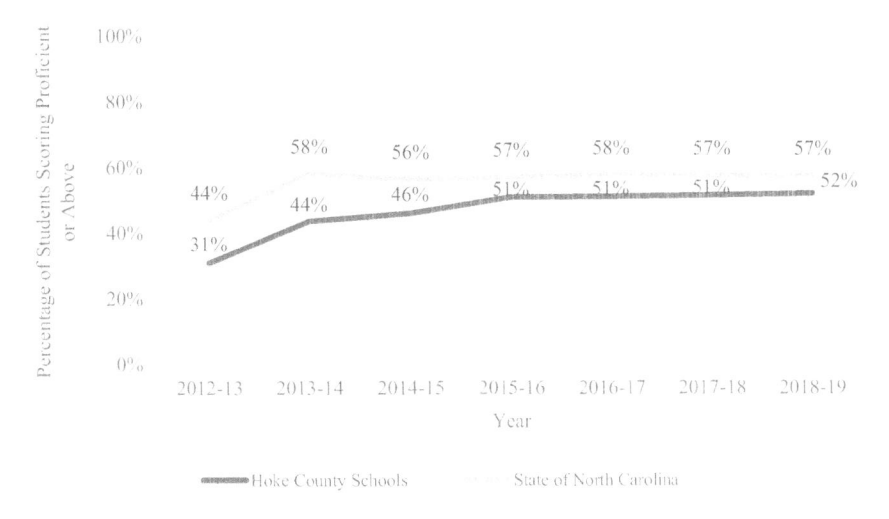

Figure 3.1 Comparison of Hoke County Schools and North Carolina Student Proficiency Rates on State Reading Tests, 2012–13 to 2018–19.

Source: North Carolina Department of Public Instruction (n.d.). Reports of Disaggregated State, School System (LEA) and School Performance Data. http://acrpt.tops.ncsu.edu/docs/disag_datasets/; Hoke County School District (2020). Testing & Accountability Data Packet; North Carolina School Report Cards (n.d.). Student Performance, 2012–13 [archived].

state reading and math proficiency trends indicate that Hoke County students are making steady improvements that outpace the rest of the state (Figures 3.1 and 3.2). Composite grade level proficiency rates refer to the percentage of students in grades 3 through 8 earning a score of 3 or above (out of 5) on a criterion-referenced math or reading exam. In 2011–12, North Carolina introduced new state tests aligned to more rigorous standards. As a result, reading and math proficiency rates statewide were especially low that year but rebounded in the following years. Hoke County proficiency rates also rebounded and progressed at a greater pace of growth than the state average. Between 2012–13 and 2018–19, while North Carolina math proficiency rates increased by about 40% (from 42% testing proficient to 59%), Hoke County math proficiency rates increased by 80% (from 30% testing proficient to 54%, nearly reaching the statewide rate). Similarly, Hoke reading proficiency rates increased by more than two-thirds from 2012–13 to 2018–19, more than double the statewide rate of growth.

Disaggregating the data reveals gains between 2012–13 and 2018–19 for each of the racial and ethnic groups in the district (Table 3.2). The greatest increases were among American Indian/Alaska Native and Black students, whose math proficiency rates doubled (from 19% to 40% and 22% to 44%,

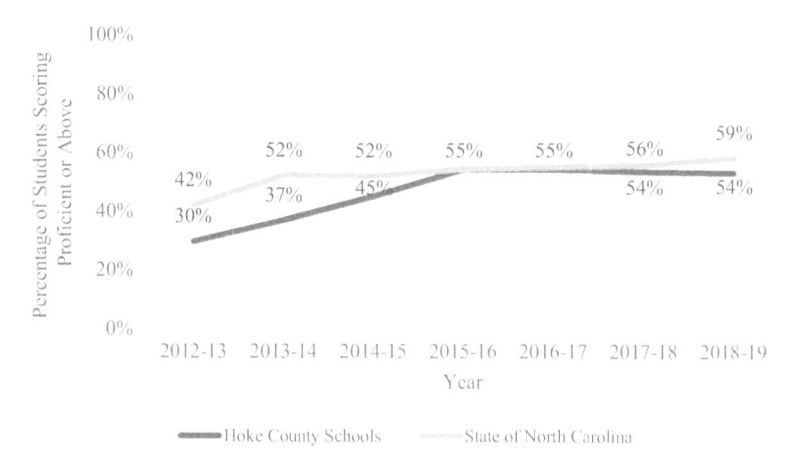

Figure 3.2 Comparison of Hoke County Schools and North Carolina Student Proficiency Rates on State Mathematics Tests, 2012–13 to 2018–19.

Source: North Carolina Department of Public Instruction (n.d.). Reports of Disaggregated State, School System (LEA) and School Performance Data. http://accrpt.tops.ncsu.edu/docs/disag_datasets/; Hoke County School District (2020). Testing & Accountability Data Packet; North Carolina School Report Cards (n.d.). Student Performance, 2012–13 [archived].

Table 3.2 Hoke County Schools Math Composite 3rd–8th Grade Level Proficiency Rates, 2012–13 to 2018–19

Race/ Ethnicity	2012–13	2013–14	2014–15	2015–16	2016–17	2017–18	2018–19
American Indian/ Alaska Native	19%	27%	33%	40%	40%	39%	40%
Asian American	71%	67%	83%	91%	82%	86%	90%
Black	22%	29%	33%	45%	44%	46%	44%
Latino/a	32%	42%	52%	58%	57%	54%	54%
Multiracial	39%	47%	48%	55%	60%	58%	57%
Native Hawaiian/ Pacific Islander	20%	N/A	60%	N/A	N/A	73%	67%
White	48%	52%	60%	68%	68%	68%	67%

Source: North Carolina Department of Public Instruction (n.d.). Reports of Disaggregated State, School System (LEA) and School Performance Data. http://accrpt.tops.ncsu.edu/docs/disag_datasets.

Note: Data for Native Hawaiian/Pacific Islander students are suppressed when fewer than 5 students were tested.

respectively). Math proficiency rates for Latino/a students increased by 68% (from 32% testing proficient to 54%).

These trends were similar for reading proficiency rates between 2012–13 and 2018–19 (Table 3.3). Again, the greatest increases were among American Indian/Alaska Native students, whose reading proficiency rate more than doubled (from 19% to 39%). Black students' math proficiency rates increased by 96% (from 23% to 45%). Proficiency rates for Latino/a students increased by 47% (from 30% testing proficient to 44%).

Although Hoke County proficiency rates for American Indian/Alaska Native, Black, and Latino/a students continue to fall below the state average, the district has supported the kind of accelerated achievement gains that will be needed to close those gaps.

Dr. Williamson promoted a district-wide emphasis on literacy, including digital literacy, that established a high bar for 21st-century teaching and learning for each and every student in Hoke County Schools. However, his long-term vision of student success begins even before kindergarten enrollment and extends beyond high school graduation. He worked with members of the district leadership team to bolster school readiness through pre-K programs and college- and career-readiness through a suite of secondary course pathways.

Every Student Prepared: Teaching for 21st Century Learning

The first priority established in the 2016–20 strategic plan relates to what the district calls 21st-century learning: "Every student will graduate from

Table 3.3 Hoke County Schools Reading Composite 3–8th Grade Level Proficiency Rates, 2012–13 to 2018–19

Race/Ethnicity	2012–13	2013–14	2014–15	2015–16	2016–17	2017–18	2018–19
American Indian/ Alaska Native	19%	32%	30%	36%	32%	35%	39%
Asian American	68%	80%	80%	78%	85%	74%	82%
Black	23%	37%	35%	41%	41%	44%	45%
Latino/a	30%	41%	46%	46%	47%	44%	44%
Multiracial	38%	50%	51%	54%	57%	57%	60%
Native Hawaiian/ Pacific Islander	<5%	N/A	80%	N/A	N/A	36%	58%
White	50%	63%	64%	70%	69%	70%	68%

Source: North Carolina Department of Public Instruction (n.d.). Reports of Disaggregated State, School System (LEA) and School Performance Data. http://accrpt.tops.ncsu.edu/docs/disag_datasets/.

Note: Data for Native Hawaiian/Pacific Islander students are suppressed when ewer than 5 students were tested.

high school prepared for work, higher education, and citizenship."[14] District educators describe 21st-century learning as focusing on critical thinking skills, project-based learning, and digital literacy. These skills align with the qualities educators seek to instill in their students: "engaged" and "active" thinkers who "own their learning." Broad and aspirational, Hoke County's vision for an inclusive 21st century consists of a continuum of learning opportunities that are relevant for meeting the challenges of today's world.

School Readiness: Investments in Pre-K Programs

When Dr. Williamson started in the district, the North Carolina Division of Child Development and Early Education had funding available for pre-K programs housed in district buildings, specifically for families at or below the 75% state median poverty level. As a high-poverty district, this was a huge opportunity for Hoke County Schools to advance school readiness. However, the district only supported six pre-K classes at that time.

Dr. Williamson asked around. He learned that, while the community and board were supportive of pre-K expansion, principals and campus leaders were reluctant to dedicate space in their buildings for pre-K classrooms. He met with principals to have, in his words, a "real conversation" that referenced the consistent and growing evidence that high-quality pre-K supports long-term academic outcomes for children from poor and deeply poor households.[15] He recalled, "I said to them, you better take a look at your third-grade scores if you don't think pre-K is a critical need."

Consequently, the number of pre-K classrooms increased from 6 in 2007–08 to 20 in 2019–20, serving 46% of the district's youngest children, over 70% of whom are children of color. The district pre-K coordinator accepts applications all year long, with the goal to recruit and identify children and families that are below the poverty level and children who have never been served in any type of preschool or daycare setting. The coordinator also collaborates with Smart Start, a state-funded program coordinated locally through the Hoke County Partnership for Children and Families.[16] Among its many programs, Smart Start offers a mobile preschool program for families with transportation barriers to enrolling their children in the district pre-K programming. The mobile preschool program also assists families to fulfill the district's health enrollment requirements, including immunizations and vision tests.

In addition to increasing the number of pre-K classrooms in the district, Dr. Williamson reported that he worked to integrate pre-K into the districtwide instructional culture "with common language and common values." He said the greatest barrier to scaffolding pre-K and elementary learning was the disconnection between Pre-K and district teachers:

> They were just disconnected. You had pre-K teachers who had never been to districtwide professional development. So, they never had that

common language [describing] what it is we are trying to do. They didn't understand [the leadership culture behind] "no random acts." Every day, I could walk into a Pre-K class and [see] something different.

Dr. Williamson pulled early education instructors into district-wide professional development and created specialized professional development for them as well. He supported the district's early educators to see themselves as teachers and instructors, rather than providing childcare services. He described his aim for early educators "to understand the standards and the instructional process." He then identified a district elementary educator with a strong academic track record to serve as the new program director. Elizabeth Mitchell, Director of NC pre-K Programs, described her work to carry forward strategic learning goals for pre-K programs:

> We take [students] as far as we possibly can in a preschool setting and make sure [instruction is] developmentally appropriate. When we do that, we're reaching the whole child, which is so important. Pre-K is all about expanding life through literacy, through math, through social/emotional skills, building relationships, interactions, and making sure those interactions are positive interactions.

Mitchell reported that all district pre-K teachers conduct home visits to build relationships with families. The district uses Teaching Strategies Gold, a formative, curriculum-embedded assessment to monitor kindergarten readiness based on a set of developmentally appropriate progressions for social-emotional, language, cognitive, physical, and academic learning.[17] To ease the transition into district kindergarten, data from these assessments are passed on to kindergarten teachers, an example of the district's theory of action to share data for decision-making.

Developing Challenging and Supportive Instruction

In 2007, the Hoke County School Board of Education collaboratively developed the vision, "We are a world-class learning organization. We engage all members of our diverse student population in rigorous and relevant schoolwork that prepares them for life in the 21st century." Subsequently, the community groups involved in strategic planning have maintained this vision while developing more ambitious goals and strategies to pursue its fulfillment.

Dr. Williamson and his leadership team established literacy as a districtwide instructional priority. This leadership move built the foundation necessary to develop and implement challenging and supportive instruction. Principal at East Hoke Middle School Antonio Covington observed, "ever since I've been in the district, literacy has been the number one focus and everything else is going to drive around that. There's no excuse for a child being illiterate." This system-wide initiative provided a strategic focus for instructional leaders and staff to align literacy skills across grade levels and subject areas to drive academic improvement. Instructional leaders leveraged the teacher-designed and research-proven framework, online tools, and resources from the Literacy Design Collaborative and Mathematics Design Collaborative. After Dr. Williamson introduced *On Common Ground: The Power of Professional Learning Communities* in the annual book club, each campus established professional learning communities to plan and implement shared literacy strategies. As instructional leaders, principals joined these sessions, supported lesson planning, and conducted regular classroom walk-throughs to provide instructional support. It became common for principals in Hoke County Schools to join the literacy walk-throughs of their colleagues, which helped seed and share instructional strategies across campuses.

Literacy was an on-ramp for developing a thinking curriculum across all of the content areas. Dr. Williamson focused his staff on developing instructional strategies for active learning involving critical thinking and problem-solving. As he noted:

> At the end of the day everything is really about instruction. You know we have to challenge kids … to think and research and reason through communication, so that the class is able to speak with confidence … to be able to reason out what that answer is. We have to take advantage of small groups that really operate the way that they should and of the prior knowledge that kids really have…. and the fact that kids like opportunities to do challenging work.

Through ongoing professional development across the grade levels and subject areas, teachers in Hoke County learned new approaches to teaching that actively engaged students, built on their experiences, and used a range of pedagogies including cooperative group work and project-based learning, with scaffolds to help students reach mastery. Teachers were expected to learn to prepare lessons, "to internalize the lessons so that they own it, and so they themselves control the classroom and help kids and meet the kids' individual needs." Teachers were enabled to collaborate and plan together, to participate in professional learning communities, to visit other buildings to look at instruction and analyze practice, and to become instructional experts. Principals were expected and enabled to facilitate these actions as they became instructional leaders.

Over time, these efforts advanced the ambitious vision of teaching and learning in Hoke County Schools by establishing consistent instructional practices across district campuses and classrooms. District leaders simultaneously monitored outcomes data to determine whether any policies and practices created obstacles for equal access to challenging and supportive instruction. The next section describes how district leaders identified and addressed learning barriers that were reinforced by programs designed to support American Indian/Alaska Native students.

All Means All: The Indian Education Department

Hoke County Schools serves a large population of American Indian/Alaska Native students (8%) relative to the state average (1%).[18] Many of the students in Hoke County who identify as American Indian/Alaska Native are affiliated with the Lumbee Tribe, which is the largest American Indian tribe east of the Mississippi, centered in neighboring Robeson County.[19] Located near the Robeson County border, Hawkeye Elementary School serves 36% American Indian students.[20] The presence of the Native community in the region predated the district by thousands of years. Maintaining cultural identity while pursuing formal education is a longstanding value in the Lumbee Tribe that has persisted through a history of discrimination and forced assimilation within educational institutions.[21]

Honoring this history, district leaders in Hoke County Schools have long operated an Indian Education Department under a Federal Title VI program. The mission of the district's Indian Education Department is to recognize and catalyze the assets of American Indian students in their educational experiences. As described on the district's website, the purpose of the Indian Education department is:

> To support programs and activities of direct assistance for meeting the diverse educational and culturally related academic needs of American Indian, and Alaska Native students so that they can achieve the same challenging state performance standards as all students.[22]

Upon Dr. Williamson's entry into Hoke County Schools, he was especially alarmed by high dropout rates and low academic performance for American Indian/Alaska Native students. These data demonstrated that the aims of the Indian Education Department were not being advanced. He observed that, in practice, participation in Indian education programs required students to frequently be 'pulled out' of regular classroom instruction to perform at various cultural exhibitions, losing significant instructional time. This resulted in systemic racial inequality: students participating in the Indian Education programs were receiving less academic support than their peers.

Through his belief in educating the whole child, Dr. Williamson knew the pursuit of cultural enrichment and academic achievement is not an either-or proposition. He took bold action, replacing the department director with an assistant principal who had a demonstrated track record of instructional leadership in Hoke County Schools. This sudden change raised concerns within the Native community, perhaps unsurprisingly, given long histories of educational exclusion and forced assimilation of Native peoples in American school systems.[23] When Dr. Williamson heard calls for his resignation based on the misperception that he did not support American Indian students, he responded with an effort to strengthen relationships with the Native community.

Dr. Williamson knew relationships require trust. He started by encouraging the new director of Indian Education to persevere. He recalled, "I made it clear to her. You have my support, 100%. It's part of our strategic plan that we are going to provide equitable opportunities for all our kids and move them [academically]." With Williamson's support, the new director launched the first-ever community meetings sharing student data as well as her department's focus and plans. She maintained these meetings monthly. She included the superintendent and the entire cabinet to ensure transparency and to field parents' questions. The meeting series shifted the narrative by sharing both historical data and new plans to invest federal dollars in strategic academic support. Dr. Williamson noted that part of the goal was to create an equitable, countywide approach that included American Indian students, instead of a more segregated discussion about their context alone. Bringing an "all means all" framing, he and his team reset the discussion:

> ... not to allow the conversations to be [focused] on Native Americans, but about how Hoke County Schools needs to serve all of our kids. You know, we shifted the conversation to [how we create] schools that serve all our kids and meet their needs. It was in those meetings that we could really share the historical data that was just critical. And so, my parents really started to see: "Yeah, they're telling the truth" [about] high drop-out rates, low performance in math and reading. We were just consistent with our message. And then we said, "the money is really to provide additional support."

Through consistent messaging and relationship-building with parents and leaders in the Native community, district leaders garnered support to reinvest Indian Education Department resources in wraparound services, including parent nights, after-school tutoring, within-classroom academic tutors, and a summer outreach program. These supplemented a renewed focus on the quality of instruction in the schools most American Indian/ Alaska Native students attended. District staff recognize that merely providing services is not sufficient; they need to ensure the services are culturally responsive. For example, Elizabeth Mitchell, Director of Indian Education, emphasized the importance of hiring tutors who are culturally responsive:

> We make sure that when the tutors are hired, they are aware of the culture of the Native Americans in the community because that's crucial to the learning process. We have found that to be very effective at making academic gains, even though we're not where we want to be.

Mitchell's remarks also demonstrate the department's focus on measurable improvements in the educational experiences of American Indian/Alaska Native students. These coordinated services and supports are showing results. As described earlier in Tables 3.2 and 3.3, American Indian/Alaska Native students have had large achievement gains. The next section describes improvements in the participation of American Indian/Alaska Native students in gifted programs and advanced courses. In addition, between 2014–15 and 2019–20, suspension rates decreased by 36% (Table 3A.5), and graduation rates rose by 16 percentage points—a 26% increase—among American Indian students (Table 3A.3). At 77%, the graduation rate of American Indian/Alaska Native students still trails the district average by 11 percentage points.[24] However, the district has made strides in supporting American Indian/Alaska Native students and continues to work to improve their opportunities and outcomes. When asked about the gains, Mitchell attributes the high expectations that educators in Hoke County Schools set for all, including American Indian/Alaska Native students and families:

> We have high expectations for our American Indian families. And we've had some great ones to go on, to graduate with honors, to graduate the highest in their class. And to come back, and what is so great is to see the students come back to serve the community in some way, and that's what it's all about.

Student Preparation for College and Careers

When Dr. Williamson arrived in Hoke County, he brought with him a vision of how school districts can prepare students for the future. Leaders in Hoke County Schools set forward-facing goals to meet the priority of "every student prepared:" (1) Students will graduate prepared for postsecondary education, and (2) students pursuing Career and Technical Education (CTE) will graduate prepared for careers.[25] Through digital literacy integration and a portfolio of college- and career-ready pathways, students in Hoke County Schools are supported to tailor their learning trajectories to graduate with postsecondary choices.

To track college readiness, district staff in the Department of Testing and Accountability monitor performance on the ACT College Admissions Assessment (ACT). The ACT, a college readiness assessment given to all students in the 11th grade, became part of North Carolina's school accountability program in 2012–13. In 2014–15, Hoke County Schools trailed the state by nearly 15 percentage points in the percentage of students achieving the state benchmark score of 17 out of 36 on the ACT (Figure 3.3). In 2018–19, the gap between the district and state in the percent of students scoring 17 or above narrowed to just 3 percentage points.

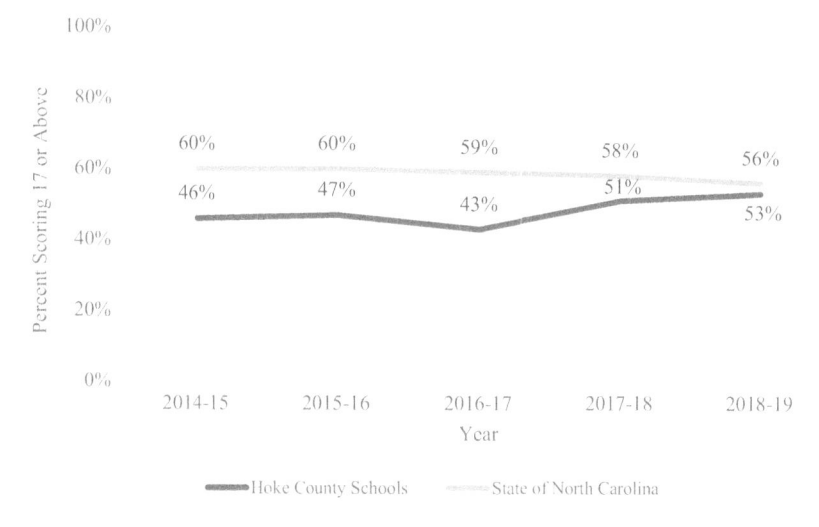

Figure 3.3 Comparison of Hoke County Schools and North Carolina Percentage Meeting or Exceeding State Benchmark on ACT College Entrance Exam, 2014–15 to 2018–19.

Source: North Carolina School Report Cards, https://www.dpi.nc.gov/data-reports/school-report-cards.

Between 2014–15 and 2019–20, the percent of students scoring 17 or above on the ACT has increased for each racial group (Table 3A.2). Although gains were made unevenly over this period, overall, the percent of students meeting this benchmark increased from 41% to 50% for American Indian/Alaska Native students, 32% to 41% for Black students, and from 46% to 50% for Latino/a students. When asked about the practices that have supported these gains, Hoke County Schools district leaders credited their ongoing work to expand digital fluency and access to college-ready curriculum through AP coursework and an early college program.

Digital Literacy Integration

As an aspect of pursuing a "world class education," Dr. Williamson championed digital literacy integration that prepares students for careers in the global economy. This effort began with long-range goals set in 2009 to provide up-to-date technologies for teachers, administrators, and staff; train teachers on how to incorporate technologies into instructional strategies; and provide students with the understanding of how and where technology is applicable in careers. His rationale was that student success in the 21st century requires technological fluency, which can be harnessed in the classroom to foster student engagement in authentic demonstrations of learning, encourage collaboration, and personalize academic experiences.

To advance this priority, Dr. Williamson asked Executive Director of Digital Teaching and Learning Dawn Ramseur to rethink and expand the work of the district's Information and Technology Department. His vision was that the newly named Office of Digital Teaching and Learning would carry the mission of literacy forward into the 21st century so that digital literacy would be part of each student's portfolio of skills. Ramseur oversaw substantial investments in digital learning aligned to the district's fourth strategic priority: "every school will have up-to-date technology systems to serve its students, parents, and educators."[26] In 2014, Ramseur and her team secured a \$2 million Department of Defense grant. This grant supported the new Office of Digital Teaching and Learning, including the 2016–17 launch of a 1-to-1 program that provides a laptop or tablet for all students from second grade through high school. According to Ramseur, however, the new Office of Digital Teaching and Learning was meant to do more than distribute hardware, its mission was to be a source of instructional leadership:

> The tail can't wag the dog, right? Technology can't make instructional decisions; they need to be supported. The first thing I did was change the alignment as Dr. Williamson had suggested. There is a need for technology to be under the instructional piece. There has to be this umbrella where we recognize our goal here is instruction, and technology is a support piece for students and teachers. Now, technology is under the instructional umbrella; it was not originally.

Before implementing a district-wide digital literacy program, Ramseur recognized that:

> It was going to be impossible for me to support the entire district. We got a lot of devices, but you can't put devices in teachers' hands without showing them what to do with them. We wanted to be sure the teachers were ready.

She focused first on establishing a Digital Teaching and Learning Team responsible for providing instructional leadership. Ramseur staffed a team of six former classroom teachers to lead and manage the Office of Digital Teaching and Learning. The online software available to students comprises an extensive digital toolbox. Members of the Digital Teaching and Learning team have trained and supported teachers to use free and customizable online software, aligned to the district's commitment to building capacity from within. Teachers can access several professional development opportunities, also open to district administrators and parents. One member of the Digital Teaching and Learning team explained:

> We regularly provide training, create videos, and publish resources for our community stakeholders who need assistance with the many topics surrounding digital teaching and learning. Whether you're a parent who needs help with your student's device, an administrator who needs a refresher, or a teacher who wants to catch up on the last professional development session you were unable to attend, this space is for you!

Establishing digital literacy as a core capacity for all students is no small feat in Hoke County, where the infrastructure for reliable, affordable on-line access is not available in many households. Ramseur explained how her office works to eliminate, rather than reinforce, socioeconomic barriers to learning:

> We knew that we have students who didn't have access to internet, so that meant we [worked closely with families to provide] access to free internet. We bought a number of hotspots for families. We recognize that we have to use lots of different modalities.

To get students online, the district provides information on free internet services through direct outreach to families, posts on their website, and advertisements on local radio stations. Ramseur said these broad efforts to share information promote digital literacy for all learners and families—no one is left behind.

Access to Advanced Coursework

One of the key leadership moves by Dr. Williamson and his colleagues was to expand access to advanced coursework. Hoke County Schools offers advanced programming through an Academically and Intellectually Gifted (AIG) program in district middle schools and an AP program in district high schools. The Director of the AIG and AP programs, Linden Cummings, identified a systemic need to increase the racial diversity in the district's advanced courses when he came on staff in 2008. As he recalled:

> When I came to Hoke County as the coordinator for the Academically and Intellectually Gifted program, there were about 300 students in the program. I would say about 85% of them were White students. I went around to all the schools and asked the principals, "What are some things we can do to improve the program?" One of the things I heard loud and clear is that we needed to do something about the identification of more students of color to make the program more reflective of the demographics of the community. So, I got to work.

Last year, we had 821 gifted kids. So, we went from 300 to 821 last year. This year, we were at 730 [due to COVID-related pauses in testing]. We had 295 White, 145 Black, 153 Hispanic, 75 multiracial, 22 Asian, and 37 American Indian. So, we've come a long way.

To increase racial diversity in the AP program as well, district leaders created an open-door policy, enabling any student to enroll in AP courses. Across North Carolina, students typically start taking AP courses in their junior year. In Hoke County Schools, students can enroll in a subset of the 18 district-offered AP courses as early as their freshman year. The district's secret to AP readiness is establishing strong academic pipelines in middle schools. In middle school, students are automatically enrolled in advanced coursework with the option to "opt out" rather than "opting in." This draws in more students than traditional teacher recommendations or a self-selection process that tends to limit enrollment. In Hoke County Schools, the district removed cost barriers to AP participation by purchasing all course materials for students, including textbooks. Hoke County Schools was the first district in the state to cover the cost of AP exams, an investment that district leaders have continued annually for roughly 200 students, with no maximum number of tests per student.

In addition to increasing access to AP courses, district leaders are seeking to ensure the AP courses are empowering learning experiences by supporting the professional development of teachers. As members of the North Carolina AP Partnership, district educators can access free professional development for AP coursework. This benefit extends to middle school teachers, who participate in pre-AP workshops to strengthen the pipeline into secondary AP coursework.[27] AP teachers are also eligible for scholarships to the National AP Annual Conference, where they can further develop practices to sharpen students' critical thinking and enhance their fluency as college-level readers and writers.[28] These efforts have meaningfully advanced equitable learning opportunities for students of color by diversifying the racial composition of students engaging in AP coursework, while performance in AP courses continues to climb to meet state averages.

The expansion of the AP program is a powerful example of how district leaders enhance the learning of all students but also, in a very concrete way, promote racial equity. AP course enrollments have risen in Hoke County Schools, across racial groups (Table 3.4).

In the school year 2001–02, Hoke County Schools offered four AP courses, enrolling a total of 39 students. Nearly 80% of students taking AP courses were White, with some Black (18%) and Asian American (3%) peers. By school year 2019–20, the district had increased to 256 AP enrollments across more than 12 courses. Compared to 2001–02, 2019–20 AP

Table 3.4 Hoke County Schools Demographics and AP Enrollment, 2001–02 and 2019–20

Race/Ethnicity	2001–02		2019–20	
	Demographics	AP Enrollment	Demographics	AP Enrollment
American Indian/ Alaska Native	14%	0%	2%	7%
Asian American	1%	3%	2%	3%
Black	49%	18%	34%	31%
Latino/a	5%	0%	22%	23%
Multiracial	0%	0%	11%	7%
White	30%	79%	26%	30%

Source: Public Schools of North Carolina Statistical Profile. https://www.dpi.nc.gov/districts-schools/district-operations/financial-and-business-services/statistical-profile; North Carolina School Report Cards, https://www.dpi.nc.gov/data-reports/school-report-cards (thru 2019–20).

Note: Students may be enrolled in multiple courses.

enrollments were more racially representative of the district demographics, comprising 31% Black, 30% White, 23% Latino/a, 7% American Indian/ Alaska Native, 7% Multiracial, and 3% Asian American students.[29]

Participation and success on AP examinations have also increased in Hoke County Schools. In 2013, the district had an AP exam participation rate of 7% of all high school students, with 141 total test-takers.[30] In 2020, the district had an AP exam participation rate of 12% of all high school students, with 281 total test-takers. The final score for each AP exam is reported on a 5-point scale. The University of North Carolina System designed its AP credit acceptance policy to promote student success in higher education. Under this policy, students who earn a score of "three" or higher on their AP exams will receive credit from all 16 universities within the system. Because the state funds these exams, students essentially earn free credits toward a bachelor's degree for every AP exam score of "three" or higher.

As Figure 3.4 shows, Hoke County nearly tripled the share of AP test-takers scoring a 3 or above between 2013 and 2020, reaching 37% by 2020. This is especially noteworthy since Hoke County does not restrict who is allowed to take the courses and exams, whereas most districts reserve these courses for only selected students. Both the district and state experienced a drop in AP exam participation rates in the spring of 2020 due to testing disruptions related to the COVID-19 pandemic.

Although these data are not available in a form disaggregated by student race/ethnicity, they are a promising indicator of student access to

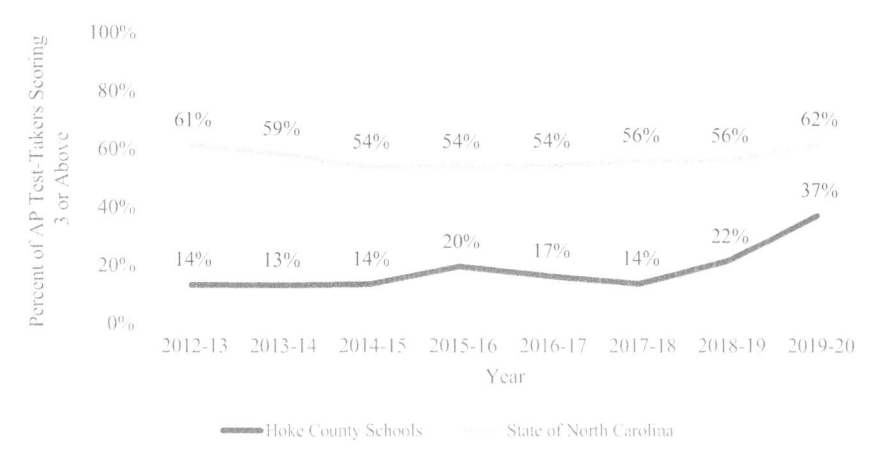

Figure 3.4 Hoke County Schools Percentage of AP Test-Takers Scoring 3 or Above, 2012–13 to 2019–20

Source: North Carolina Department of Public Instruction, SAT and AP Test Results, https://www.dpi.nc.gov/districts-schools/testing-and-school-accountability/school-accountability-and-reporting/north-carolina-sat-and-ap-reports#advanced-placement-ap-reports.

opportunity. As AP participation increased and became more representative of the district's racial/ethnic composition, overall district pass rates increased.

SandHoke Early College

As part of Dr. Williamson's vision to transform Hoke County Schools into a "world class learning organization," he established the SandHoke Early College High School in 2007 through a collaboration with the Sandhills Community College. SandHoke Early College High School was among the first early college high schools opened in North Carolina. Through the five-year early college program, SandHoke graduates fulfill requirements to receive both a high school diploma from Hoke County Schools and an Associate in Arts or Associate in Science degree from Sandhills Community College. Seventy percent of the 500 students in the early college are students of color.

Once enrolled, SandHoke students begin a personalized high school program featuring class sizes of roughly 15 students, academic advisories, and seminars designed to develop academic and social-emotional skills to ease the postsecondary transition. SandHoke students begin building credits toward an Associate in Arts degree in their sophomore year, with the aim of completing the Associate in Arts degree at the end of their fifth, "super-senior" year. The program involves a physical transition into college: after completing coursework at the early college high school campus, seniors and super seniors transfer to the nearby Sandhills Community College campus. Outcomes demonstrate the success of the SandHoke Early College High School; since 2016–17, the average four-year cohort graduation rate has been above 95%.[31]

The partnership with Sandhills Community College supports Hoke County Schools graduates to enroll in postsecondary (see Table 3.5). In aggregate from 2009 to 2016, SandHoke Early College graduates enrolled in postsecondary education within 12 months of graduation on par with the state average and at a higher rate than the district's other high school, Hoke County High School. Disaggregated by race, all groups at SandHoke except White students enrolled in postsecondary education at higher-than-state-average rates, some by significant margins. For example, 85% of American Indian/Alaska Native SandHoke graduates enrolled in postsecondary education within 12 months of graduation, compared to 47% from Hoke County High and 51% across the state. Similarly, Black and Latino/a Sand-Hoke graduates were also more likely to enroll in postsecondary education (63% and 49%, respectively) than their counterparts at Hoke County High (50% and 37%) and across the state (59% and 44%).

Career and Technical Education Pathways

A critical part of Dr. Williamson's vision was to break down the educational silos that track students into academic and vocational programs, which can

Table 3.5 Postsecondary Enrollment for Graduating Classes 2009–16 by Race/Ethnicity

Race/Ethnicity	SandHoke Early College High School	Hoke County High	North Carolina
ALL	63%	48%	63%
American Indian/ Alaska Native	85%	47%	51%
Asian American	N/A	67%	72%
Black	63%	50%	59%
Latino/a	49%	37%	44%
Multiracial	74%	43%	62%
White	60%	49%	67%

Source: North Carolina School Report Cards. https://ncreports.ondemand.sas.com/src/?county=Hoke

Note: Percentages represent public high school graduates enrolled in postsecondary education within 12 months of graduation. Data for Asian American students are suppressed when counts are fewer than 20.

result in dividing students according to questionable measures of ability and all too often by race and family income.[32] Today, students can experiment with a variety of career and college options. In a school district where poverty and deep poverty are prevalent, preparing students to be successful long after high school graduation is a mission that drives how the district's faculty and leadership develop curriculum. Director of CTE Dr. Dana Chavis explained that her department cultivates future-facing learning opportunities that prepare graduates to directly enter the workforce:

> What we do try to do is project out. And when you're looking seven years down the road or ten years down the road and you have students that will be graduating, you want those students to have an opportunity to immediately go to work in a profession that's actually going to be available for them.

As participants in a statewide Career & College Promise Program, district leaders collaborated with Sandhills Community College and local businesses to establish a program called the Workforce Continuing Education Pathways. This program enables students to earn "a state or industry-recognized credential aligned with a high school career cluster, preparing them to enter the workforce." Determining which choices are most likely to result in a well-paying local job is not left to chance. Director of CTE Dr. Dana Chavis explained how the district connects to the world of business:

> It's important to be connected to the business world in Hoke County, but also in the surroundings counties. We know that typically our students, if they're going to move, they're not going to move too far away. They may move to another part of North Carolina, but they'll probably stay pretty much close to home. We listen to the business world because they're the ones that know what's coming and what their needs are. The reason why we have certified production technician at the high school is because the manufacturing plants said, "We have got to get work. We don't have anybody to work with our machinery." We said, "Okay." The businesses brought in all this equipment, and we marketed it to the students.

District middle schools offer exploratory CTE courses in computer science, engineering, and business and entrepreneurship. In high school, introductory courses begin in 9th and 10th grade, and advanced specialization courses are available in 11th and 12th. CTE pathways include agriculture, business, finance and marketing, career development, computer science and information, family and consumer science and information technology, health science, technology, and engineering and industrial classes that include plumbing and heating, ventilation, and air conditioning.

Chavis reported that in 2018–19, more than 90% of students enrolled in a CTE course earned a credential. This approach to career and technical training supports postsecondary readiness by breaking down the barriers between the world of work and how the district develops programs and learning opportunities.

Safe and Productive Learning Environments

Academic excellence is a marker of a "world class learning organization," and educators in Hoke County Schools know that meeting high academic standards requires a community of care and compassion. One of the strategic priorities in the district reads, "every student will be healthy, safe, and responsible."[33] This section describes the work of district leaders to establish systemwide supports for a safe and productive learning environment, which the district formally defines as:

> …one where learners feel physically, emotionally, and socially comfortable. Students feel they are protected by caring and thoughtful teachers and members of their community. A safe learning environment is focused on academic achievement, maintaining high standards, fostering positive relationships between staff and students, and promoting healthy social and emotional development.[34]

Efforts to create and sustain safe, instructionally supportive classroom environments have coincided with measurable improvements in opportunity and outcomes for students of color: in addition to the academic gains presented in the prior section, graduation rates have increased and suspension rates have decreased for all racial and ethnic groups in the district. In 2014–15, Hoke County Schools had a four-year cohort graduation rate of 75% compared to 86% statewide (Figure 3.5). By 2019–20, the district's four-year cohort graduation rate rose to 88%, reaching the state average.

In this same period, disaggregated district graduation rates show gains of more than 10 percentage points for every racial group. Between 2014–15 and 2019–20, graduation rates rose by 16 percentage points among American Indian/Alaska Native students, 16 among Latino/a students, and 12 among Black students (Figure 3.6).

Staff reported that their efforts to keep students on track to graduation included both strengthening academic supports, described earlier in this report, and efforts to decrease the use of exclusionary discipline that results in loss of learning time and disengagement. Indeed, research has shown that suspensions correlate strongly with dropping out.[35]

The short-term suspension rate in Hoke County Schools decreased from 18 suspensions per 100 students in 2015–16 (the first year of data available) to 11 suspensions per 100 students in 2019–20. In the same period, the

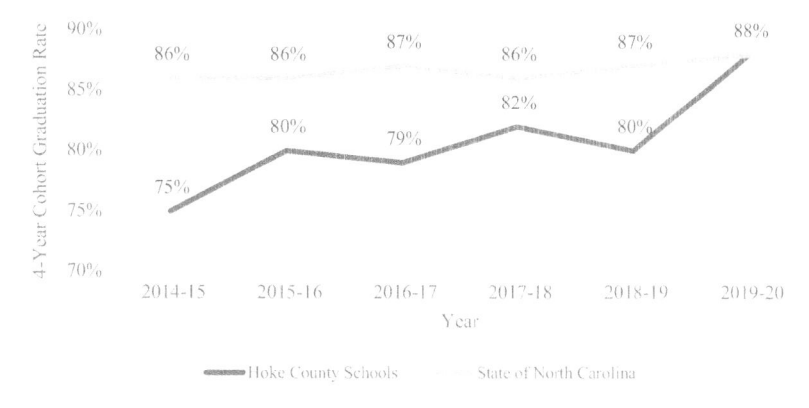

Figure 3.5 Comparison of Hoke County Schools and North Carolina 4-Year Cohort Graduation Rates, 2014–15 to 2019–20.

Source: North Carolina School Report Cards, https://www.dpi.nc.gov/data-reports/school-report-cards.

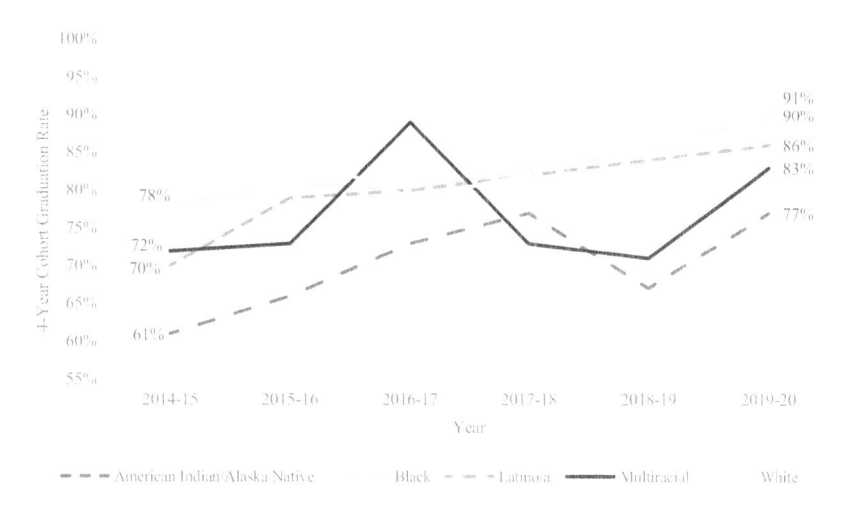

Figure 3.6 Hoke County Schools 4-Year Cohort Graduation Rates by Race/Ethnicity, 2014–15 to 2019–20.

Source: North Carolina Department of Public Instruction. (2020). Longitudinal 4-Year and 5-Year Cohort Graduation Rates through 2020. https://www.dpi.nc.gov/longitudinal-4-year-and-5-year-cohort-graduation-rates-through-2020.

Note: Disaggregated data are not available for Asian American and Native Hawaiian/Pacific Islander student groups.

total number of days missed due to short-term suspensions decreased from nearly 4,000 to less than 2,500. The data also show a persistent, racialized pattern in short-term suspensions (see Figure 3.7).

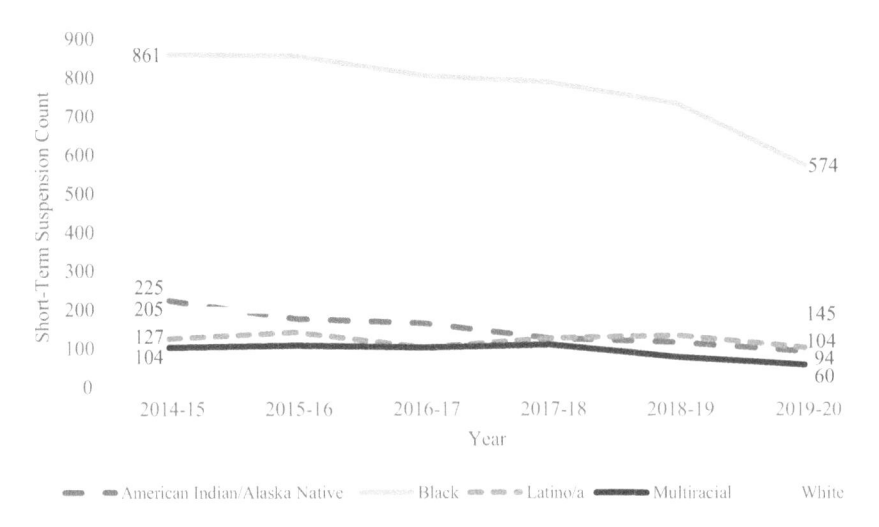

Figure 3.7 Hoke County Schools Short Term Suspensions (Count) by Race/ Ethnicity, 2014–15 to 2019–20.

Source: North Carolina Department of Public Instruction (n.d.). Discipline, ALP, and Drop-out Annual Reports. https://www.dpi.nc.gov/data-reports/dropout-and-discipline-data/ discipline-alp-and-dropout-annual-reports#2019-20.

Consistent with national trends,[36] suspension rates were disproportionately high for Black students in Hoke County from 2014–15 to 2019–20 (Table 3A.5). During that time, Black students comprised about one-third of the county's students. However, in 2014–15, over half of the 1,523 total short-term suspensions were issued to Black students (861 short-term suspensions). In 2019–20, at 574 suspensions, Black students still received over half of the district's 979 suspensions. The district, however, has made strides in reducing disparities in discipline rates. Between 2014–15 and 2019–20, short-term suspensions dropped by nearly 60% for American Indian/Alaska Native students and by one-third for Black students. These drops in suspension rates outpaced changes in statewide suspension rates, which dropped by 36% for American Indian/Alaska Native students and by 30% for Black students. The district issued no expulsions from 2013–14 to 2019–20 and only two long-term suspensions during that period.

Relationships in Support of Learning

Instructional strategies centered on student engagement through positive relationships are at the heart of efforts to ensure each school and classroom in the district is a safe and productive learning environment. As part of his leadership strategy to hold adults responsible for the learning in the district, Dr. Williamson messaged an oft-repeated phrase that "relationships matter." Members of his cabinet team and school leaders connected the instructional strategies driving academic achievement in Hoke County Schools to concerted efforts to establish communities of learning that are safe, productive, and affirming for each and every learner.

Principal of West Hoke Middle School Mary McLeod expressed why positive relationships with students and families, many of whom have experienced generational poverty, are central to her educational mission: it is the responsibility of adults in the district to "treat them with dignity and respect." She explained that mutual respect is the foundation for meaningful learning (Box 3.1).

Box 3.1   The Science of Positive Relationships and Learning

Research on brain science has shown that positive relationships support the development of neural networks that are critical for learning and managing behavior.[37] Educators who foster responsive, affirming relationships with learners are better able to recognize and ameliorate the effects of adverse childhood experiences by teaching skills related to calming, self-expression, and healing necessary for resilience and holistic student success.[38] The following vignette summarizes one principal's example of best practices:

In the morning bustle of students arriving at school, a teacher observes one of his students cutting through the throng. The student bypasses the usual stops on her morning routine: the breakfast cart and idle chatter of her peers. Instead, she slings her backpack under her chair and slouches with her head on her desk. She appears tired and disheveled. The teacher reads her tone, posture, and one-word greeting as a need for connection, not a sign of disrespect. The teacher responds quickly from a place of care. He crouches by her desk and privately checks in on how she is feeling. When she says that she is tired, he makes it clear that he understands. With encouragement, she gets settled and ready for class. Later that day, she confides in him that she had a rough night and needed that extra encouragement to get going in the morning. He thanks her for pushing through and makes a note to check in with other adults in her support networks at school and home.

Adults' Roles in Establishing Positive Relationships

Creating safe and productive learning environments in Hoke County starts with establishing a pervasive, supportive culture. Leaders, teachers, and support staff in Hoke County Schools are expected to understand the context of schooling in the district and establish asset-based relationships with students and families. In Hoke County Schools, staff help each other understand students better. They discuss the differences in life experiences between the adults and learners head-on. Forty-six percent of the district's teachers are White; 74% of the student population are students of color. Many Hoke County teachers enter the district without prior professional or life experience in communities experiencing poverty or racial discrimination. Because of this, teachers enter the district with knowledge gaps and misconceptions about what life is like for many of their students. A district administrator explained, "We have a tendency [to think] that our frame of reference is the real one and the only one that exists." Another teacher recognized that, "Sometimes, we ourselves are the barrier for our learners."

To address staff misconceptions about poverty and race, the district aims to forge an asset-based culture—embodied in the "Hoke County Way"—that guides the interactions between students, families, and adults. One district administrator described how this culture is built:

> District staff start every year teaching the "Hoke County Way." That's what can really impact your equity in the classroom. If staff don't understand, if they say, "I can't teach low performing students," you need to recognize that issue right away. We have to be able to have those real tough, real crucial conversations with people about their mindset. It's not that they're bad people; it's just they've lived so differently. Whatever experiences they bring, you might have to open them up a little bit more. "Yeah, [your students] might be in poverty, but that's not their potential."

The "Hoke County Way" hinges on two understandings: first, every child can learn, and second, every child's family is doing everything they can to support them. These understandings are the foundations of a district-wide culture that holds the adults accountable for creating safe schools and classrooms. Principal of Turlington High School Joel Brewington described a safe school and classroom environment as one in which: "Every student who is going through Hoke County is going to have a teacher who cares about them tremendously, cares about their future, and cares about their success." School leaders set expectations and offer in-the-moment supports for instructional staff to establish safe and productive classrooms, encouraging behaviors that build persistent, caring, and trusting relationships with students (see "Stepping in the Gap the Hoke County Way"). In this way, educators in Hoke County Schools cultivate caring relationships with students that enable them to, in the words of another leader, "keep an ear to the pavement" and quickly respond to any barriers that get in the way of learning (Box 3.2).

In Hoke County Schools, positive school climate is not the result of chance but is intentionally created based on a whole-school commitment to support all students with empathy and systemwide supports. More than a sentiment, positive and asset-oriented relationships are systemically reinforced through the implementation of a MTSSs and additional programs to support physical and mental well-being.

Multi-Tiered System of Supports

To advance the district priority that "every student is healthy, safe, and responsible," district leaders adopted a MTSS that systematized their focus on relationships that support learning.[39] Dr. Williamson explained that this change was driven by a look at the data on "exceptional children," a state-defined designation for students with different educational needs than the average child, including physical, mental, or social disabilities. [40] He recalled, "the identification numbers for [exceptional children] were just too high, and [it was] that same story based on behavior, not based on true

---

Box 3.2 'Stepping in the Gap' the Hoke County Way

The following vignette summarizes an example Principal of West Hoke Middle School Mary McLeod provided when asked how her staff creates safe classroom environments for learners:

> A teacher noticed a marked shift in the demeanor of one of her students. He was getting easily frustrated with himself and others during class. She requests a meeting with the family to check in and discuss the ideas for helping get the student back on track. The teacher receives a voicemail after hours explaining that family members can't make it to the school. The teacher consults her principal, who says, "We can't assume and don't ever make a child feel as though their parent doesn't care because they can't come to the school." The principal and teacher decide to return the family's call together in the evening. While talking, they discover that the county's limited access to reliable transportation is what's preventing an in-person meeting. The principal flexes her schedule to provide a ride both to and from the family-teacher conference. She calls this 'stepping in the gap' to support student success.

assessment and [addressing the] real needs" behind perceived misbehavior. He acknowledged:

> We [were] wasting time with kids because of our beliefs. [Our teachers made assumptions] early on that [certain students] can't learn, can't do complicated work, can't be problem solvers. So [we were] really just biding the time and waiting for kids to fail.

It was difficult for teachers to hear they were not addressing students' real needs. Dr. Williamson reported that his teachers "took it personally," which he considered a sign of their passion and commitment. He responded to frustration with a clear message: educators should be frustrated because the district had not yet provided the training they needed to change. With the introduction of MTSS, he provided educators the awareness and tools needed to own their decisions about student engagement and academic performance moving forward.

MTSS established a consistent and research-backed process for district educators to track and respond to the instructional needs of students as they arise, replacing individual judgment calls with valid assessment. Dr. Williamson characterized the shift as moving from intervening to preventing academic disengagement. He said the real challenge was shifting established practices to "help individuals come to grips with the truth: a lot of behaviors we're seeing are because of a lack of relationship with the kids. That's on you, not the kids." MTSS set the foundation for a renewed focus on reengaging learners through world-class instruction. Dr. Williamson saw the work as helping teachers understand "the instructional work they needed to do, along with a true assessment of progress so that needs could be addressed." He explained,

> It took time to correct, in terms of how we address this issue daily in instructional time. How do kids learn best? Why do you think they are bored? It's because you're not engaging them. You have not done your work in terms of how kids in high-poverty [communities] learn best. They learn best through an applied curriculum, through mentors that care and engage them in conversation, and they learn from each other. That was a major change.

This major change required concerted professional development for the teachers across the district. The MTSS infrastructure included a dedicated MTSS coordinator and facilitator who provides monthly trainings for assistant superintendents and directors, monthly administration, coaching support to MTSS representatives at each campus, and ad-hoc progress monitoring and support to campus teams.[41] Bridget Parnell-Hayes, Principal of Hawk Eye Elementary School, emphasized the importance of professional learning to implement MTSS:

The level of support is continuous. It's a true team effort. It is hugely important with the new teachers to have conversations about MTSS and how we're looking at individual students and what their needs are and how to best meet them.

A district leader echoed the importance MTSS places on transforming the behavior of adults, not students:

We are looking at the teacher first. What interventions are the teachers bringing before they're sending that student to the office or writing that student up? We have to look at that teacher's behavior. How did they react to that situation? Did they blow up that situation? Did it cause that student to do that?

The strategy and supports for districtwide MTSS implementation appear to be gaining success; it has coincided with declines in suspension rates and increases in achievement for all students in Hoke County Schools and especially students of color.

Programs to Support Physical and Mental Wellbeing

As a high-poverty district, MTSS implementation has helped instructional staff identify learning needs that extend beyond the classroom environment. The 2016–21 strategic plan establishes strategies for administrators, instructional staff, and support services to promote health, nutrition, and counseling services that are foundational for academic learning.[42] Director of Student Support Services Peggy Owens reflected on the district's approach to addressing the harm caused by community-level stress on children's ability to learn: "We are constantly asking 'what is it that we can do in order to set up our students?' Because the student is right there in the center." This emphasis on placing the student at the center reflects the pervasive leadership culture that believes all students can learn, which means adults are responsible for promoting physical and mental well-being.

The Hoke County Schools Child Nutrition Services Department promotes students' physical well-being as foundational for learning. The department's website states simply, "Students cannot learn if they are hungry." Department staff coordinates participation in national programs to provide school breakfast, lunch, and afterschool snacks for all students. All district students, regardless of family income, can access three meals a day at no charge and without the obstacle of an application process. In addition to nutritional services, staff in the Department of Student Services coordinate a range of health programs, including immunizations, medication administration, and health screenings for students. A team of 12 school nurses coordinates these health programs. Staff in the Student Services Department also coordinate with the Hoke County Health Department and Department of Social Services in their work to provide families access to area physicians outside of schools, regardless of their insurance coverage.

District staff promote students' social and emotional well-being through a Mental Health Program, which coordinates a Mental Health Service System with multiple levels of integrated supports between the schools and community. The district employs 16 full-time school-based counselors dedicated to supporting the affective and cognitive development of students at all grade levels. Every school is staffed with at least one counselor: the high school has five counselors, a college and career coordinator, a scholarship coordinator, and three dropout prevention specialists, which are funded locally.

Resource Equity

> The district vision is to level the playing field. It's giving all students an opportunity for success. I think we do that throughout the professional development we have for our administrators in the district, the teachers in the district, and then making sure that technology is available to all students.
>
> — Mary McLeod, Middle School Principal

Leveling the Playing Field

The conviction in Hoke County Schools that 'all means all' is evident in the district's approach to resource allocation. Hoke County Schools seeks to ensure that its resources are equitably distributed between every campus, classroom, and student. Budgets follow values. By ensuring equal access to educational materials, teacher qualifications and experience, and extracurricular activities across campuses, the leadership in Hoke County Schools creates educational opportunity for students of color and students from poor and deeply poor households. District-level leaders said their practice of considering resource equity in financial decision-making was an important strategy for ensuring strategic priorities are met as written for every student. In a 2015 article for EducationNC, reporter Mebane Rash noted:[43]

> An interesting thing has happened in Hoke County. While many school districts have implemented magnet programs, year-round schools, and other choices that allow different schools to offer fit to different students and families, the Hoke County Schools have moved to equalize the offerings at each school so they can sell every school as a great school.

Financial resources are limited in Hoke County Schools. In 2020–21, the pupil expenditure in the district was $10,038 through a combination of local (10%), state (80%), and federal (10%) funding.[44] As already stated, its local funding is less than half of that generally available in the state, and although it has higher need students than the state average, its combined federal, state, and local funding continues to be less than the state average. To transform their system, district and site-level leaders were encouraged to become entrepreneurial and advocate for their schools. School leaders are active in the community, always ready to make a pitch for fundraising. Principal McLeod explained,

> As building leaders, you have to have an elevator speech ready about your school at all times. You have to be able to describe your school in the community. I think we're all pretty savvy at it, supported by district initiatives with our board of education and commissioners. All those entities work together to make sure Hoke County gets what it needs.

Various community partnerships were necessary for securing the resources the district's children need.

- Local businesses and faith-based organizations: campus leaders of a school located in downtown Raeford, one of Hoke County's urban hubs, coordinate with businesses and faith-based organizations to provide community meals and organize drives for material resources, including clothes and holiday gifts.
- The Hoke County Partnerships for Children and Families: founded in 1994, this non-profit strives towards the mission of "helping children and families by providing a foundation to develop self-assurance for life through education and resources." This organization partners with campuses across the district.
- Whole-child support: the school board built partnerships that provide whole-child support for learning. These span the areas of childcare (e.g., need-based scholarships and directory of referrals), healthcare (e.g., pediatric development therapy, early childhood speech intervention, and mental health supports), and other social services (e.g., nutritional programs, car seat safety classes, and book giveaways).

As another means to pull more resources into the district, leaders actively pursue funding above and beyond the per-pupil revenues provided by state, local, and federal governments. For instance, the district has a close relationship with Fort Liberty, enrolling children from military families in many of its schools. Because of this, the Department of Defense takes an interest in the district's educational programs. To advance their goal of digital literacy for every learner, Hoke County received a Department of Defense grant totaling $1.2 million to increase access to STEM-related courses for military-connected, female students and students from underrepresented populations. District leaders used that grant to develop project-based STEM and health science curriculum that supports learners to leverage technology to address issues related to public health issues.

District leaders mobilized behind efforts to ensure their students access educational programs and opportunities that prepare them for the future. This was made possible by the new leadership culture that Dr. Williamson brought to the district. School leaders were given the freedom to experiment and connect with the Hoke County community. The Principal of Rockfish Hoke Elementary School, Shawn M. O'Connor, explained, "the autonomy that's granted to us as co-leaders from our superintendent to make decisions [and] to work hard works in the best interests of our students." He continued, "We have a spectacular superintendent who allows us to run our schools the way we need to run them. I think it makes our jobs easier to move quickly."

Investing in People

A basic assumption of the district's board, leadership team, teachers, and staff is that, to achieve the district's strategic goals, the district must invest in people. In the words of Dr. Williamson, "we invest in people, not programs." He described the district's approach to budgeting as straightforward and prudent: leaders in the district understand that "more isn't always better" and opt to "stay the course" through frugal investments in culturally responsive and research-based professional development aligned to strategic priorities. The guiding mantra of the district's leadership culture is that improvements are not random. Systemic planning will lead to consequential and lasting investments that result in greater access to learning opportunities for all students, especially students of color. Money is invested in the people who live and work in the district every day: students, staff, and leaders.

Investing in Students

As described earlier, the district invests in empowering learning experiences and safe classroom environments that are correlated to greater student achievement. To better understand how these reforms play out in the lives of the children requires getting a feeling for what these investments mean on a day-to-day basis. Principal of Upchurch Elementary School Alfred Hammond describes what "all means all" means to her and her students:

> I believe that all students can learn regardless of where they come from, who they are, or who their parents are, if they're provided with true, meaningful learning opportunities. I live by this. Students are not defined by their zip code or their race or their economic status. It's what we do each and every day. When we talk about equity, we talk about funding and resources. […] I don't care what school district you are in. We all

require the same thing. No one has enough of everything, of anything, is what I found to be true. [In Hoke County,] we take the funding and resources that we have, and we try to provide our students with opportunities to help them to be successful. We developed a data club because the club provides students with opportunities to be leaders and to do things outside of their current environment. We have a robotics plan for each school in the district. As a county, we are doing different things to make sure that our students, regardless of funding and regardless of resources, are provided with the opportunities and the things they need in order to be successful when they go to the next level.

Investing in students is the district's North Star. Investing in staff is how the district can reach its North Star.

Investing in Staff

The third strategic priority from the 2016–20 plan reads, "every student, every day will have access to excellent educators."[45] Stabilizing and diversifying the district's teaching force so that every student is taught by excellent educators requires a major investment. In this section we touch on two areas of investments the district is making: (1) recruitment and (2) retention through early career supports and professional development for instructional staff.

In 2021–22 the district employed 604 full-time teaching positions, which resulted in a student/teacher ratio of 14 teachers per student, similar to the North Carolina average. Maintaining this student/teacher ratio, however, was not achieved easily. In 2019–20, the total teacher attrition rate in Hoke County Schools was 22%, compared to an overall state attrition rate of 8% and a mobility rate of 5%.[46] Hoke County Schools is located in the Sandhills Region of North Carolina, which in 2019–20 had the highest regional teacher attrition rate (9%) in North Carolina.[47] District leaders reported that most of the turnover in Hoke County Schools is due to relocation, either teachers seeking better pay or military spouses moving for new assignments. High turnover rates exact a cost to district budgets while also depressing student achievement.[48]

Attracting teachers who stay in the district is a demanding task. Superintendent of Human Resources Dr. Donna Thomas explained, "Whew. We do a lot of recruiting." She said, "[Teachers] are only here for a few years and then they pick back up, so it's like a revolving cycle." She added that North Carolina does not have a lot of teacher candidates right now, which drives the demand for attracting teachers from out of state.

In addition to stability, diversity is key to an excellent teacher workforce. A large body of evidence demonstrates that teachers of color contribute to all students' social, emotional, and academic development, with research showing particularly strong benefits for Black students taught by Black teachers.[49] Hiring and retaining teachers of color is essential to ensure the teacher workforce can create a culturally responsive environment for students. According to Dr. Thomas, leaders in Hoke County Schools pursue this goal with a high degree of intentionality:

> We definitely pay attention to [the racial composition of the teaching force]. Our priority is to hire the best person for the position, no matter what. In 2018–19, there was a study done of every district in North Carolina, and we were one of the top districts for [teacher diversity]. We know that it's important.

As this quote from Dr. Thomas indicated, the effort to diversify the district's teaching force has yielded promising results: from 2014–15 to 2019–20, the share of teachers of color in the district increased from 43% to 53% (Figure 3.8). Dr. Thomas reported that her team has been increasingly looking toward career-changers and graduates of historically Black colleges and universities as candidates for sustainable and racially diverse teacher pipelines.

As previously noted, retaining educators can be just as challenging as recruiting them. One factor that contributes to educator retention is the level of support they receive upon entering the workforce. In Hoke County, a team of personnel support coordinators conducts new teacher orientations

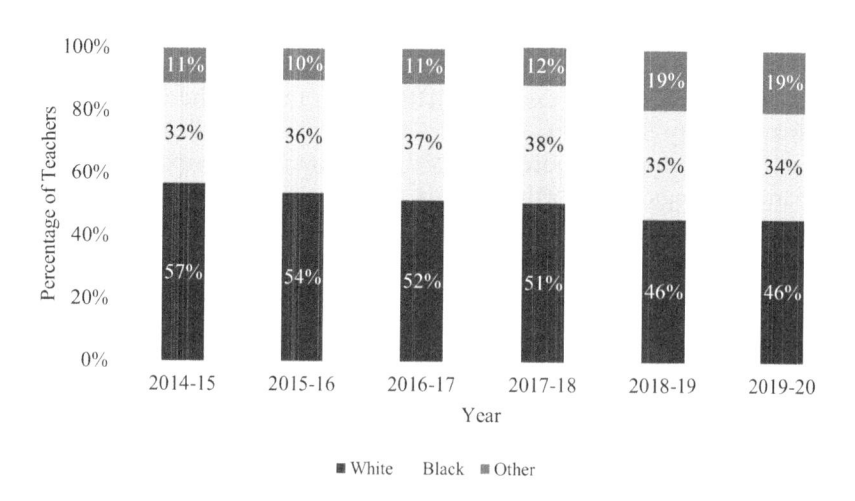

Figure 3.8 Hoke County Schools Teacher Demographics, 2014–15 to 2019–20.

Source: North Carolina Department of Public Instruction (n.d.). Public School Statistical Profile, Personnel Summary, https://www.dpi.nc.gov/districts-schools/district-operations/financial-and-business-services/statistical-profile.

Note: "Other" is defined as not Black and not White.

and induction programming for certifying staff. Personnel support coordinators also train and support a team of mentors at each campus—academic coaches at the elementary level and instructional facilitators at the middle and high school level—who provide day-to-day feedback and support for novice teachers. Personnel Support Coordinator Molly Patterson described how Hoke County invests in instructional mentorship:

> [Personnel support coordinators] meet with our mentors several times throughout the year to provide them with professional development on ways that they can support beginning teachers. [Our mentors are] in roles where they have to truly be a mentor, a support[er], and a listening ear for the beginning teachers. [We] meet with [each mentor and] their beginning teachers monthly. They [also] see them daily, especially our academic coaches are in and out of classrooms providing feedback and support.

Patterson continued, emphasizing the importance of strong, supportive relationships to develop and retain novice teachers:

> Our goal is to be in each of our schools weekly to see our teachers, especially teachers that have the most need. We really are there to build relationships with our teachers and to provide them with constructive feedback, just little bits at a time, and supporting them with small changes [and] helping them find solutions. [...] We really focus heavily on the relationships that we're building with these teachers and hoping that it's making some sort of positive impact on them wanting to stay and keeping them here with us.

Hoke County also views professional development and housing as means to retain excellent educators. The district supports a suite of professional development opportunities, including paying for out-of-state teachers to obtain a North Carolina teaching license. Due to the lack of housing development in the county, many new teachers in the district faced a commute of nearly 25 miles from Fayetteville. In 2013, Hoke County Schools built housing for district teachers. The Echo Ridge Apartment Complex has 24 units that are located centrally in Raeford—putting district teachers in the heart of the community they serve. A company donated the land for the apartment complex, and the State Employees Credit Union Foundation provided a $2.5 million loan at 0% interest for the project.[50] In 2020, a multiracial group of the district's employees—Asian American, Black, Latino/a, and White—lived in this building.

Investing in Leadership

In Hoke County Schools, leadership matters. The work to support and sustain a high-quality, diverse team of leaders is ongoing. Assistant Superintendent of Pre-K-Elementary Curriculum and Instruction Dr. Debra Dowless said:

In our district, we do an awful lot of professional development in support of our principals and our assistant principals, [who] monitor what's going on in classrooms and give me feedback. The principals have to be the instructional leaders. We work with them. We walk side by side within their classrooms. We train them. Because, at the end of the day, if the principal doesn't buy in to what we're trying to support and they don't understand why we're doing this, it never takes flight in the building.

In 2020, the school-level leadership team was comprised of fourteen principals, eight of whom came up through the district's leadership network. These data exemplify the district's commitment to developing talent from within, often expressed in the district as "growing your own." By investing in people, district leaders exercise their belief that talent development, supported by thoughtful recruitment, is the way to build a sustainable "world class learning organization." For example, the district budget includes funds for staff to further their education and work toward their administrative credential by providing tuition reimbursement up to $750 per class. District leaders can pursue master's programs focused on instruction and school administration that are supported by the North Carolina Principal Fellows Program, a grant-funded program in school administration that is available through the Sandhill's Regional Consortium in partnership with Pembroke University.

The district has also focused on growing a diverse leadership cohort. From 2014–15 to 2019–20, principals of color in Hoke County Schools increased from 36% to 64% (see Figure 3.9).

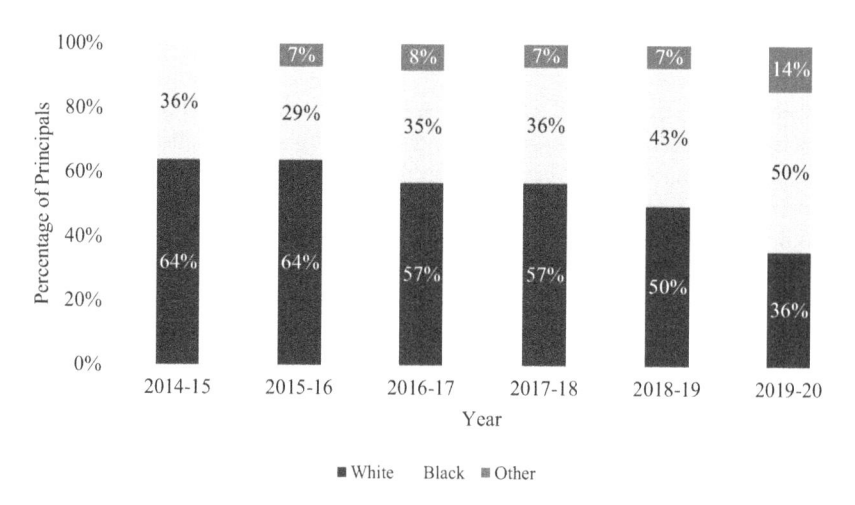

Figure 3.9 Hoke County Schools Principal Demographics, 2014–15 to 2019–20.

Source: North Carolina School Report Cards. https://www.dpi.nc.gov/data-reports/school-report-cards.

Note: "Other" is defined as not Black and not White.

By distributing district resources strategically based on student need and by obtaining much-needed outside resources, leaders in Hoke County Schools supplement its relatively low level of funding from the state, local property taxes, and the federal government to fund a wide variety of programs and learning opportunities staffed by qualified teachers and leaders. The Hoke County experience gives evidence to the proposition that money matters, but how it is spent also matters, particularly when it comes to a fair and equitable distribution of funds between schools and in supporting the learning mission of a district.

Lessons Learned

> One of the things that the superintendent shared was that we would not have any random acts with the leadership team. […] Our work as leaders in the district must be intentional as it relates to predictability and repeatability and sustainability. We're at a point that we're looking at sustaining the work and how do we do that with integrity and commitment.
>
> – Hoke County Schools district leader

Under the direction of Dr. Williamson, district and school leaders in Hoke County Schools have acted with intentionality, integrity, and commitment to move from the brink of state takeover toward pursuing a world-class education for each and every learner. This section reviews the leadership moves that have facilitated improved opportunities and outcomes for students of color. The explicit and effective equity leadership described in this small, rural, racially diverse district in the upper South is not the norm in public school districts across the United States. When asked to state the hallmark of Hoke County Schools in one word, members of the district leadership team enthusiastically responded with terms such as *purpose, relationships, expectations, diversity, commitment, longevity, and mindset.* These words are not empty or casual; they describe a concerted leadership strategy behind the Hoke County Way. Key features of this leadership strategy include establishing an empowering, aspirational framework for equity; cultivating a widespread equity consciousness that supports equitable resource allocation; leveraging data analysis for continuous improvement; and building a continuity of leadership that enables Hoke County Schools to stay the course.

Leadership in Hoke County Schools established a shared framework for equity and excellence that is empowering and aspirational. Dr. Williamson introduced a new core value that "all students can learn" and therefore student success should not be predetermined by social identifiers, including race and socioeconomic status. He institutionalized this core value through iterative strategic planning, which both invested the community in the aspirational vision of a "world class education" and outlined a roadmap of the goals, strategies, and measurements to get there. District educators cultivate future-facing educational opportunity as they enact the strategic plan. They do this by providing ambitious instruction that promotes digital fluency and postsecondary readiness and by dismantling barriers to learning previously embedded in district practice. Dr. Williamson has garnered widespread community buy-in for the equity framework through regular, proactive engagement with families, community members, board members, school-level staff, district administrators, and local industry leaders.

Through the conviction that "all means all," leadership fostered an equity consciousness that supports equitable resource allocation and attention to individual students in Hoke County Schools. District leaders message support for "all students" as a strategic way of pursuing equity that can be heard, felt, and acted upon in a racially diverse community with historical and persistent inequities. The slogan, "all means all," sets common expectations for success while diversifying the means to achieve them, acknowledging that no two learners are alike. It also compels educators to honor the lived experiences of students, especially children and families living in poverty, through empathy and understanding, as well as skillful instruction that engages students and supports their distinctive needs to pursue challenging learning goals for all. Educators in Hoke County Schools establish asset-based relationships with students and their families through regular engagements with families out in the community, including home visits. School leaders also coach staff, particularly new teachers from outside the community, to develop equity consciousness through ongoing, direct conversations about their beliefs and assumptions and provide them with mentoring and professional development to build their teaching skills. A MTSSs also enables students to receive the academic and behavioral supports they need to succeed.

This shared equity consciousness garners widespread support for bold initiatives, including the reallocation of resources. When Dr. Williamson arrived in Hoke County, he noticed that educational experiences were highly variable across the district's 14 schools. He worked with the board to equalize these investments. He also invested in people, budgeting for extensive professional development to build consistent instructional practices focused on literacies (traditional and digital), critical thinking, and problem-solving and rooted in positive relationships. In this way, district leaders established continuity that seeks to ensure that every student receives a "world class education." The simultaneous efforts to develop equity consciousness and invest resources are mutually reinforcing.

By engaging in shared analyses of district and school outcomes, leadership secured backing for an ambitious set of reforms that built over time. Dr. Williamson established a culture of systems thinking and data-driven instructional decision-making. District leaders regularly monitor and share outcomes in data talks with school leaders, which allows them to respond proactively to underperformance with resources and growth, not blame or punishment. Leaders have established the expectation, time, and support necessary for educators to improve their practice.

Leaders leveraged sustained improvements as the foundation for strategic equity initiatives. Each of three five-year strategic plans took up critical issues that the community agreed needed attention, set goals for progress, and provided a vision and a focus for the efforts of everyone in the district. The first strategic plan in 2006 transformed a collection of schools into a system with shared practice; the second in 2010 improved that practice to outpace learning outcomes in the state, and the third in 2016 established even more ambitious goals to deliver a 'world-class' education. All major initiatives are driven by the conviction that instruction should center on positive relationships and high academic standards.

The continuity of leadership in Hoke County Schools supported sustained equity improvements that deepened over time. The improvements in Hoke County Schools were not a flash in the pan; community buy-in, investment, and strategic planning built over time under the leadership of Dr. Williamson. Over the course of his 15-year tenure, Dr. Williamson worked to establish strong teacher and leader pipelines and distributed leadership to bolster the equity strategy that has outlived his time in the district. He has been succeeded by two longtime district educators and administrators, Dr. Debra Dowless and Dr. Shannon Register, whose leadership has further advanced the mission and vision they helped to establish as part of his cabinet.

The findings of this study align with what research tells us are essential areas of policy and practice for advancing racial equity in school settings: a clear, ambitious vision; access to deeper learning; safe, healthy, and inclusive school environments; meaningful partnerships; human, financial, and material resources; and systems for gathering, communicating, and using data to drive progress.[51] These domains promote racial equity, a condition in which student success is not predetermined by student race.

This case study presented improvements in Hoke County Schools that foster racial equity across multiple measures of academic opportunity and outcomes (Appendix 3A). Strong improvements and reduced racial disparities are visible in reading and math achievement, college readiness indicators, graduation rates, and college-going, with Hoke County meeting or nearing state averages in all these areas.

Building on the wisdom of practice and continuous improvement, the leaders in Hoke County Schools have arrived at successes through hard work, reflection, and questioning. Leaders and staff recognize that while there is no one path toward racial equity, there are certain practices and policies that emerge when the conviction that all students can learn drives a shared mission and vision.

Appendix 3A: Hoke County Schools Data Tables

Table 3A.1 Comparison of Hoke County Schools and North Carolina Composite 3–8th Grade Proficiency Rates, 2012–13 to 2018–19

Site	Subject	2012–13	2013–14	2014–15	2015–16	2016–17	2017–18	2018–19
Hoke County Schools	Math	30%	37%	45%	55%	55%	54%	54%
	Reading	31%	44%	46%	51%	51%	51%	52%
State of North Carolina	Math	42%	52%	52%	55%	55%	56%	59%
	Reading	44%	58%	56%	57%	58%	57%	57%

Sources: North Carolina Department of Public Instruction (n.d.). Reports of Disaggregated State, School System (LEA) and School Performance Data. http://accrpt.tops.ncsu.edu/docs/disag_datasets/; Hoke County School District (2020). Testing & Accountability Data Packet; North Carolina School Report Cards (n.d.). Student Performance, 2012–13 [archived].

Note: Composite proficiency rates are defined as the percentage of students meeting the state proficiency level.

Table 3A.2 Hoke County Schools Percentage of Students Meeting or Exceeding State Benchmark on ACT College Entrance Exam by Race/Ethnicity, 2014–15 to 2019–20

Demographic	2014–15	2015–16	2016–17	2017–18	2018–19
North Carolina Average	60%	60%	59%	58%	56%
HCS Average	46%	47%	43%	51%	53%
HCS American Indian/Alaska Native	41%	36%	29%	35%	50%
HCS Black	32%	37%	30%	43%	41%
HCS Latino/a	46%	43%	43%	58%	50%
HCS Multiracial	36%	48%	45%	50%	56%
HCS White	68%	70%	73%	66%	73%

Source: North Carolina School Report Cards, https://www.dpi.nc.gov/data-reports/school-report-cards.

Table 3A.3 Hoke County Schools Four-Year Cohort Graduation Rates by Race/Ethnicity, 2014–15 to 2019–20

Race/Ethnicity	2014–15	2015–16	2016–17	2017–18	2018–19	2019–20
ALL	75%	80%	79%	81%	80%	88%
American Indian/ Alaska Native	61%	66%	73%	77%	67%	77%
Black	78%	81%	80%	83%	85%	90%
Latino/a	70%	79%	80%	82%	84%	86%
Multiracial	72%	73%	89%	73%	71%	83%
White	78%	85%	79%	82%	78%	91%

Source: North Carolina Department of Public Instruction. (2020). Longitudinal Four-year and Five-year Cohort Graduation Rates through 2020. https://accrpt.tops.ncsu.edu/docs/cgrdisag_datasets/.

Table 3A.4 Hoke County Schools Short Term Suspensions, 2013–14 to 2019–20

Year	Total Number of Short-Term Suspensions	Number of Short-Term Suspensions Per 100 Students	Total Short Term Suspension Days
2013–14	1,282	N/A	N/A
2014–15	1,523	N/A	N/A
2015–16	1,487	18	3,977
2016–17	1,374	16	3,731
2017–18	1,344	16	3,507
2018–19	1,259	14	3,535
2019–20	979	11	2,460

Source: North Carolina Department of Public Instruction. Discipline, ALP, and Dropout Annual Reports. https://www.dpi.nc.gov/data-reports/dropout-and-discipline-data/discipline-alp-and-dropout-annual-reports#2019-20; NC Department of Public Instruction (n.d.). Statistical Profile Online. https://www.dpi.nc.gov/districts-schools/district-operations/financial-and-business-services/statistical-profile.

Table 3A.5 Hoke County Schools Short Term Suspensions by Race/Ethnicity, 2014–15 to 2019–20

Race/ Ethnicity	2014–15	2015–16	2016–17	2017–18	2018–19	2019–20
American Indian/Alaska Native	225	178	167	128	117	94
Asian American	1	3	2	6	0	2
Black	861	857	807	788	734	574
Latino/a	127	143	105	128	136	104
Multiracial	104	109	104	112	80	60
White	205	197	189	182	192	145
Total	1,523	1,487	1,374	1,344	1,259	979

Source: NC Department of Public Instruction. Discipline, ALP, and Dropout Annual Reports. https://www.dpi.nc.gov/data-reports/dropout-and-discipline-data/discipline-alp-and-dropout-annual-reports#2019-20 (accessed 5/2021); NC Department of Public Instruction (n.d.). Statistical Profile Online. https://www.dpi.nc.gov/districts-schools/district-operations/financial-and-business-services/statistical-profile.

Notes

1 From its founding in 1922 until 2023, Fort Liberty boasted the name of a Confederate general. Price, J. (2023, June 1), *WUNC. As Fort Bragg becomes Fort Liberty, Army leaders promise the base won't forget its history.* https://www.wunc.org/military/2023-06-01/as-ft-bragg-becomes-ft-liberty-army-leaders-promise-the-base-wont-forget-its-history

2 Deep poverty is defined as households living with incomes at or below 50% of the Federal Poverty Level, or less than $12,300 per year for a family of four. North Carolina Justice Center. (2018). https://www.ncjustice.org/publications/rates-of-deep-poverty-are-rising-in-nc-and-nation/

3 Hoke County Schools. (2020). *2019–2020 individual schools information* [Pamphlet].

4 Triplett, N. P. & Ford, J. (2019). *E(Race)ing inequities: The state of racial equity in North Carolina public schools.* Charlotte, NC: Center for Racial Equity in Education.

5 Roy, E., & Ford, J. (2019). *Deep rooted: A brief history of race and education in North Carolina.* Charlotte, NC: Center for Racial Equity in Education.

6 Cordasco, F. (Ed.). (1974). Toward equal educational opportunity: The report of the select committee on equal educational opportunity, United States Senate (No. 2). Ams Pr Inc.

7 Leandro v. State of North Carolina, 488 SE2d 249 (NC: Supreme Court, 1997). Triplett, N. P. & Ford, J. (2019). *E(Race)ing inequities: The state of racial equity in North Carolina public schools.* Charlotte, NC: Center for Racial Equity in Education.

8 WestEd, Learning Policy Institute, & Friday Institute for Educational Innovation at North Carolina State University (2019). Sound Basic Education for All:

An Action Plan for North Carolina. San Francisco, CA: WestEd. https://www.wested.org/resource/leandro-north-carolina/

9 Public School Forum of North Carolina. (2020). Local school finance study. https://www.ncforum.org/local-school-finance-study/

10 *Per pupil expenditures in North Carolina.* Data Source: Public Schools of North Carolina, State Board of Education, Department of Public Instruction, Statistical Profile: Per Pupil Expenditure Ranking. https://datacenter.kidscount.org/data/tables/2271-per-pupil-expenditures?loc=35&loct=2#detailed/10/5063/false/2043,1769,1696,1648,1603,1539,1381,1246,1124,1021/872,1534,1535,1533/4746

11 Rash, M. (2015). The Hoke County Way: No excuses. EducationNC. https://www.ednc.org/the-hoke-county-way-no-excuses/

12 Hoke County Schools. (2016–21). *Strategic plan: Preparing today's students for tomorrow's world.*

13 Hoke County Schools. (2016–21). *Strategic plan: Preparing today's students for tomorrow's world.*

14 Hoke County Schools. (2016–21). *Strategic plan: Preparing today's students for tomorrow's world.*

15 WestEd, Learning Policy Institute, & Friday Institute for Educational Innovation at North Carolina State University (2019). Sound basic education for all: An action plan for North Carolina. San Francisco, CA: WestEd. https://www.wested.org/resource/leandro-north-carolina/.

16 Hoke County Partnership for Children and Families. (n.d.). Enhancing opportunities and inspiring young minds. https://www.hokechildren.net/wordp/

17 Teaching Strategies. (n.d.). Move beyond measurement: Drive differentiated, effective instruction. https://teachingstrategies.com/solutions/assess/gold/

18 North Carolina Department of Public Instruction (2020). Public schools of North Carolina statistical profile. https://www.dpi.nc.gov/districts-schools/district-operations/financial-and-business-services/statistical-profile

19 Lumbee Tribe of North Carolina (n.d.). *History and culture.* https://www.lumbeetribe.com/history--culture

20 Hoke County Schools. (2020). *2019–2020 individual schools information* [Pamphlet].

21 Members of the Lumbee Tribe secured funds and land to establish their own school in the fall of 1887. That school developed into Pembroke College for Indians, the only state-supported institution offering four-year degrees between 1939 and 1953. Today, it is part of the University of North Carolina system. Lumbee Tribe of North Carolina (n.d.). *History and culture.* https://www.lumbeetribe.com/history-and-culture

22 Hoke County Schools. (n.d.). Indian Education. https://sites.google.com/a/hcs.k12.nc.us/indian-education/

23 Garcia, R. L., & Goldenstein Ahler, J. (1992). Indian education: Assumptions, ideologies, strategies. In Jon Reyhner (Ed.), *Teaching American Indian students* (pp. 13–32). Oklahoma: University of Oklahoma Press; Reyhner, J., & Eder, J. (1992). A history of Indian education. In J. Reyhner (Ed.), *Teaching American Indian students* (pp. 33–58). Oklahoma: University of Oklahoma Press.

24 North Carolina School Report Cards. https://www.dpi.nc.gov/data-reports/school-report-cards

25 Hoke County Schools. (2016–21). *Strategic plan: Preparing today's students for tomorrow's world.*

26 Hoke County Schools. (2016–21). *Strategic plan: Preparing today's students for tomorrow's world.*

27 Hoke County Schools. (2019). *Local Academically or Intellectually Gifted (AIG) plan, 2019–2020.* https://www.dpi.nc.gov/media/7734/open

28 Hoke County Schools. (2019). *Local Academically or Intellectually Gifted (AIG) plan, 2019–2020.* https://www.dpi.nc.gov/media/7734/open

29 Public Schools of North Carolina Statistical Profile, https://www.dpi.nc.gov/districts-schools/district-operations/financial-and-business-services/statistical-profile; North Carolina School Report Cards (through 2019–2020). https://www.dpi.nc.gov/data-reports/school-report-cards.

30 The participation rate is defined as the number of AP test-takers divided by final average daily membership for grades 9–13. North Carolina Department of Public Instruction, SAT and AP Test Results, https://www.dpi.nc.gov/districts-schools/testing-and-school-accountability/school-accountability-and-reporting/north-carolina-sat-and-ap-reports#advanced-placement-ap-reports

31 North Carolina Department of Public Instruction. (2020). Longitudinal 4-Year and 5-Year Cohort Graduation Rates through 2020. https://www.dpi.nc.gov/longitudinal-4-year-and-5-year-cohort-graduation-rates-through-2020.

32 Oakes, J. (2005). *Keeping track: How schools structure inequality.* New Haven, CT: Yale University Press.

33 Hoke County Schools. (2016–21). *Strategic plan: Preparing today's students for tomorrow's world.*

34 Hoke County Schools Student Support Services. (n.d.). Safe learning environment. https://sites.google.com/hcs.k12.nc.us/sss/programs/school-mental-health-program/safe-learning?authuser=0

35 Leung-Gagné, M., McCombs, J., Scott, C., & Losen, D. J. (2022). *Pushed out: Trends and disparities in out-of-school suspension.* Palo Alto, CA: Learning Policy Institute. https://doi.org/10.54300/235.277

36 Losen, D. J., & Martinez, P. (2020). *Lost opportunities: How disparate school discipline continues to drive differences in the opportunity to learn.* Palo Alto, CA/ Los Angeles, CA: Learning Policy Institute; Center for Civil Rights Remedies at the Civil Rights Project, UCLA.

37 Cantor, P., Osher, D., Berg, J., Steyer, L., & Rose, T. (2018). Malleability, plasticity, and individuality: How children learn and develop in context. *Applied Developmental Science*, 23(4), 307–37. https://doi.org/10.1080/10888691.2017.1398649; Osher, D., Cantor, P., Berg, J., Steyer, L., & Rose, T. (2018). Drivers of human development: How relationships and context shape learning and development. *Applied Developmental Science*, 24(1), 6–36. https://doi.org/10.1080/10888691.2017.1398650.

38 Darling-Hammond, L., Flook, L., Cook-Harvey, C., Barron, B. J., & Osher, D. (2019). Implications for educational practice of the science of learning and development. *Applied Developmental Science*, 24(2), 97–140. https://doi.org/10.1080/10888691.2018.1537791. Learning Policy Institute & Turnaround for Children. (2021). *Design principles for schools: Putting the science of learning and development into action.*

39 Hoke County Schools. MTSS Implementation Site. https://sites.google.com/hcs.k12.nc.us/hoke-county-schools-mtss-imple/home

40 North Carolina Department of Public Instruction. (n.d.). Students with disabilities. https://www.dpi.nc.gov/students-families/parents-corner/students-disabilities

41 Hoke County Schools. MTSS Infrastructure (flyer). https://sites.google.com/hcs.k12.nc.us/hoke-county-schools-mtss-imple/home

42 Hoke County Schools. (2016–21). *Strategic plan: Preparing today's students for tomorrow's world.*

43 Rash, M. (2015). The Hoke County Way: No excuses. EducationNC. https://www.ednc.org/the-hoke-county-way-no-excuses/

44 *Per pupil expenditures in North Carolina.* Data Source: Public Schools of North Carolina, State Board of Education, Department of Public Instruction, Statistical Profile: Per Pupil Expenditure Ranking. https://datacenter.kidscount.org/data/tables/2271-per-pupil-expenditures?loc=35&loct=2#detailed/10/5063/false/2043,1769,1696,1648,1603,1539,1381,1246,1124,1021/872,1534,1535,1533/4746

45 Hoke County Schools. (2016–21). *Strategic plan: Preparing today's students for tomorrow's world.*

46 In 2019–20, the attrition rate (8%) and mobility rate (5%) contribute to an average effect of LEA-attrition rate for the state of 13%. Public Schools of North Carolina (2020). Report to the North Carolina General Assembly: 2019–20 State of the Teaching Profession in North Carolina.

47 Public Schools of North Carolina (2020). Report to the North Carolina general assembly: 2019–2020 state of the teaching profession in North Carolina.

48 Carver-Thomas, D., & Darling-Hammond, L. (2017). *Teacher turnover: Why it matters and what we can do about it.* Palo Alto, CA: Learning Policy Institute; Ronfeldt, M., Loeb, S., & Wyckoff, J. (2013). How teacher turnover harms student achievement. *American Educational Research Journal, 50*(1), 4–36.

49 Carver-Thomas, D. (2018, April 19). *Diversifying the teaching profession: How to recruit and retain teachers of color.* Palo Alto, CA: Learning Policy Institute. https://learningpolicyinstitute.org/product/diversifying-teaching-profession-report

50 Rash, M. (2015). The Hoke County Way: Problem solved. Education North Carolina. https://www.ednc.org/the-hoke-county-way-problem-solved/

51 Hyler, M. E., Carver-Thomas, D., Wechsler, M., & Willis, L. (2020). *Districts Advancing Racial Equity (DARE) tool.* Palo Alto, CA: Learning Policy Institute.

4 "Consistent and Courageous"

Building Racial Equity Infrastructure in Jefferson County Public Schools

Desiree Carver-Thomas, Marjorie Wechsler, Larkin Willis, and Wesley Wei

Introduction

> [Jefferson County Public Schools] is officially a majority-minority school district. As such, the means by which we allocate resources, train our teachers, and implement [our strategic plan] is tantamount. I am proud of this work and the team that helped bring this much-needed lens in focus. I appreciate being a part of a district that is willing to unapologetically and aggressively shift from equality to equity and diversity to inclusion.
>
> —John Marshall, JCPS Chief Equity Officer[1]

Tucked into a bend of the Ohio River that borders Indiana, Jefferson County Public Schools (JCPS) encompasses Louisville, Kentucky—the commonwealth's largest city—and the city's surrounding county. JCPS is the largest school system in Kentucky, with 168 schools, over 6,800 certified teachers, and roughly 100,000 students.[2] Like many other metropolitan districts of its size, JCPS serves a student body made up of a majority of students of color (Table 4.1). It similarly has regions of concentrated wealth and others that are socioeconomically depressed, which fall largely along lines of race and ethnicity. The Black population, primarily from low-income families, is concentrated in Louisville's West End, while the White population, primarily more wealthy, is concentrated in the surrounding county.[3]

Despite its demographic, economic, and geographic similarities to other large districts, JCPS's explicit and action-oriented commitment to equity sets it apart from many of its peers. In the sections to follow, this case details the district's efforts to acknowledge and address head-on significant racial and ethnic disparities in student access to opportunity and achievement outcomes. Building on a legacy of reform beginning with desegregation in the 1970s, JCPS has struggled toward racial equity with resilience and tenacity. At many junctures, district leaders have reassessed and redirected its efforts in the face of opposition or barriers, including when its desegregation

Table 4.1 JCPS Student Demographics, 2021–22

Demographic	Percent
White	39
Black	37
Latino/a	13
Multiracial	6
Asian American	5
American Indian/Alaska Native	0.1
Native Hawaiian/Pacific Islander	0.1
Free and reduced-price lunch	68
English learners	13

Sources: JCPS Current Enrollment by Race and Gender (2021–22) https://assessment.jefferson.kyschools.us/publicDatasets/PublicResources.aspx?id=511359, Kentucky Department of Education School Report Card Datasets Students/Teachers or Student Membership, https://www.education.ky.gov/OpenHouse/data/Pages/Historical-SRC-Datasets.aspx

(accessed 3/27/2025); Kentucky Department of Education School Report Card Datasets Learning Environment, https://www.education.ky.gov/ Open-House/data/Pages/Historical-SRC-Datasets.aspx (accessed 3/27/2025).

plans were overturned by the Supreme Court in 2007 as part of the *Parents Involved* case. Through many administrations, the district has had to reevaluate and re-articulate a vision for equity that drives policy change and programmatic investments.

Over the course of this past decade, JCPS leaders have articulated an explicit vision for addressing persistent racial disparities in student opportunities and outcomes and created an equity office that has had significant authority to enact that vision. Even as the superintendency changed hands during that time, from Dr. Donna Hargens to Dr. Marty Pollio, the district leadership and broader JCPS community maintained a steadfast commitment to advancing racial equity. And when its efforts were not fully successful, the district redoubled and redirected its efforts. Indeed, as the district began to develop a vision and plan for racial equity, a 2017 state audit found widespread racial disparities that demanded a corrective action plan, putting the district at risk of a state takeover. Rather than change course, district leaders pushed forward and accelerated their efforts to put an increasingly impactful racial equity plan into effect.

As a result of its persistent efforts, JCPS is making strides in providing students of color equitable opportunities to learn and was released from the state's corrective action plan in 2020. As will be described in more detail in this case,

- Between 2018–19 and 2019–20, the proportion of Black administrators in the district nearly tripled, increasing from 17% to 47% of JCPS administrators.
- Between 2011–12 and 2021–22, the four-year cohort graduation rate[4] increased from 68% to 85% for JCPS students overall, an increase of 25%. In the same period, graduation rates for Black JCPS students increased from 63% to 84%, an increase of 33%, which exceeded the statewide and districtwide rate of growth over the same period. Graduation rates for Latino/a students also increased modestly during this period from 73% to 75%.
- Between 2017–18 and 2021–22, the proportion of graduates meeting the state of Kentucky definition of postsecondary readiness increased from 50% to 68% and increased for every group. The readiness rate nearly doubled for Black graduates.
- Between 2012–13 and 2018–19, the number of students taking Advanced Placement exams increased by nearly 60% for Black students and by more than 120% for Latino/a students.
- Between 2017–18 and 2021–22, access to gifted and talented education programs increased for JCPS students overall and especially for Black and Latino/a students. In 2022, 8.3% of Black students were identified for gifted and talented education, an 11% increase from four years earlier.
- Between 2018–19 and 2019–20, the number of disciplinary actions, including suspensions and expulsions, experienced by Black students dropped by nearly 20%.

Although JCPS district leaders recognize that they still have considerable work to do, these data points suggest that their efforts are beginning to pay dividends. This case describes these efforts and the leadership moves that have sustained these efforts for more than a decade. The case illustrates how JCPS leaders have managed to deepen and expand a commitment to racial equity where it could have easily stagnated or been pushed to the wayside. Further, the case demonstrates how a focus on strategic, structural reforms has allowed the district to pass the baton of racial equity from one superintendent to the next.

Organization of the Case

In the remainder of this introduction, we describe the history of racial equity leadership in JCPS and how it has shifted since the 1970s. In the first section, "Leading for Racial Equity," we describe the key leadership moves that enable JCPS leaders to successfully drive forward efforts that advance racial equity. This section describes the overarching vision, framework, policies, and processes that guide the district's approach to designing and implementing racial equity reforms. The remaining sections of the case detail the major features of the district's strategy for addressing racial disparities. "Driving Action Through Data Transparency" describes how JCPS leaders analyze and share data on student opportunities and outcomes. This section details, for example, the development of the district's equity scorecard and how it has motivated critical shifts in district policy and practice. "Expanding Learning Opportunities for the Whole Child" discusses how JCPS takes a whole child approach to expanding access to academic opportunities. Specifically, the district shifted to more rigorous and experiential deeper learning by supporting culturally responsive teaching, increasing access to college and career pathways and other transformative school models, and providing positive behavioral supports and restorative practices. Investing in people describes how JCPS is able to move its racial equity work forward through a rich suite of professional growth opportunities that develop capacity related to racial equity while recruiting new teachers and leaders. Finally, we conclude with lessons learned for districts, leaders, and other educators.

JCPS Racial Equity Reform, Past to Present

JCPS has a decades-long history of taking action—both voluntarily and by court order—to correct its history of racial discrimination and provide greater opportunities for students of color.

The Courts Set the Foundation for Racial Equity

As in many parts of the US at the time of the Supreme Court's 1954 ruling on B*rown v. Board of Education,* Jefferson County had two largely segregated school districts—Jefferson County School District (JCSD) and Louisville Independent School District (LISD). By 1971, there was little progress on the desegregation front, with JCSD serving primarily White students and LISD serving primarily Black students.[5] That year, several civil rights organizations filed suit against the districts in a case that was eventually heard by the U.S. Court of Appeals. The court ruled that "all vestiges of state-imposed segregation must be eliminated within each school district in the county."[6] The court ordered JCSD and the LISD to merge into one district, which is now known as JCPS.

In the following years, JCPS's equity work focused on desegregating its student body at the school level. In 1972, the district opened its first magnet school, the J. Graham Brown School, which is still in operation.[7] At the time, magnet schools were an emerging strategy to achieve voluntary desegregation by providing options for unique and rigorous specialized instruction, often designed to attract White students to schools in urban, majority-Black neighborhoods.[8]

In addition, by court order, the district began full implementation of a desegregation plan in the 1975–76 school year. Each elementary, middle, and high school was required to enroll a certain percentage of Black students, and the district designed a comprehensive busing program to transport a total of more than 22,000 Black and White students traveling to 165 different schools.[9] Although the plan led to integrated schools, it resulted in Black children being bused out of their neighborhoods at a higher rate than White students.[10]

Initially, the district's desegregation plan was rejected by a large segment of the population, with 98% of majority-White suburban residents disapproving of the plan in surveys conducted at the time.[11] On the second day of the 1975–76 school year, with the desegregation plan in full effect, thousands of residents engaged in violent attacks, leading to the arrest of more than 500 White protestors.[12]

Louisville Mayor Harvey Sloane, a leader in the desegregation efforts, eventually called the Kentucky National Guard to support the desegregation plan. The following week, Black students were escorted to classes by armed guards, while Sloane rode buses with Black students to show his support. In spite of this contentious beginning, Jefferson County residents began to accept the desegregation efforts in the new combined district.

The District Takes the Mantle for Racial Equity

Even after active court supervision of the district ended in 1978 and the court desegregation order ended in 2000, JCPS has continued to refine its student assignment policies to prioritize desegregation and better meet the needs of all students.[13] During the 1991–92 school year, the district adopted Project Renaissance, a managed choice plan that ended mandatory busing and "emphasized parental choice and racial composition guidelines at each school level."[14] Families were asked to rank the schools they would like their students to attend, but the district made the final assignment of students to schools to ensure each campus enrolled between 15 and 50 percent Black students in elementary school, with similar guidelines at the middle and high school levels.[15]

A group of parents challenged the district's student assignment policy in a case that was eventually merged with a challenge to Seattle School District and heard by the Supreme Court in 2007. In a divided opinion on *Parents Involved in Community Schools vs. Seattle School District No. 1*, the court struck down the JCPS desegregation policy, arguing it relied too heavily on race. The court ruled that even though there is a government interest in maintaining school diversity, race alone cannot determine student assignment. Ironically, while the court's decision in *Brown vs. Board of Education* set the foundation for racial equity in JCPS, the *Parents Involved* decision threatened to undermine the district's progress.

Undeterred by the court's ruling, in 2008, JCPS developed a new student assignment policy that classified student enrollment zones using census data, including the average household income, average education level of the census block group, and the racial and ethnic population. Under Superintendent Sheldon Berman, schools were required to have 15 to 50 percent of their students from enrollment zones that have a student of color population of more than 48%, an average household income of below $41,000, and an average education level of below high school with some college.[16] The specific enrollment zones and demographic requirements have shifted over time, but the district retains this race-conscious approach to assigning students to schools.

In addition, the district continues to provide a robust magnet school program that includes nearly two dozen schools at the elementary, middle, and high school levels, as well as magnet programs within more than 30 traditional schools as an equity approach.[17] Furthermore, under a new proposal, JCPS will allow for all students, including students in the predominantly Black West End neighborhood, to have more and better school options near home. West End students will still have the option of attending schools in other parts of the county outside of their neighborhoods as well.[18]

JCPS Shifts Racial Equity Efforts Beyond Student Assignment

Though the history and legal challenges surrounding student assignment in JCPS are well documented, the district's reform efforts toward racial equity have diversified and strengthened since the *Parents Involved* decision. These equity efforts have been supported and led not by any one leader, but by a collective public will for greater racial equity. In the hometown of Muhammad Ali, renowned boxing legend and prominent voice for Black civil rights, district staff expressed that there is a strong expectation that all JCPS leaders center racial equity. Indeed, one staff member noted it would be "political suicide" not to. The local newspaper, the *Courier-Journal*, plays a role in holding the district accountable with regular reporting on JCPS policies and their impacts. The newspaper's investigative reporting on disparities in bussing and student access to magnet schools, for example, presaged a set of sweeping changes to the student assignment policy and magnet schools program that the district began in 2023.[19]

Notably, the JCPS Board of Education has been a key voice of public sentiment, with Board Chair Diane Porter leading the call for racial equity. Since 2010, Porter has represented JCPS District 1, which encompasses Louisville's West End, a primarily Black neighborhood and one of the city's poorest areas.[20] Porter is a lifelong member of the JCPS community, beginning with her education, as she describes, at Virginia Avenue Elementary School "during the time that the district was clearly segregated." Her affiliation continued through her time as a JCPS teacher and as the "first African American female principal for vocational schools" to her leadership as a central office administrator. On the Board of Education, she has been a strong advocate for racial equity, with Chief Equity Officer John Marshall describing her as "an oak tree in this work." The board's commitment to racial equity has manifested, in part, in hiring equity-minded district leaders, including both former superintendent Dr. Donna Hargens and her successor, Dr. Marty Pollio. According to Porter, the board has generally approved of district efforts to advance racial equity. In Porter's words, "we move forward together."

The district hired Dr. Donna Hargens for the superintendency in 2011, ushering in greater efforts on racial equity beyond school integration and student assignment. These efforts included attracting and hiring equity-oriented cabinet-level leaders and district staff; delegating authority to these leaders to implement and enforce new practices; and codifying their influence through funding and policies. Rather than operating from the superintendent's desk alone, Dr. Hargens positioned other members of district leadership to cooperate across offices and divisions and to operate as an extension of the public sentiment within the broader Jefferson County community about the need to address racial inequities.

Further, Dr. Hargens built the infrastructure for racial equity systems that would outlive her tenure as superintendent. In 2012, she hired a cabinet-level chief equity officer, at the time one of few in the nation, in response to persistent racial disparities across multiple domains, including academic achievement, disciplinary actions, and opportunities to learn. Chief Equity Officer John Marshall continues to lead the district's Diversity, Equity, and Poverty (DEP) Programs Division, which spearheads the district's efforts on racial equity in close coordination with other JCPS divisions and school leaders.

In 2018, Dr. Marty Pollio took up the superintendency and the mantle of racial equity leadership. Building on the values and infrastructure Dr. Hargens put in place, Superintendent Pollio has worked to infuse the work of racial equity into every decision the district makes. In 2020, the killing of Breonna Taylor, a Black Louisville resident and emergency room technician, by White police officers spurred widespread protests in Louisville and across the country and prompted further calls for JCPS to take action against racial injustice. As Superintendent Pollio put it:

> Louisville, Kentucky was the center of racial and social unrest. Breonna Taylor was a Jefferson County Public Schools student. Coming back from that and the impacts of the pandemic caused us to really double down on the work we had done over the past 12 to 18 months.

In alignment with appeals from the broader community and with the support of the school board, Dr. Pollio has expanded the district's infrastructure for racial equity by implementing a series of policy changes and dedicating resources to those efforts, described in the rest of this case. In turn, the district's commitment to racial equity has grown more intentional, widespread, and integrated across departments.

The district's racial equity efforts are not done merely out of compliance or on the whims of a single actor, but rather are a collective, concerted effort to proactively address the inequities throughout JCPS. The progression from the district's historical focus on student assignment to the variety of policies today represents a maturing of the racial equity vision that has only become clearer and more developed, despite leadership changes. The energy and momentum behind the charge to resolve persistent inequities have thus equipped JCPS leadership to weave racial equity into the fabric of the district.

As we illustrate throughout the case, evidence shows this approach is making a difference. The district's gains, while modest, suggest that JCPS is on the right track toward more equitable educational opportunities and outcomes. The districtwide commitment to racial equity and corresponding innovative strategies in JCPS set an example for other districts interested in addressing disparities and striving for racial equity in their systems.

Leading for Racial Equity

Even in a district that has demonstrated a decades-long commitment to school integration, advancing racial equity is challenging work that requires strategic leadership. According to JCPS staff, despite considerable community investment in racial equity, they have pushed up against limited resources, reluctance among others within the district community, and organizational issues that can place racial equity work in a silo. Over the course of a decade, JCPS leaders have developed strategies to move racial equity efforts forward in ways that address these challenges while working to improve these conditions. District leadership strategies include articulating an explicit vision for racial equity that they support with research and data; investing in racial equity by building the staffing capacity to support sweeping changes from the classroom level to the central office; and setting an expectation that every staff member is accountable to that racial equity vision by developing policies and providing tools and practices for implementation.

Moving Equity from the Margins to the Center

The district began building its capacity to lead racial equity work in earnest when Dr. Hargens created an Equity Division and hired Chief Equity Officer

John Marshall in 2012. According to Dr. Marshall, there are districts "from Maine to LA" with equity officers, but few that had structured the role quite the way JCPS had at the time he was hired. Dr. Marshall reports directly to the superintendent, has a team of program staff, and oversees a host of units under the DEP division: foster care, compliance and investigations, site-based decision-making, homeless and migrant students, and community engagement, among others. While in some districts racial equity work is hidden in the human resources department or lumped with recruiting teachers of color, in JCPS racial equity work and its staff are front and center. Indeed, the DEP division has the responsibility and authority to support other district departments, such as Human Resources or the Curriculum Design and Learning Innovations department, with improving their policies and practices to advance racial equity. Dr. Marshall noted, "there are not too many organizations that have someone challenging the practices and ills of the district." Forthright reflection about equity challenges is key to the district vision for advancing racial equity, and they have hired the staff to take on that work.

Importantly, Dr. Hargens empowered Dr. Marshall to lead decision-making in the district and stood by his side as he took on that leadership role. She also encouraged him to "manage up," or influence her approach to racial equity work. According to Marshall, she acknowledged that he was well positioned to lead with authority, saying, "John, you're from Louisville. You're a Louisville native. You came up in the city, your research is on this work, and you're now the chief equity officer." Hargens encouraged Marshall to make decisions on behalf of the district and the superintendent. As Marshall put it:

> She would say, "Make a decision for the district and all these kids." It forced me to be a leader. And without apology, she stood up and said, "This is what we're going to do." And when certain areas in the community resisted, she didn't back down and hand it [back to me]. She said, "We made a decision. This is what's right." She let me manage up, and not so she could stay out of the fray. She let me manage up and stood right beside me to initiate some of those first initial things.

Under the leadership of Superintendent Pollio, the district has increased the size of the DEP staff, along with growing the division's purview of responsibilities. Dr. Marshall explained that when he was hired, his division started with 4 staff members. As of 2023, he managed a team of 54 that included "anti-racist specialists...foster homeless care, migrant and immigrant refugee supports... the multicultural specialist... an executive administrator... [and] a teacher residency program for minorities," among others. According to Marshall, Pollio has supported the growth of the division, arguing that DEP "'is just as much a department as [human resources] and finance and academics.'"

Notably, both Dr. Hargens and Dr. Pollio have steadily built the district's bench of equity-minded education leaders, including Black educators with deep ties to the community, many of whom have remained in the district and have kept the district's racial equity efforts moving forward.

With a robust staff at DEP, the team endeavors to help teachers, staff, and the community at large develop racial equity mindsets and practices that will translate into improved opportunities and outcomes for students of color. When asked what the greatest challenge to racial equity is in the district, Georgia Hampton, former Director of Compliance and Investigation, replied, "Our expectations. Expectations of our students, expectations of our teachers, and so forth." The premise of the JCPS racial equity vision is that by changing those expectations and developing a racial equity mindset among all district staff and community members, the district can achieve improved opportunities and outcomes for students of color. As described throughout this case, district leaders work to shift mindsets and practices through setting policy and investing in staff professional development.

Setting a Vision for Racial Equity

A vision for racial equity sits at the center of all of the work in JCPS. JCPS leaders have articulated an explicit focus on racial equity that guides decision-making in the district. Further, JCPS leaders build support for this vision by aligning it to the district's longstanding values and communicating the need for this vision through research and data.

In light of persistent racial disparities in student learning opportunities and achievement, under the leadership of Dr. Hargens in 2015, district leaders began the process of creating a strategic plan to guide the district over the next five years. They solicited input from all stakeholders: district staff across departments, school board members, school personnel, and the broader community. The result was *Vision 2020: Excellence with Equity* (full text available in the Online Materials Package), which outlined the district's core values, goals, and strategies for making progress toward the district's overall vision:

> All Jefferson County Public Schools students graduate prepared, empowered, and inspired to reach their full potential and contribute as thoughtful, responsible citizens of our diverse, shared world.

One of the core values in *Vision 2020* is equity, which JCPS defined as follows:

> All students receive an education that gives them what they need to thrive through differentiated supports focused on removing social factors as a predictor of success.

Although the word "racial equity" does not appear in *Vision 2020*, the document recommends strategies targeted to "gap groups," defined as those students in the following demographic groups: "African American, Hispanic, Native American, With Disability, Free and Reduced-Price Meals, [and] Limited English Proficiency."

In 2018, Superintendent Pollio built upon the vision set out in *Vision 2020* when he introduced three pillars to guide the implementation of the district's strategic plan. One of those pillars was racial equity, thus making the district's commitment even more explicit and focused on addressing persistent racial disparities in JCPS.

In interviews, JCPS leaders noted that they have encountered some opposition to their racial equity focus, both among other district staff and in the broader community. In response, a significant aspect of their work is developing a persuasive communication strategy to advocate for their racial equity vision, whether at board meetings, community forums, or in other district communications. JCPS leaders do this by explaining how their initiatives connect to long-held racial equity values in the community, how they further the district's stated commitments and goals, and how they are motivated by compelling research and district data.

JCPS leaders appeal to the district's legacy of working toward integration when discussing racial equity initiatives. In a board discussion about establishing a Males of Color Academy, for example, one board member grappled with how the project squared with the district's commitment to integration, stating, "we've tried to preach and sell diversity for all these years." As will be described in more detail later, JCPS leaders explained to the school board and broader community how the Academy furthers, rather than detracts from, support for student diversity in the district. JCPS leaders garner support for racial equity initiatives by positioning them as part of the district's ongoing racial equity legacy.

JCPS leaders also use data and research to drive support for their racial equity vision. Dr. John Marshall began his tenure as Chief Equity Officer, spearheading an initiative to share district data with the JCPS community in order to motivate the district's vision. The DEP division released the *Envision Equity Scorecard* in fall 2013, which shared data on key indicators disaggregated by school poverty levels and student race. From there, Marshall and other JCPS leaders were able to point to deep racial disparities in educational opportunity and outcomes as evidence of a need for bold solutions. Similarly, Dr. Dena Dossett, the district's Chief of Accountability, Research, and Systems Improvement Division, explained that research is instrumental in making the case for the district's racial equity vision. Her division produces detailed literature reviews and evaluations of district proposals and initiatives to demonstrate, in part, their relationship with racial equity. For example, the division conducted a study on the relationship between students' sense of belonging and their engagement and other outcomes.

They tracked data using an annual student survey and found that Black girls reported the lowest levels of a sense of belonging in the district. Then, according to Dr. Dossett, they collaborated with the DEP division to understand "what type of services and experiences can we help put in place to address that?" These investigations of district data both help to guide district decision-making and provide concrete justification for the district's racial equity priorities.

Implementing Policies and Practices for Racial Equity

JCPS leaders recognize that developing a vision for racial equity is not an endpoint but rather a beginning. The consequential work comes in operationalizing that vision, beginning with the Racial Equity Policy developed by district leaders and approved by the school board. Securing that foundational policy opened the door to creating a series of policies and practices that make the district's commitment to racial equity real. JCPS leaders emphasize that these efforts have not been without challenges. To the contrary, Superintendent Pollio argues that "it takes a lot of courage," especially leading the only large, liberal-leaning district in a predominantly conservative state. These challenges, though, have also come from within the district. Superintendent Pollio acknowledged that this pushback makes the work difficult, but persistence makes it possible:

> We don't have everybody on board. When you have 17,000 employees, you're not going to… But what you have to do, I believe, is just be consistent and courageous, and make the case and continue to make the case. More than anything, it is making sure not just to do lip service to it, or the relatively easy things. It's the courage and the ability to just continue to play that long game, to keep pushing hard.

It is clear that JCPS leaders have been playing the long game as they have built the infrastructure to support more and more expansive and substantive racial equity leadership over a decade.

In 2018, the school board unanimously passed a racial equity policy, *District Commitment to Racial Educational Equity*.[21] The policy builds on the district's *Vision 2020* plan by setting explicit goals for educational access and achievement outcomes for students of color and calls for system-wide plans across five areas: diversity in curriculum, instruction, and assessment; school culture and climate; programmatic access to educational opportunities; staffing and classroom diversity; and central office commitment to racial educational equity.[22] The holistic and multifaceted nature of this policy demonstrates the district's commitment to moving past rhetoric to drive action across all the core areas of the district's operations.

The DEP division spearheaded the process of crafting the policy and, as will be discussed, its accountability measures, and involved a myriad of community members, including educators, school leaders, parent and teacher association members, and students. This level of collaboration set up the Racial Equity Policy to become an integral source of authority woven into future district policies.[23]

By enshrining racial equity into district policy, JCPS leaders were ensuring that the district's commitment to racial equity will be longstanding and not easily shifted by a change in leadership or staffing. As Superintendent Pollio explained:

> It's cemented. This is not something that next summer a new superintendent could roll in and say, 'Okay, we're not doing that anymore.' It's in policy. And in order to stop doing that, a future board and superintendent would have to say, 'we would like to stop doing that or change it.'

One major shift demanded by the Racial Equity Policy was to generate a wider commitment to racial equity, particularly from the central office. Superintendent Pollio explained that before the policy was passed, the district placed much of the onus of racial equity onto school staff:

> The racial equity work before we passed the Racial Equity Policy was about disproportionality in discipline and achievement gaps between Black and white students, and it was really focusing on schools. Where we turned as a result of the Racial Equity Policy was, if we're going to be successful [at improving student outcomes], we have to have a comprehensive look at everything we do, every division, every department, everybody being invested. It needs to be woven through everything we do, from budgeting, to facilities, to hiring. If the outcomes were going to come to us, it was going to be everybody in the boat, doing the work.

Shifting the imperative for racial equity from the school level alone to the district level allowed the district to make sweeping policy changes that leaders believed to be challenging but necessary. To operationalize their commitment to racial equity, the district developed a racial equity plan that articulates each chief's racial equity goals with specific outcome metrics that they track and report on monthly. The district, for example, developed a student-weighted equity funding formula. Superintendent Pollio explained:

> Instead of every student is worth $3,000, we have to say, a special education student, an immigrant student, a student of poverty, a homeless student, are all multipliers of that formula. That's an equity formula.

Similarly, when it came to building and renovating facilities, rather than simply going down a list of school needs as had always been done, district leaders created an equity index that took into account both racial equity and building need.

Building on the expectation that all staff commit to advancing racial equity, JCPS leaders created a host of tools and processes to support this shift. For example, Superintendent Pollio noted that "every administrator in the district has in their yearly growth plan a racial equity growth plan. You have to identify something in which you are going to improve with racial equity." These growth plans reached all corners of the central office, ranging from finances and facilities management to human resources and curriculum development. In addition, as will be described in detail later, applicants hoping to become new administrators in the district are assessed using a racial equity screener that evaluates evidence that they have driven racial equity work forward in their previous roles.

The district also created the Racial Equity Analysis Protocol (REAP), a district instrument with about a dozen questions that school and district leaders use when making decisions that impact students (available in the Online Materials Package). According to Superintendent Pollio, the purpose of the tool is for teams to ask, "Are we making a decision that has racial equity in the forefront? Are there unintended consequences to this that may, somewhere down the line, have a negative impact on students of color?" For example, the instrument asks teams to consider, "Have stakeholders, particularly those most impacted by this decision, been meaningfully informed or involved in the discussion of the proposal?" and "What root causes may be producing and perpetuating racial inequities associated with this issue? Does this policy/practice/initiative deepen these inequities or improve them?" District leaders complete a REAP with every major decision, and Superintendent Pollio estimates that "thousands of REAPs have been done."

For decision-making at the school level, the REAP stands alongside a suite of district anchor documents developed by the DEP Division. The Racial Equity (ARE) Tool supports school staff to incorporate "more racially equitable practices into curriculum, instruction, and pedagogy" (available in the Online Materials Package).[24] The DEP division advises teachers to use the tool in their weekly professional learning community meetings to develop all unit and lesson plans. The Equity Monitoring Progress Tool (EMPT) allows school staff to evaluate how their school sites are progressing on a series of racial equity metrics. The EMPT asks staff to assess progress on student access to opportunities, educator diversity, the amount of cultural competence training offered, and shifts in curriculum. Based on the assessment of their site's progress, school leaders craft racial equity plans that guide areas for further focus and development. School leaders use these tools in a cycle of continuous improvement as they reevaluate their site's progress and reconsider how to meet their goals. Figure 4.1 demonstrates how these tools work together.

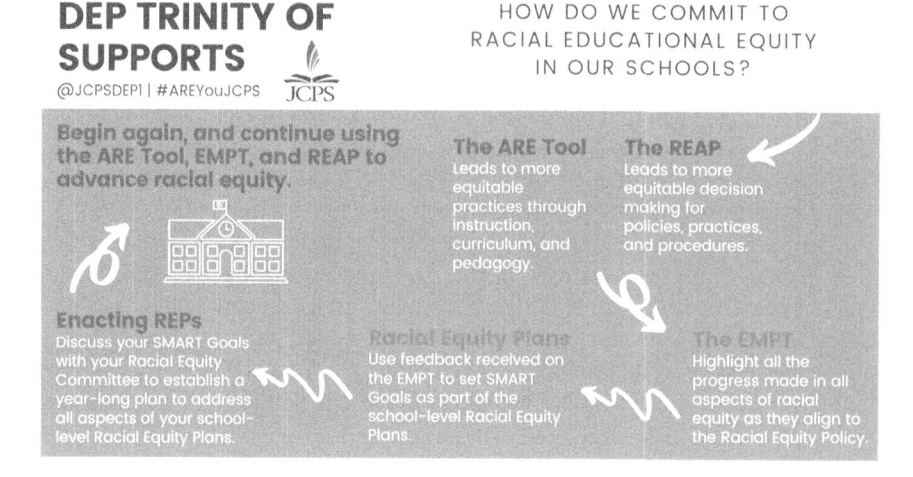

Figure 4.1 Diversity, Equity, and Poverty Division Trinity of Supports.

Source: Jefferson County Public Schools (n.d.). Affirming racial equity tool guidebook. https://docs.google.com/presentation/d/1wnjsL8n7esUlEArCy12m3cCIZHatA41cVF4p 0iZATZM/edit#slide=id.g1402f19bcef_2_58 (accessed 5/23/2023).

JCPS also has a process for monitoring data districtwide to assess progress on racial equity metrics and make decisions. As will be described in the following section, every six weeks the Accountability, Research, and Systems Improvement Division provides data on the district's "vital signs," a series of academic and culture and climate metrics.

At the same time, the district has had to contend with constraints that limit the capacity of DEP, forcing Pollio to balance competing priorities. On one hand, he acknowledges the need to sufficiently build the DEP division in order to properly support district staff to implement the sweeping changes the district has been demanding. He noted, for example, that

> we've expected our schools to do so much more. [For example], the Equity Monitoring Progress Tool [is for] schools identifying areas in which they need improvement, setting goals, and tracking those goals. There has to be support for schools to do that.

On the other hand, Pollio noted that district leadership tries to "ensure that most of our dollars are going to school budgets and not to Central Office. So that's a consistent battle that's not just in DEP, but everywhere. There's only a finite amount of dollars." With the district contending with a teacher shortage like many other districts in the country, Pollio explained that he had to make the difficult decision to send 95 resource teachers, including DEP staff, back to the classroom. In his words, "we can't have resource teachers sitting at the district office in a cubicle while we have a vacancy with kids sitting in desks... So, it does look like you're making a cut to DEP, but we're making a cut everywhere." JCPS leaders recognize that expanding the expectations around racial equity also demands expanding the district's staff capacity to support shifts in practice while balancing competing district priorities.

JCPS has strategically developed policies and practices to realize the district's racial equity vision. The Racial Equity Policy, in particular, has been instrumental in motivating the district to develop a host of additional policies and practices that touch each and every corner of district decision-making.

Driving Action Through Data Transparency

Most of Dr. John Marshall's visitors notice one thing when they walk into his office: elephants. The surfaces in his office are adorned with dozens of elephant figurines collected from his travels. When it's time to get down to work, Dr. Marshall reaches into a sack by his desk, pulls out an elephant, places it squarely on his desk, and says, "Let's talk about the elephant in the room." The elephant in the room is racial inequity, a condition that some in the community disregard, according to Marshall, preferring instead to focus on disparities across socio-economic strata. However, Dr. Marshall and other JCPS administrators acknowledge racial inequity head-on by gathering, analyzing, and sharing data related to the opportunities and outcomes for student groups in the district. Over the years, as data collection and transparency grew into cornerstones of the JCPS approach to racial equity, district leaders equipped themselves with tools and evidence that grounded their decision-making to resolve documented racial inequities.

Beginning in 2013, district leaders began intentionally organizing and sharing data on several indicators to take account of racial equity in the district. Though the data transparency efforts were met with internal and external challenges, concerted action from leadership to share the data broadly with district staff, families, and community partners helped the district's DEP division advocate for program funding, build support, and enact policy change. Further, the decision to maintain an explicit focus on racial equity over a decade has equipped the district with the necessary data and policy backing to accelerate and refine their racial equity efforts.

The Launch of the Envision Equity Scorecard

After Dr. John Marshall was hired in 2012, he launched a team of three staff members to develop a powerful "instrument for organizational and community learning and change." An advisory group of over a dozen stakeholders aided the team. The advisory team included teachers as well as district administrators in data evaluation, finance, human resources, student assignment, and DEP programs. It also included professors from local universities and a healthcare organization leader. The mission of the equity scorecard team was:

> To raise the collective awareness about current system inequities in order to promote systemic district change on the basis of internal and community-wide collaboration to ensure ALL of our children receive excellent, equitable, and dignified educational experiences, opportunities, and outcomes.[25]

Guided by this mission, the team released the first JCPS *Envision Equity Scorecard* in Fall 2013. The scorecard shares key indicators disaggregated by school poverty levels and student race. JCPS initially selected four "Domains of Equity"—discipline, literacy, college and career readiness, and school climate and culture (Figure 4.2)—aligned with the district's strategic plan. The equity scorecard team made the intentional decision to focus on a narrow set of domains and indicators "…fundamental in driving societal inequities that are also highly connected."[26]

District leaders overseeing the scorecard designed it to be accessible to a broad audience, making the data available as a technical report, a lay-friendly pamphlet, and online to encourage data sharing and consumption. The scorecard is organized by domains, which include explanations of why the domain is important as well as graphics and key statistics that point to inequities captured by the data. For example, as seen in Figure 4.3, the Discipline domain includes a text box that states, "sixty-six percent of

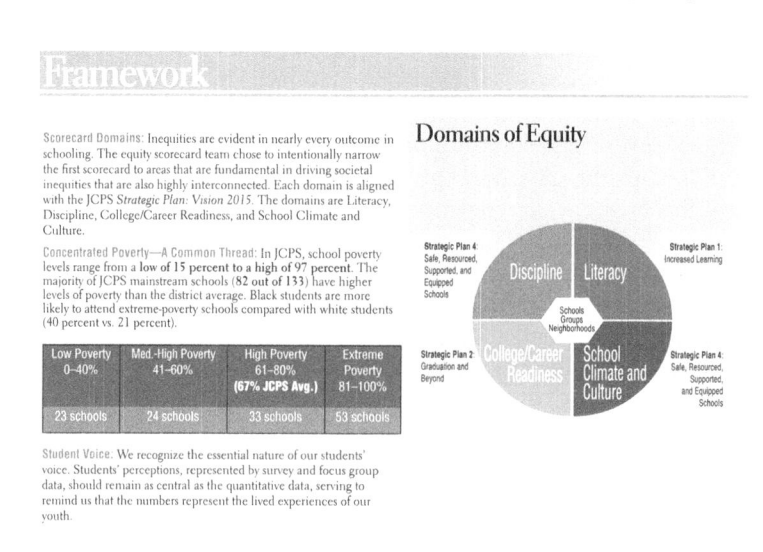

Figure 4.2 Envision Equity Domains.

Source: Jefferson County Public Schools (2013). Envision equity scorecard. https://issuu.com/jcps-ky/docs/eesingpgs.

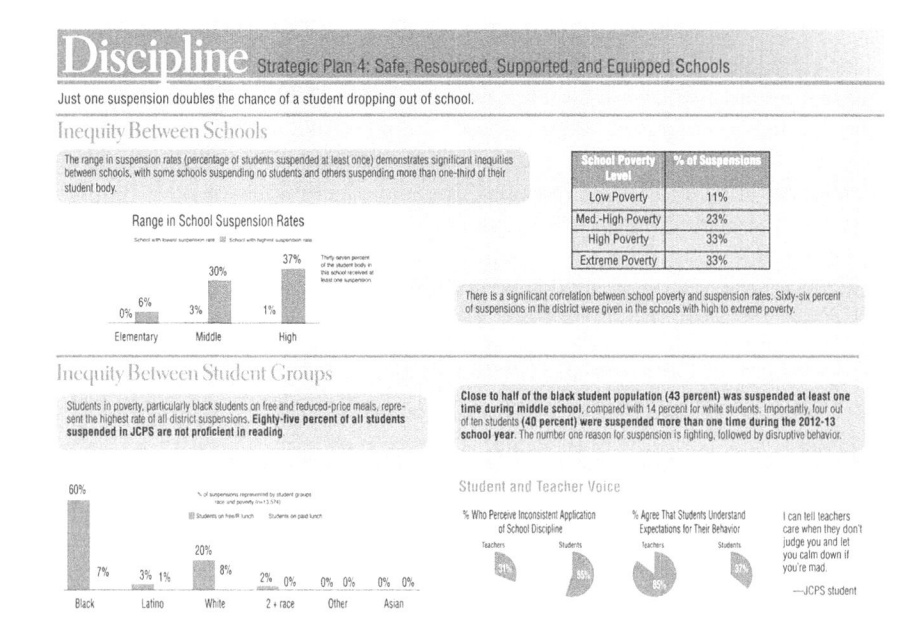

Figure 4.3 Envision Equity Scorecard: Discipline, 2013.

Source: Jefferson County Public Schools (2013). Envision equity scorecard. https://issuu. com/jcps-ky/docs/eesingpgs.

suspensions in the district were given in the schools with high to extreme poverty." In other cases, these boxes offer opportunities to unpack the complexities of equity. For example, a text box that accompanies a graph on reading proficiency rates points out that socio-economic status alone cannot explain the district's low reading proficiency rates for Black students. Dr. Marshall argues that the disparity in test scores across socio-economic status and race is evidence that "we can't just default to poverty. We have to put race at the center of this when we talk about our goals." The scorecard does just. In this way, the equity scorecard shines a light on deep and troubling inequities while also highlighting the potential for improvement.

Rather than a one-off initiative, JCPS leaders have made the Envision Equity Scorecard central to maintaining the district's focus on resolving documented racial inequities. From the inception of the equity scorecard, its purpose has been to inform school communities and drive decision-making. The authors of the scorecard assert that it is

> an organization learning and change mechanism that can become integrated into the language and culture of our institution to enable and support access and equity commitments for many years to come. Its value and impact will be ongoing, not short term or static.

JCPS has made progress on that charge by continuing to iterate on the scorecard, contributing to district action to ensure that the scorecard was, according to Dr. Marshall, "not a project: its value is ongoing and long-term." In addition to the original four domains (discipline, literacy, college and career readiness, and school climate and culture), district leadership has included two additional domains that implicate racial equity: Attendance, including disproportionate rates of chronic absenteeism, and Opportunities & Access, which tracks data on student educational access such as teacher turnover and rates of gifted and talented identification.

Data as a Tool for Community Engagement

Dr. Marshall recalls that when the equity scorecard was first released in November 2013, it "came with heat." According to him, the pushback came from both some sectors of the community and some district staff. Although Marshall did not describe the pushback in detail, the literature on racial equity leadership indicates that education leaders commonly encounter challenging reactions to their racial equity efforts.[27] However, Dr. Marshall's leadership move was to be as transparent as possible in communicating both the data and its purpose across the full spectrum of the community, from the "grassroots to the silver spoons." He and his team work diligently to engage parents in the work of the district and support parents to understand ways in which they can support their children's success, whether with data from the equity scorecard or otherwise. This support is accomplished in a variety of ways, most notably in a parent involvement series. "We're trying to connect parents to the information they need to be effective in their child's academic experience," stated Delquan Dorsey, the Parent Engagement Coordinator at JCPS. John Marshall expanded, "One thing we do [through the] parent involvement series, [is] keep everyone informed of the status of our inequities and what parents can do to make sure their child doesn't fall on the wrong side of the equity gap."

In addition to the parent involvement series, Dr. Marshall devised a bold plan to host community summits about the district's inequities, which, he said, were unapologetically transparent and eschewed education jargon:

> We just said Black kids are getting suspended more, now here's the data. We said students of color and poor kids are not reading at the same level, now here's the data. Boys of color are not feeling accepted in school. Here's the data. We just said it.

The purpose of these community forums was not only to share data with communities but also to partner with them to work toward solutions. Dr. Marshall remembers asking at community summits, "What can you do to help?"

The community summits were met with resistance from some community members, but Dr. Marshall says, "we just pushed through it." He credits that to the leadership of former Superintendent Hargens, who "100% supported" the transparency of community summits on inequities. Despite the challenge of presenting data in a way that had not been done before, "it helped that as the superintendent entered the district, she talked about transparency. And she didn't back away from that." This transparency, in turn, supported Dr. Marshall's ability to engage with his community and built trust in ways that centered community members. As he noted,

> [W]e have rebuilt trust, not with the entire community…but rebuilt trust with the marginalized community. There are people calling, "how do I get there to support?" That comes with a lot of door knocking, sitting inside the church house, sitting with grandmama. And we do all of that.

By identifying and speaking candidly about discrepancies between the district vision and reality, staff emphasize that they are able to use data as fuel for their efforts and to communicate the urgency of student need. For example, as will be described later, data demonstrating dramatic disparities in suspension rates enabled the district to attend to the root conditions for suspensions by changing student behavior supports and policies. In addition, some staff have been able to use data to show the progress they are making through programs and initiatives. Charles Davis, former coordinator of DEP programs, put it this way: "I keep communicating that our theory of action can work. I can show you results. I'm constantly building the case for our work." As a result, his programming received dedicated funding from the general budget, unlike in prior years. Dr. Marshall also uses the data in his meetings with the mayor of Louisville to find common regions of need and develop solutions together. By developing a comprehensive data system with a racial equity lens, JCPS is able to push forward a host of racial equity initiatives across several domains (e.g., teaching and learning, teacher recruitment and preparation, student health, and behavior support).

Even after the superintendency transition from Dr. Hargens, Dr. Pollio continued to use scorecard data to garner buy-in and gauge progress toward racial equity. Dr. Pollio's superintendency centered around ensuring that he and other district leaders had "the ability, the courage, the tenacity to stand up to make the case, to change hearts and minds, to ask the tough questions." In a poignant example, he shared that after the killing of Breonna Taylor in Louisville, "there was a lot of support for [racial equity]. But, as predicted, in about 12 months, we've been getting significant pushback because of all of that political [discourse]." Still, Dr. Pollio's steadfast approach to advancing racial equity was supported not just by community engagement but also by data. The equity scorecard established the tone to analyze and share all district data through an equity lens and afford narrative power to the lived experiences behind the numbers on the scorecard.

A Focused Approach to Equity Data

District leadership, including Dr. Dena Dossett, the district's Chief of Accountability, Research, and Systems Improvement Division, noted that JCPS and the Louisville community have their hands on a wealth of data; the challenge then was to make sure that they were focusing on the right data-informed activities that could drive improved racial equity outcomes. As demanded by the district's racial equity plan, Dr. Dossett and her division continue to improve and publish the Equity Scorecard—now online—which tracks progress made toward the five central tenets of the Racial Equity Policy. These five tenets include twenty-two unique metrics ranging from the percentages of students of color who are transition-ready to the percentages of contracts with minority and women-owned business enterprises. In addition, the division also reports on the district's "vital signs" every six weeks, which include, for example, rates of student growth on formative assessments and disciplinary rates. Dr. Dossett explained that, despite collecting and sharing the district's progress on this wide range of metrics on a regular basis, JCPS leaders were not seeing the shifts in key outcomes that they might have expected:

> To be transparent, we weren't seeing the data change in the way that we needed to see the data on key metrics, particularly around proficiency.... Looking at the data is the easiest rationale to say that we need to try something different.

Dr. Dossett and other JCPS leaders identified the problem with their approach. The leadership team had been meeting monthly to discuss progress on each of their division's racial equity plans, but "it's really just a report-out on activities, without a strong connection to outcomes based on that activity... How do I know what [I did] made a difference in student outcomes?"

In the face of persistent racial gaps across various metrics, including in suspensions and proficiency rates, Dr. Dossett and other district leaders sought to rethink and retool their approach to defining racial equity activities and metrics. Dr. Dossett worked with other chiefs to narrow down the metrics to the key data points they want to see change. With chiefs and other district staff, she systematically re-evaluated each metric and sought to gauge whether each metric had a clear connection to the district's racial equity goal. She probed other district leaders with a series of questions:

- Does this activity center racial equity and directly contribute to this racial equity goal? If so, how does it center racial equity?
- During this activity, will racialized students be impacted? If yes, how?
- Will your staff be made aware of this activity and expectations that [racial equity] should be centered?
- What quantifiable data will you use to monitor that activity?

In these conversations, she mentions that:

> if you can't directly tie it to racial equity, then that's not a strategy that we want to put in our racial equity plan.… I'm excited about being able to clearly connect our strategies to our impact on racial equity and having a logic model that helps people tell their story in a very easy and succinct way.

Through these processes, Dr. Dossett's leadership moves to refine and right-size the district's data-based approach to racial equity work increased their ability to focus on data that provides actionable insights focused on student outcomes.

Expanding Learning Opportunities for the Whole Child

JCPS leaders strive to provide all of the district's students with a world-class education that prepares them with core academics, but also "to be good communicators, problem solvers, collaborators, and more."[28] This vision aligns with the research on whole child education, which recognizes and builds upon the connections between children's social, emotional, cognitive, and academic development, as well as their physical and mental health.[29] In JCPS, whole child education encompasses a shift to providing more rigorous and experiential deeper learning, including through culturally responsive teaching, providing positive behavioral supports and restorative practices, and supporting students physical and mental health needs.[30]

Though causation can't be confirmed, the district's shift to a whole child educational approach has coincided with growth in the district's graduation rates and rates of college and career readiness, as well as declines in exclusionary discipline rates.

Between 2011–12 and 2021–22, the four-year cohort graduation rate[31] increased from 68% to 85% for JCPS students overall, an increase of 25% (Table 4.2). In the same period, graduation rates for Black JCPS students increased from 63% to 84%, an increase of 33%, which exceeded the districtwide rate of growth over the same period. Graduation rates for Latino/a students also increased modestly during this period from 73% to 75%.

Not only have graduation rates been increasing, but the percentage of students demonstrating postsecondary readiness has also increased (Table 4.3). The state of Kentucky defines postsecondary readiness as meeting one of several college or career readiness metrics, including meeting a benchmark score on a college admissions exam, earning college credit through an approved course or exam, completing the required hours for an apprenticeship, or earning an industry-recognized certification. Districtwide, the proportion of high school graduates identified as postsecondary ready increased from

Table 4.2 JCPS Four-Year Cohort Graduation Rate by Racial/Ethnic Group, 2011–12 to 2020–21

Race/Ethnicity	2011–12	2012–13	2013–14	2014–15	2015–16	2016–17	2017–18	2018–19	2019–20	2020–21
ALL	68%	77%	81%	79%	80%	81%	82%	82%	84%	84%
American Indian/ Alaska Native	N/A	N/A	N/A	N/A	N/A	N/A	71%	N/A	N/A	80%
Asian American	91%	86%	91%	88%	92%	90%	92%	92%	95%	94%
Black	63%	74%	79%	77%	77%	78%	79%	79%	82%	83%
Latino/a	73%	73%	80%	78%	75%	76%	76%	79%	77%	76%
Multiracial	20%	73%	72%	84%	84%	78%	79%	81%	84%	86%
Native Hawaiian/ Pacific Islander	N/A	N/A	N/A	N/A	100%	80%	N/A	91%	80%	82%
White	72%	78%	82%	80%	82%	83%	84%	84%	86%	87%

Source: JCPS District Data (2019–2021), https://www.jefferson.kyschools.us/departments/data-management-research/data-books; Kentucky Department of Education School Report Card Datasets, https://www.education.ky.gov/Open-House/data/Pages/Historical-SRC-Datasets.aspx (accessed 3/27/2025)

Note: The four-year cohort graduation rate is defined as the number of students who graduate in four years with a regular high school diploma divided by the number of students who entered high school four years earlier, adjusting for transfers in and out, émigrés, and deceased students. Data are suppressed for student groups with a sample size smaller than ten.

50% to 68% between 2017–18 and 2021–22. At the same time, the postsecondary readiness proportion nearly doubled for Black graduates, increasing from 31% to 54%. For Latino/a students, the proportion deemed postsecondary ready increased from 44% to 63% in the same period.

With a greater emphasis on supporting students' access to meaningful learning, the district has seen considerable growth in students of color accessing advanced coursework, including gifted and talented education and Advanced Placement classes. Between 2012–13 and 2018–19, the number of students taking Advanced Placement exams increased by nearly 60% for Black students and by more than 120% for Latino/a students (Appendix 4A). In addition, between 2018 and 2022, rates of gifted and talented identification increased by 11% for Black students and by 27% for Latino/a students (Appendix 4A).

Table 4.3 Percentage of High School Graduates Identified as Postsecondary Ready

Race/Ethnicity	2017–18	2021–22
American Indian/Alaska Native	N/A	N/A
Asian American	59%	86%
Black	31%	54%
Latino/a	44%	63%
Multiracial	56%	72%
Native Hawaiian/Pacific Islander	N/A	90%
White	64%	79%
Total	50%	68%

Source: Kentucky Department of Education School Report Card Datasets (2017–18 and 2021–22), https://www.education.ky.gov/Open-House/data/Pages/Historical-SRC-Datasets.aspx (accessed 3/27/2025)

Note: The state of Kentucky defines postsecondary readiness as meeting one of several college or career readiness metrics, including meeting a benchmark score on a college admissions exam, earning college credit through an approved course or exam, completing the required hours for an apprenticeship, or earning an industry-recognized certification. Data are suppressed for student groups with a sample size smaller than ten.

There is also evidence that the district's shift to restorative practices, described in more detail later in this section, may have contributed to a decline in exclusionary discipline rates. Between 2011–12 and 2018–19, there were drastic increases in the number of disciplinary actions experienced by Black students (Figure 4.4). As suggested by district staff, some of this increase may have been attributable to improved reporting standards. Between 2018–19 and 2019–20, the number of disciplinary actions experienced by Black students dropped by nearly 20%. Disciplinary actions dropped to nearly zero in 2020–21 while schools shifted to remote learning at the height of the pandemic. Although they rebounded the following school year, the number of disciplinary actions for Black students in 2021–22 was about 30% lower than in 2019–20. These outcomes are consistent with research showing that implementing restorative practices can reduce suspension and expulsion rates and, in turn, improve school climate outcomes and academic achievement.[32]

JCPS takes a whole-child approach to expanding learning opportunities by using data to motivate bold solutions, providing culturally responsive, deeper learning experiences, prioritizing positive behavior supports, and providing wraparound services through community partnerships.

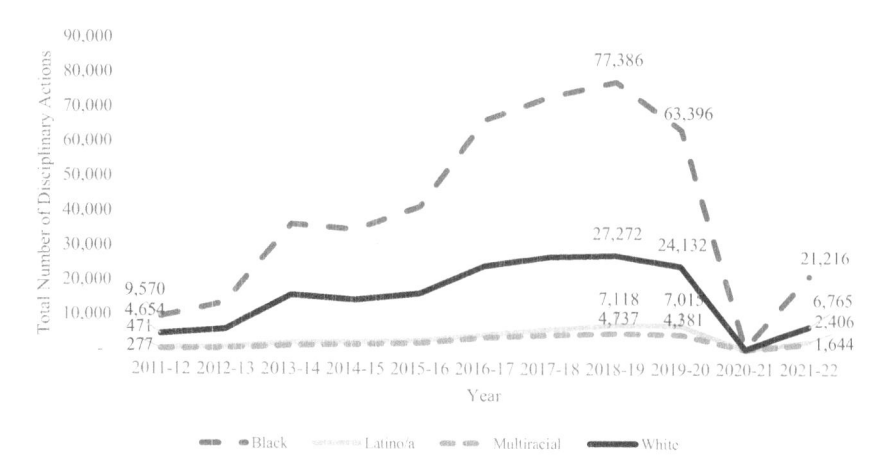

Figure 4.4 JCPS Total Disciplinary Actions (Counts) by Racial/Ethnic Group, 2011–12 to 2018–19Source: Kentucky Department of Education School Report Card Datasets (2011–21). https://www.education.ky.gov/Open-House/data/Pages/Historical-SRC-Datasets.aspx

Note: Disciplinary actions include expulsion, out-of-school suspension, removal, restraint, and seclusion.

JCPS Shifts Focus to Deeper Learning

In classrooms where deeper learning is the goal, rigorous academic content is paired with engaging, experiential, and innovative learning experiences. Such experiences equip students with the skills to find, analyze, and apply knowledge in new contexts and situations and prepare them for college, work, civic participation in a democratic society, and lifelong learning in a fast-changing and information-rich world.[33]

In 2018, after Dr. Pollio transitioned into the superintendency, he led JCPS educators and community partners on a ten-month process of teaching and learning redesign. District leadership initiated this journey in response to data that showed increasing achievement gaps and what they stated were "unacceptable" reading and math proficiency rates on state and national exams that showed "clear evidence that many of our students were not ready for key transitions in their educational journeys."[34] Further, the district's racial equity plan stated that the Chief Academic Officer and Chief of Schools would "ensure that each school has systems in place to support students in becoming transition ready."[35]

The result of this intensive work was the Backpack of Success Skills (referred to as the Backpack), one of the district's three pillars, alongside racial equity and culture and climate. The Backpack is "a P-12 innovative educational initiative to ensure every single student within JCPS receives an education in which academic achievement and personal development go hand in hand."[36] The heart of the Backpack is its Five Success Skills:

1. Prepared and Resilient Learner
2. Globally and Culturally Competent Citizen
3. Emerging Innovator
4. Effective Communicator
5. Productive Collaborator

As part of the initiative, each student builds a digital portfolio of learning artifacts that tracks individual student progress from pre-kindergarten to twelfth grade on the Success Skills, providing evidence of their readiness to progress from elementary school through college and career. Their readiness is assessed during student-led conferences at "Backpack Defenses" in 5th, 8th, and 12th grades.

The Backpack emphasizes student choice and voice, as well as rich, meaningful learning experiences, which are often neglected for students of color in favor of remediation or rote, low-level cognitive skills. Upon completing her Backpack defense, Marion C. Moore High School senior, Ariana, described how the Backpack defense provides an authentic opportunity for students to showcase their growth and accomplishments:

> It's about looking at the student as a whole really, and giving them the opportunity to present what they have done these four years, beyond a test score…These Backpacks are a way to show the work that is not always tested: writing pieces, performance pieces, maybe just personal growth…to show that you're ready to go onto the next step in the world.[37]

The Backpack also refers to the instructional framework that guides how teachers plan lessons, teach students, and assess student learning to develop the Five Success Skills. According to the then-Chief Academic Officer, Carmen Coleman, who helped devise the Backpack, transforming student assessment was really about transforming teaching and learning:

> Our theory of action was simple: if students were required to show tangible evidence of mastering those Success Skills each year, then they must have learning experiences that would lead to those artifacts. And as one of our third-graders said early on when he was learning about the Backpack, "Worksheets won't make good artifacts."[38]

Indeed, when the district launched the Backpack initiative, they highlighted examples of deeper learning projects already happening in JCPS schools that would make strong Backpack artifacts: students educating the community on a civic issue of their choice, publishing a youth poetry anthology, and collaboratively engineering a catapult using physics and math concepts.[39]

To ensure that each aspect of the Backpack is implemented with fidelity, instructional leads, instructional coaches, and deeper learning resource teachers on the Curriculum Design and Learning Innovation team provide support for teachers to enact the learning experiences students need to produce evidence of learning in their Backpacks. For example, Curriculum Design and Learning Innovation staff have developed detailed curriculum frameworks across grades K to 12 in the four core subject areas, as well as in visual and performing arts, health and physical education, and world languages, totaling over 100 individual curriculum frameworks. These frameworks and resources, which include unit plans and lesson ideas, are designed to "ensure equitable and culturally responsive experiences for all students" while also facilitating "implementation of [project-based learning], deeper learning, and personalized learning."[40]

Deeper Learning is Culturally Responsive

At the same time that the Backpack provides greater access to deeper learning for all students, the district's Vision 2020 and Racial Equity Policy demand that the district also better meet the needs of historically underserved students of color. Dr. Marshall articulated the importance of culturally responsive practices in JCPS, noting, "Culturally responsive teaching, in a nutshell, is reaching students where they are and allowing their cultures to be a part of the pedagogy and curriculum." Research indicates that culturally responsive teaching strategies can support positive relationships in the classroom and improve student achievement outcomes.[41]

JCPS leaders work districtwide to shift mindsets and practices toward culturally responsive deeper learning through in-depth and ongoing professional learning. Starting in 2015, guided by *Vision 2020*, JCPS began offering equity institutes and what John Marshall calls "a battery of professional development opportunities," as well as a speaker series focusing on racial equity and culturally responsive teaching, in particular. One example is a JCPS "Does the Work" Cohort, through which "Participants will learn how racism factors into their daily lives and will discover ways in which to be antiracist in their classrooms, schools, and the community."

In 2018, in compliance with the Racial Equity Policy, JCPS division chiefs worked together to incorporate culturally responsive practices into the district's racial equity plan and across its divisions, such as "[leveraging] teachers to demonstrate and design culturally responsive lessons."[42] As previously mentioned, the DEP division developed the Affirming Racial Equity Tool to support teachers in incorporating culturally responsive practices in regular lesson and unit planning.

With the support of the Racial Equity Policy and resources from the DEP division, JCPS educators are piloting innovative courses that center culturally responsive practices. For example, with feedback from members of the district's Black Student Unions, in 2018, the JCPS social studies team developed a curriculum for an elective called Developing Black Historical Consciousness. Aligned to the Racial Equity Policy, the purpose of the course is to "investigate Black histories representative of and centered on Black perspectives and voices in order to represent Black people's full humanity."[43] Beginning with investigations of ancient African civilizations and ending at present day, essential questions in the curriculum include:

- How free were Black Americans during Reconstruction? (1865–77)
- How did Black Americans create a culture of Black joy in the 1920s?
- How did Black Americans persevere during times of uncertainty? (1930–45)

Consistent with the district's commitment to providing resources to support implementation, JCPS has built a team of equity-oriented curriculum leaders who create tools and support teachers to shift their mindsets and practices toward deeper learning and culturally responsive practices. One limitation, however, is that working with these curriculum leaders is primarily voluntary, and according to JCPS leaders, teachers who may need this professional development are often those who do not elect to participate.

JCPS leaders are also expanding opportunities for advanced learning by assessing students through a culturally responsive lens. Multiple district leaders pointed to the intentional efforts and outcomes of rethinking their gifted and talented identification strategies. According to Dr. Dossett, the gifted and talented qualifications were "stringently considered on how well you do on one particular assessment." Acknowledging the racial disparities in identification rates, beginning in 2018, JCPS leaders expanded the definition of gifted and talented to align with the state's definition, which includes screening students for high potential in not just academic aptitude, but also in psychosocial or leadership skills and the visual or performing arts. The realignment also informed the decision to switch the district's identification screener to one that was deemed less culturally biased, a move that increased gifted and talented identification among emergent bilingual students and students of color.

Professional Pathways with the Academies of Louisville

Aligned with the district's expansion of deeper learning opportunities through the Backpack of Success pillar, JCPS has thoughtfully built career academies over the course of a decade, known as the Academies of Louisville. Initially conceived in partnership with Ford Next Generation Learning in 2012 (Box 4.1), JCPS developed a plan to provide every student access

Box 4.1   Ford Next Generation Learning: Partnering with Communities for Deeper Learning

Cultivating personalized, real-world learning environments takes work. Just ask Kristin Wingfeld, JCPS Director of School and Business Partnerships, who explained that the launch of a career academy "really has to be, and it is being, heavily driven by the community." JCPS partners with local businesses to ensure their career academies position students to pursue high-skill, high-wage careers needed in Louisville. Working closely with the Metro Chamber of Commerce and Louisville Workforce Development Board to design sector-themed pathways, career academies connect students to area industries with demonstrated demand. This approach serves students who go directly from high school into the workforce as well as those bound for a post-secondary degree. Further, JCPS requires participating school leadership to poll their communities, gathering input from teachers, students, and families to determine the best-fit professional themes. Members of the DEP division sit on the academy launch team, considering the relevance and accessibility of programming decisions for all students.

After aligning business and student interests, the process isn't over. Companies like Ford and others involved in designing and funding academies coordinate with JCPS to provide ongoing support as participating schools transition into smaller, cross-disciplinary learning communities. Teachers prepare for work-based instruction through innovative professional development. Specifically, collaborative teaching teams participate in sector-aligned externships to develop experiential skills and knowledge in the field to later incorporate into project-based curriculum.

The curriculum engages students in practical learning tasks to build authentic knowledge and skills related to their field. For example, students in one school built their own assembly line and presented their final product to a team of Ford engineers. In another school, student inquiry around sustainability launched a pilot project designing solar go-karts. Cristy Rogers, then Director of College and Career Readiness, described deeper learning within career academy programming:

> We are deeper learning. When we talk about the whole child and soft skill development, and communication skills and teaching the whole child through passion projects and taking a child and finding their interest, and then helping grow that organically, and learning through authentic learning experiences. It is…project-based. That is the model that helps drive [our] platform for personalized, passion-driven…high-level interest projects.

Table 4.4 Percentage of High School Graduates Identified as Postsecondary Ready with High Demand, Kentucky vs. JCPS Academies of Louisville 2021–22

Race/Ethnicity	Kentucky	Academies of Louisville
Black	53%	56%
Latino/a	66%	75%
White	80%	81%
Total	76%	72%

Source: Data provided by Jefferson County Public Schools by request. Data were not available for all racial/ethnic groups.

to "career academies," professional pathways within local high schools that offer meaningful, personalized, real-world learning experiences with the goal of increasing student engagement, performance, and college and career readiness.[44]

Dr. Marshall noted that the program has since grown to include several other industry partners because he "saw an appetite from industry… We just thought it'd be a seamless marriage to really expand that investment in the community." Since the launch of the academies, these partnerships now involve large companies like GE, Norton Healthcare, Yum!, and Amazon, as well as minority and women-owned business enterprises. To date, the Academies of Louisville have been integrated into 15 high schools that serve nearly 20,000 students.[45] These schools offer career pathways in finance, biomedical science, teaching, aerospace engineering, and a host of other fields.[46] Students graduate with industry exposure, junior and senior year internships, and the opportunity to earn college credit and participate in apprenticeships.

District data indicate that Black and Latino/a Academies of Louisville students were more likely than their peers in the state to graduate with industry-recognized certifications, licensures, or credentials identified as being in high demand (see Table 4.4).

Out-of-School Enrichment and Supports

In addition to developing transformative school models, JCPS increases student access to opportunity by offering programs that address the most immediate needs of children, both during and outside the typical school day. The district's Racial Equity Plan stipulates that the Chief Academic Officer, Chief Equity Officer, and Chief of Schools will "improve community access to after-school activities and enrichment" and "increase the number of students of color participating in extended learning time programs."[47]

For the most part, these programs are offered free of charge and are focused on creating rich yet educational experiences outside of the traditional school day, including after school or during the summer, or outside of the school building, such as in career-focused settings. According to Marshall, "the programs we put out are ways of creating access, ways of keeping students engaged." Furthermore, JCPS board chair Porter explained that these opportunities are "a way of providing a safe environment for our students… Students want to feel safe and engaged and involved…Now we have broadened [education] to try and embrace our students not just in the classroom."

The DEP division runs one such program in the summer called "Literacy &." There is literacy & yoga, literacy & karate, literacy & chess, literacy & archery, and literacy & hip hop, among others. This summer camp deliberately connects literacy instruction to an enrichment activity, using high-interest, age-appropriate books. Students have two teachers, one a certified educator who focuses on the literacy component and another, a community member who is an expert in the enrichment activity. During the program, students read books about the enrichment activity and learn literary concepts such as foreshadowing or similes and metaphors. They spend the other half of the time engaged in the enrichment activity.

In another effort to meet the needs of children, JCPS coordinates with homeless shelter directors to identify students experiencing homelessness and provide them access to summer camps. The district also places teachers and resources inside some city shelters. The district runs a camp at St. Vincent de Paul, for example, that includes a focus on literacy and numbers, field trips, and other enrichment activities such as cooking.

As a result of these efforts, the district has seen considerable growth in the share of students accessing extended learning opportunities, especially among Black students. Between 2018–19 and 2021–22, the share of JCPS students participating in extended learning time activities more than doubled from 3% of students to 7%. During the same period, the participation rate for Black students increased from 4% to 12%. Increasing access to extended learning time, particularly for students of color, continues to be a goal in the district.

From a Code of Conduct to Student Support and Restorative Practices

Introducing structures that support positive student behavior is paramount to a whole-child approach and ensuring students' academic success. Motivated by *Vision 2020* and stark disparities in the district's suspension rates, JCPS worked to remove subjectivity from its disciplinary policies and shifted its stance on student discipline from one of punishment to one of support.

Relatedly, the district adopted another initiative, Positive Behavioral Interventions and Supports (PBIS), which also has the goal of reducing exclusionary discipline and maximizing instructional engagement.

According to the district's 2013 equity scorecard, 60% of the district's suspensions were of Black students on free or reduced lunch. Students were far more likely than teachers to believe that school discipline was inconsistently applied and far less likely to agree that students understand expectations for their behavior. The scorecard links disciplinary data to literacy achievement, noting that 85% of all students suspended were not proficient in reading. Further, overall, Black students were less likely to report feeling a sense of belonging at school compared to other racial and ethnic student groups.

In response to these data, the district launched an effort to understand the disproportionality in suspensions. New to her position, then Assistant Superintendent for Academic Achievement, Katy Zeitz reviewed over 900 discipline narratives representing each grade level. What Zeitz found in her review was the blatant, inconsistent application of the district's code of conduct. For example, the behaviors for which teachers cited students for "deliberate disruption" ranged from a refusal to follow teacher instructions (perhaps an annoyance but not a dangerous behavior) to setting off a smoke bomb (a potentially very dangerous behavior). As Zeitz said, "[Teachers] could do whatever because it was tough to monitor."

Further, the students more likely to be cited for infractions and receive more severe consequences were students of color. As John Marshall described:

> Two years ago, inward facing, we realized there was subjectivity in our suspensions, specifically around disruptive behavior. Disruptive behavior is a systemic, inward-facing problem in that it allowed teachers to have variability of judgment about what disruptive behavior was, from chewing gum to throwing a desk. That variability always fell harsher on students of color. And that was in every school. Disruptive behavior for one student might be detention, and for the same infraction it could result in suspension… On TV I [have publicly announced that] our code of conduct perpetuates racism and subjectivity.

The district response to these disparities in disciplinary action is a prime illustration of the JCPS approach to leading for racial equity. District leaders leveraged clear and compelling data to motivate a change in district policies, then partnered with a wide swath of stakeholders to rewrite the JCPS code of conduct. This policy change included removing the infraction "interference with staff" from the district's code of conduct. As Zeitz explains, "If a kid is starting a fight or using profanity, let's call it that. So, nothing arbitrary. So that code [interference with staff] is gone." The goal was to remove subjective infractions entirely and replace them with specific, observable infractions.

At the same time, district leaders also sought to shift staff mindsets about discipline from punitive to restorative. As Zeitz commented, "Our previous code of conduct was very punitive. This is not what we're trying to do, which is keep kids in school." Signaling this shift, the district changed the title of the guiding policy document from its "Code of Conduct" to the "Student Support and Behavior Intervention Handbook" (SSBIH), which was developed collaboratively by students, parents, educators, and community leaders.

The introduction of the revised district policy describes the district's new approach to discipline:

> The SSBIH ... seeks to provide a clear picture to guide all JCPS stakeholders in the fair and equitable application of behavior support systems provided by the district ... The handbook is intended to be instructive, not punitive; is based on the principle of positive and preventive responses (e.g., interventions and skill building); and is aimed at addressing the causes of inappropriate behavior, resolving conflict, meeting students' needs, and keeping students in school.[48]

In furtherance of the district's commitment to positive student support, in 2016–17 JCPS embarked on bringing restorative practices and PBIS to its schools in an integrated fashion. In contrast to zero-tolerance discipline policies focused on punishment and sanctions that often unfairly target students of color, restorative practices aim to foster more safe and equitable school environments by nurturing community building and conflict resolution and addressing the root causes of student misbehavior. As noted on the district's website, "Restorative Practice is not a program. It is a philosophy focusing on repairing harm, restoring relationships, and responsibility. Restorative Practice gives students a voice—communication and problem-solving skills that will help them pursue appropriate solutions to future problems."[49] PBIS is a three-tiered system for providing students with instructional, behavioral, social, and emotional supports that are tailored to their needs.[50]

In 2017, the district partnered with the International Institute for Restorative Practices and the Midwest PBIS Network to bring restorative practices and PBIS to ten schools per year over three years. The effort continued to be supported by the district's 2018 Racial Equity Plan, which called on the Chief Academic Officer and Chief Equity Officer to "Provide training for staff to positively impact disproportionality [in disciplinary rates]," including training in restorative practices and "proactive behavior supports."[51]

All staff in the participating schools—bus drivers and food services staff included—attended a two-day training to learn about the restorative justice framework and how to operationalize it. In addition, several school principals and district behavior support staff participated in more intensive training, including the opportunity to become licensed trainers.[52] This approach to bringing restorative practices and PBIS to schools is designed to correct previous implementation attempts in which some principals lacked commitment and inconsistently applied positive interventions and supports. As Zeitz described:

> We were using [PBIS] incorrectly and not offering a true opportunity or any accountability to principals on equitably implementing it. When you just throw something at principals, you get an inconsistency, especially across 160 schools.

Early evaluation data indicate that the implementation of restorative practices in JCPS is linked to improvements in behavior referrals and reports of student engagement. In the first two years of the district's restorative practices and PBIS rollout, implementation fidelity, as measured across several metrics, ranged from 22% to 80%.[53] High-fidelity implementation mattered for student outcomes. Behavior referrals dropped in about 80% of high-implementing schools compared to a drop in just 30% of low-implementing schools. In addition, across all restorative practices and PBIS schools, teachers reported a 5-percentage point increase in a measure of student engagement between the first and second year of implementation. Given the importance of high-fidelity implementation, JCPS has taken a targeted approach to supporting schools in adopting restorative practices. The district requires that schools apply to become a restorative practice school. Leaders at accepted schools spend an entire school year developing their behavior systems and capacity for training staff in new methods. The next summer, all school staff—teachers, classified staff, administrators, and bus drivers—engage in training.

Launching WEB DuBois Academy, a School for Boys of Color

The district's approach to expanding student opportunities by advocating for a Men of Color Academy encapsulates much of the district's whole child approach to expanding learning opportunities: using data to motivate bold solutions; providing culturally responsive, deeper learning experiences; prioritizing positive behavior supports; and providing wraparound services through community partnerships. The district's effort to open this school also illustrates the challenge of tailoring resources for students furthest from opportunity. District leaders were able to advocate for this academy by coupling the district's stated commitment to racial equity with compelling data and the often-marginalized community voices that articulated a need for transformative school models.

Spotlight: Men of Color Academy Work Session

Walking up to the podium at a special work session for the JCPS Board of Education, then board chair Chris Brady scanned the packed rows of attendees, cleared his throat, and brought the full house to attention. He introduced the day's topic: to review the plan for a new program developed by a work group convened under the district's Young Men of Color Initiative.[54] Having studied district data, engaged communities throughout the district, and consulted with experts for over a year, the work group was ready to share their plan before a board vote in two weeks to determine if the district would develop a new Men of Color middle school program.

The work group launched the conversation by presenting data from the district's Equity Scorecard. The presentation slides flashed through a series of data points that confronted the audience with an alarming snapshot: male students of color in JCPS were underperforming across many measures of student success. District data revealed a 20-point difference in reading and math proficiency rates, suspension rates three times that of white peers, and the lowest sense of belonging among all student groups (Table 4.5). Board member Chris Kolb voiced the consensus in the room: "I don't think

Table 4.5 JCPS Districtwide Males of Color Comparison

Grade	Student Group	Percent P/D Reading	Percent P/D Math	Number Out-of-School Suspensions
2014–15 (5th Grade)	White Males	58.84%	62.53%	39
	Non-White Males	34.78%	38.05%	152
2015–16 (6th Grade)	White Males	54.17%	54.59%	327
	Non-White Males	31.66%	28.95%	1,072

Source: Slides presented at Males of Color Academy Work Session, June 13, 2017. Full presentation available at: https://portal.ksba.org/public/Meeting.aspx?PublicAgencyID=89&PublicMeetingID=20315&AgencyTypeID=.

Note: "P/D" stands for proficient or distinguished. These labels correspond to meeting or exceeding grade-level expectations on end-of-grade state exams. "Percent P/D" refers to the percent of students earning proficient or distinguished scores.

anybody could look at the data and come to any other conclusion: we are failing the vast majority of our African American students."

Prior to the meeting, the work group shared these data widely in meetings held with district families, community organizations, business leaders, and external experts, many of whom filled the room. The work group reminded board members of the longstanding district commitment to action in addressing problems facing male students of color. The work group returned to these data as they framed their plan for the JCPS Males of Color Academy. Board member Diane Porter explained how the data express a clear call to action:

> Data clearly state we have a problem in Jefferson County. To quote James Baldwin: before we can fix something, we have to face it. … To keep doing what we are doing means the same results. These scores are not what our students deserve. We can claim it, we can fix it, we can be passionate about our students.

The presentation then turned over to Dr. Marshall, who answered the call to "do something different" by introducing their proposal for an academy designed for male students of color. The academy, he explained, will be founded on the idea that access to rich, deeper learning curricula and practices can boost both engagement and performance. To that end, the Males of Color Academy will consult with literacy experts to develop culturally responsive curricula. He stated, "the greatness of African Americans did not start in the stage of slavery. [The curriculum will] allow boys to see greatness in themselves and the culture from where they come." The Males of Color Academy, Dr. Marshall explained, will incorporate inclusive instructional practices that address unique student learning needs. Board member Stephanie Horne illustrated this concept by describing her recent visit to a model school in Lexington, Kentucky, the Carter G. Woodson Academy:

> I have two boys and know how boys can get disengaged in school as they get older. [Visiting the school, I was] really excited to see kids all over the floor, loud, doing projects—it was fabulous—lots of Socratic method and project based learning. In the middle of math class, they got up to do push-ups to give them a little break. Then, the kids were right back there, engaged. My boys would have loved it.

This image provided some board members with a convincing approach to address a clear need but raised concerns among others. Will the academy be able to retain the students who need it the most? The work group responded by detailing their provisions for offering student supports through an explicit focus on male social and behavioral development. To address the high suspension rates among males of color in the district, the academy would feature restorative practices. Dr. Roszalyn Atkins, dean of students at the Carter G. Woodson Academy and lead consultant in the work group, vividly depicted this structure by describing its form in the model school: "Kids get a second chance; we don't just kick them out. We don't just suspend you. We try everything before we get to that suspension." Board member Linda Duncan noted that students dealing with the greatest challenges often lack necessary supports outside of school to stick with such an immersive program.

The work group was ready with a response: the design of the academy includes continual support through meaningful partnerships with family and other community members that provide supplemental programming. The work group added that they had already recruited five faith-based and other community groups to offer additional cultural and educational experiences outside the academy. These organizations agreed to provide (1) enrichment programs for 4th and 5th grade prospective attendees; (2) tutoring for Males of Color Academy scholars; and (3) community-based out-of-school activities for young men of color, including, but not limited to, those enrolled in the academy.

Pointing to the limited enrollment of the academy—150 students in its first year—a board member then asked how the program would "move the needle" on a problem pervasive to the entire district. Dr. Marshall responded that this capacity for student success applies to all schools in the district. Serving as a demonstration school, the Males of Color Academy would "dispel the myths about reaching and teaching our boys" by welcoming teachers from other schools and districts to see their practices at work. As a lab school, the academy would incubate innovative curricula, teaching strategies, and disciplinary structures that may be observed, tested, and scaled across the district. As board member Kolb described, instead of being a school "over there," the academy would aim to set an example for equitable practices across JCPS.

A robust discussion of the academy's first-year budget—about $760,000—highlighted the resources necessary to support the launch of such a project. The work group presented a set of non-negotiables: diverse learners, an experienced principal, mandatory Saturday programming, space for 150 students, one-to-one technology, extracurricular activities, countywide transportation, and a full staffing budget. Also, school staff required additional professional learning on equity, deeper learning, restorative practices, and cultural studies beyond the traditional district development. Board member Kolb stressed the importance of these concrete investments: "If we vote to approve, we need to understand what [the academy] needs to be successful."

Though many members seemed enthusiastic, the idea of an academy serving male students of color raised some concerns. Board member Linda

Duncan asked the work group to reconcile the Males of Color Academy with the district's historic efforts to integrate students across racial and ethnic lines:

> It's a turn for us. It's a concern for me, when we've tried to preach and sell diversity for all these years. We turn and say, it's not really diversity that's important. We can have an all African American school, Hispanic, males of color school and that's not contrary to what we've done.

There was an air of suspense as audience members leaned in for the response. Dr. Marshall acknowledged, in a measured tone, that this initiative would require the district to rethink the meaning behind the goal of "diversity," explaining that there is great diversity among students of color. He said:

> We have to think about diversity as more than race: geographic areas, census data on median household income, adult educational attainment, and race. We can build a school that fits within that [diversity and assignment plan] in this program. Part of what we need to do, and will be doing, is define diversity moving forward.

Board members recognized this turn will be difficult and considered the inevitable questions from county legislators and district legal counsel. Board member Porter spoke up, appealing to the urgent need in the district to support an initiative for boys of color: "To not support this, I would not be doing what I was elected to do." The data and experiences presented in the work session showed the costs of inaction are too high for JCPS. Dr. Atkins addressed the room:

> I wore black on purpose. Let me tell you why: I see pastors tired of burying young African American men. Tired of waking up the next day to say, "who's going to be next?" I mourn all the boys we missed that are already dead. We have a chance now to do something different. Schools can make a difference.

Two weeks later, on June 27, 2017, the JCPS board voted yes. The Males of Color Academy, later dubbed the WEB DuBois Academy, opened its doors to its first cohort of 156 6th graders in the fall of 2018.[55]

Outcomes at the WEB DuBois Academy

Since the school opened in 2018, it has begun to live up to its promise. Nearly 90% of students are Black boys, but enrollment also includes Latino/a, White, Asian American, and multiracial boys. In 2021–22, nearly half of the academy's teachers were Black, compared to 14% of teachers in JCPS middle schools overall. In 2021–22, about 17% of the academy's Black students were identified for gifted and talented education compared to 7% of Black middle school students in the district. Black boys eligible for free and reduced-price meals were suspended at about half the rate of their peers in JCPS as a whole (Table 4.6). For example, in 2019–20, 10.3% of WEB DuBois Black students eligible for free and reduced-price meals were suspended at least once, compared to more than a quarter of their peers in JCPS middle schools.

The academy has shown modest but promising academic outcomes compared to the district as a whole. The school's first year of state test data (2018–19) showed that Black students eligible for FRPM in the academy were less likely to earn a passing math or reading score (proficient or distinguished) than Black students eligible for FRPM across JCPS Middle Schools (Table 4.7). However, in 2020–21, amid the immense difficulty of the pandemic, DuBois Black students eligible for FRPM tested on par with their district peers in math, and slightly more earned passing scores than their peers in reading.

Table 4.6 Suspension Rate for FRPM-Eligible Black Students (2019–20, 2021–22)

Year	*WEB DuBois*	*JCPS Middle Schools*
2019–20	10.3%	25.6%
2021–22	17.6%	30.1%

Source: Jefferson County Public Schools. (2022). Envision Equity School Profile: WEB DuBois Academy. https://assessment.jefferson.kyschools.us/DMC/ee/eeSchoolProfile?schoolID=199&gradeLevelID=2 (accessed 6/7/2022).

Note: Suspension Rate is defined as the number of unique students suspended at least once divided by the total student population. Data from 2020–21 are excluded due to the pandemic.

Table 4.7 Percentage of FRPM-Eligible Black Students Scoring Proficient or Distinguished on K-PREP Math and Reading State Exams (2018–19, 2020–21)

Year	*Math*		*Reading*	
	WEB DuBois	*JCPS Middle Schools*	*WEB DuBois*	*JCPS Middle Schools*
2018–19	14.1%	15.9%	21.2%	29.1%
2020–21	4.2%	4.6%	19.9%	17.4%

Source: Jefferson County Public Schools. (2022). Envision Equity School Profile: WEB DuBois Academy. https://assessment.jefferson.kyschools.us/DMC/ee/eeSchoolProfile?schoolID=199&gradeLevelID=2 (accessed 6/7/2022).

Note: Proficient and Distinguished are passing scores equivalent to levels 3 and 4, respectively, on a scale of 1 to 4. Data from 2019–20 are excluded due to the pandemic.

Community members have been enthusiastic about the success of the DuBois Academy, building momentum that led to the 2020 launch of the Grace M. James Academy of Excellence, a sister school to the WEB DuBois Academy. JCPS Board Chair Diane Porter recalled the fervor among the community around these initiatives:

> It's about educating our students. And one of the things I will say with the DuBois Academy, they had an open house when it first started…. I have been to a lot of meetings like that, [but] I have never seen that many people fill that auditorium to hear about the DuBois Academy. And it was not just the mothers and the fathers. It was the grandmothers, the grandfathers, the aunts, and the uncles. They were extremely excited about it and are still excited about both [the WEB DuBois Academy and Grace M. James Academy of Excellence], and the growth of those programs.

Investing in People

The JCPS Racial Equity Plan calls for the district to advance racial equity by hiring, retaining, and developing the capacity of a diverse and high-quality staff. It stipulates that the Chief Academic Officer and Chief Equity Officer will provide professional development on topics ranging from restorative practices to cultural competence.[56] As a result, JCPS leaders have created systems to ensure that racial equity is considered for staff hires at every level and also provide a series of professional development opportunities in support of their multiple efforts to transform teaching and learning.

Some of these initiatives come with hefty price tags, which Dr. Marshall argues demonstrates the district's commitment to racial equity. The leadership decision to financially invest in these programs was done not only to "A, show buy-in, but B, to make sure we have some stake in the game. We're not just saying we want it. We're so serious about it, we're going to pay for it."

Intentional Hiring Practices

The district has developed policies and practices to hire more diverse and equity-oriented school leaders, growing its proportion of Black administrators between 2019 and 2022 from 17% to 47% of administrators. It has also developed the Louisville Teacher Residency to create a pipeline of fully prepared teachers of color. The Louisville Teacher Residency has prepared 50 new teachers for the district and counting.

Hiring for Racial Equity Leadership

As previously noted, under the leadership of Superintendent Pollio and in alignment with the district Racial Equity Policy, JCPS developed a set of policies and practices to attract and hire school leaders who can support advances in racial equity. For example, the DEP division developed a hiring screener to assess the racial equity dispositions and achievements of applicants to school leadership roles. As Superintendent Pollio put it:

> You have to show not only that you're willing to talk about [racial equity], but what success you've had with racial equity work... If you've been in a [school] system that has not been committed to this work, you need to be able to verbalize how you *would* do this. If you can't do that, this is not the place for you.

According to Chief Equity Officer Marshall, this change "has really upset the apple cart." Applicants who might have expected to be hired in school leadership positions due to their family ties or popularity are being passed over in favor of applicants who can show evidence of supporting racial equity work. As a result, the hiring pool for school leadership positions has gotten smaller. Superintendent Pollio explained,

> We don't get many people from outside of our district applying for school leadership jobs like we used to, because the word is out that, first of all, it's not an easy application. Second of all, if you haven't done the work, you're probably not going to get hired.

Still, JCPS leaders emphasized that the results they have seen have been worth the resistance to the change. Marshall, for example, has noticed that when "the right principal gets put in place, that school thrives or moves forward faster."

The district has also added a diversity hiring specialist to the DEP Division. According to Superintendent Pollio, this specialist "sits on every single central office administrative hire." The specialist "doesn't say you have to hire the Black candidate," but does ensure that hiring managers are considering a holistic set of criteria, including the need for greater staff diversity and the need for leaders who can advance racial equity.

Louisville Teacher Residency

Research indicates that high-quality teacher residency programs are effective at recruiting more teachers of color and preparing teachers who are effective in the classroom and stay in the profession longer than their peers.[57] In 2020, JCPS launched the Louisville Teacher Residency (LTR) in partnership with the University of Louisville to prepare future teachers for JCPS schools.[58] Through the LTR, residents complete a master's degree at the University of Louisville while engaging in a one-year intensive apprenticeship with an expert teacher at one of the district's Accelerated Improvement

Schools, schools that are in need of improvement (Box 4.2). Residents receive mentoring, coaching, and feedback and work with a cohort of peers for support and a shared learning experience. Residents earn a $30,000 stipend during their residency year in exchange for a commitment to teach in an Accelerated Improvement School for at least five years after graduation.

In LTR promotional materials, Leslie Hall, a five-year veteran in the district who started in a residency program, describes the level of support that helped him feel confident about becoming a teacher:

> In the beginning I didn't really know if being a teacher was exactly what I wanted to do, but the authentic field experience, it gets you in there and it guides you along the way. It didn't just throw everything at you, but along the way...you can learn. I think it helped me to find exactly what I wanted to do.

In a brochure for recruiting new teacher residents, Director Sylena Fishback strategically links the goals of the LTR to the district's Racial Equity Policy, writing, "Our Racial Equity Policy calls for us to attract, recruit, hire, and retain" a more racially, ethnically, and linguistically diverse staff and leadership. The LTR is designed to (1) recruit more teachers of color for JCPS through a rigorous pathway that prepares them to support student success and (2) increase retention in the district's Accelerated Improvement Schools.[59] Around half of the courses that residents take through LTR are

---

Box 4.2   Louisville Teacher Residency: The Residency Year

Summer one	**June** *Monday through Friday, evening:* Attend classes at the University of Louisville. **July–August** *Monday through Friday, full day:* Attend classes at the University of Louisville.
School year	**September–June** *Monday through Thursday:* Hands-on, clinical training in the classroom, side by side with an expert mentor teacher. *Friday:* Attend classes at the University of Louisville.
Summer two	**July** Attend planning sessions and professional development to prepare for their first day of class as a teacher-of-record in a JCPS school.

centered around race, gender, and equity, key areas of need given persistent disparities in student opportunities and outcomes.

Developing Staff Capacity

At the same time that JCPS leaders are cultivating a pipeline of new teachers and leaders who can support racial equity, they are also working to develop the capacity of the staff already in the district. Although the district cannot mandate professional development for teachers, JCPS offers voluntary learning opportunities, including an annual deeper learning symposium and a master's degree in diversity literacy, in addition to professional development opportunities already described (i.e., the annual equity institutes and professional development on deeper learning, culturally responsive teaching, and restorative practices).

JCPS leaders have also been able to offer widespread learning on racial equity to the district's school leaders. Under former superintendent Hargens's leadership, the DEP division hosted a racial equity institute for school leaders to introduce them to the district's burgeoning focus on racial equity. Since then, JCPS has been able to expand training to school leaders in partnership with the Wallace Foundation. In 2021, JCPS was one of 8 districts nationally to be selected for the Wallace Foundation Equity Centered Pipeline Initiative. The initiative provides participating districts with $8.2 million over five years to design an aligned and comprehensive equity-centered leadership pipeline, provide mentoring and training to current principals and assistant principals, and engage in continuous improvement. With the grant funding, the district has been able to provide training to principals and principal supervisors on assessing their ability to advance racial equity in their schools.

Deeper Learning Symposium

JCPS staff have committed substantial financial and human resources to advancing their goal of improving students' college and career readiness through deeper learning. The first notable investment was the organization of a Deeper Learning Symposium, which was a signal for the entire district about the shift toward this new conception of teaching and learning. "This is not a fad for us. Rather, it is a journey and commitment to co-construct a better way forward," stated the call for session proposals.

This inaugural symposium was held July 7–9, 2017, and brought together over 1,500 educators from across the district and region. It was held at the Kentucky Expo Center and was supported financially by the school board with very little philanthropic support. The symposium focused on best practices in deeper learning with a call for proposals directed at JCPS teachers as well as deeper learning experts outside the district. Attendees learned best practices for deeper learning and heard from national leaders engaged in deeper learning research, teaching, and practice. A strand that ran through the symposium was bridging the opportunity and achievement gaps for students of color, with sessions such as the following:

- Deeper Learning for All: Examining Equity in the Deeper Learning Movement
- Why I Matter: Iroquois [High School] ESL Students Partner with the SPEED Art Museum
- Cultural Resilience: Redefining Excellence through the Power of Story and Identifying the Brilliance of Students

"This is a change for our kids in our district," Alan Young, a resource teacher and project manager in JCPS who is deeply involved in the deeper learning work, noted. He explained the symposium was more than a conference. "It wasn't just what you were getting in those three days. It became felt in our classrooms with our kids…it cultivates and builds capacity." Building on the success of the symposium, the district created a position, Coordinator of Professional and Deeper Learning, who oversees the integration of deeper learning practices within the district.

The district continues to host the Deeper Learning Symposium annually and has expanded the initiative to include two additional two-hour Mini-Deeper Learning Symposia each school year. Racial equity continues to be a key strand of learning at these professional development events. In 2021, the Symposium featured, for example, Dr. Kaleb Rashad, Creative Director of the Center for Love and Justice, who shared a framework for anti-racist deeper learning.[60] The 2022 Mini-Deeper Learning Symposium call for proposals sought sessions connected to "racial equity," "activating equity," and "culturally responsive and inclusive learning."[61]

Competency, Awareness & Responsiveness to Diverse Students Program

The district also offers more intensive professional development through its Competency, Awareness & Responsiveness to Diverse Students (CARDS) Program, a partnership with the University of Louisville, "to better equip JCPS educators for teaching in the state's most diverse district."[62] CARDS funds a master's in teacher leadership and a graduate certificate in diversity literacy. The program is designed to teach participants "how to intervene to reduce the impact of structural barriers that stand in the way of inclusion and social equity."[63] At the same time, participants hone their "pedagogical expertise for the classroom."[64] Applications to the program are open to all certified teachers in the district, and seven teachers each semester are selected. Upon completion of the 30-hour program, participants commit to stay in their schools and "guide the practices of their fellow educators" for at least 3 years.[65]

In part, the program's service commitment is designed to promote teacher retention in the district's Accelerated Improvement Schools (AIS), schools that receive specialized supports and resources to improve student opportunities and outcomes. Former program coordinator Sylena Fishback explained that CARDS was "developed to incentivize teachers to stay in those [Accelerated Improvement] schools so we can pull students up while providing teachers with the foundation and arts and skills they need to master their technique." While the price tag for CARDS is high—upward of $75,000 for the district—John Marshall doesn't blink. He recognizes that each teacher sees 150 students a year, and these teachers are developing skills to be culturally responsive and more effective. As he said, "It's a different way to look at how we are spending money around equity." The district's investment in the CARDS program has paid off in high retention rates and positive reviews from principals where CARDS teachers teach. Marshall noted that, based on principal interviews, "the retention [of CARDS teachers] and the evaluations have been very, very glowing."

Despite the availability of professional development opportunities, JCPS faces ongoing challenges in developing a workforce with the knowledge and skills to provide culturally responsive, deeper learning instruction in classrooms that are welcoming of the district's diverse student body. As mentioned, many professional development offerings are voluntary, which can mean that those who self-select into those resources are those who need the training the least. A related challenge is the inequitable distribution of teachers, particularly in terms of teacher experience. High-performing schools attract the most experienced teachers, and low-performing schools see a revolving door of teachers. This means that teachers in low-performing schools take their professional learning and expertise with them when they leave, creating an ongoing challenge for developing equitable educator capacity at the school level. Christy Rogers, then-Director of College and Career Readiness, wondered, "Do you pay people more money to stay? Do they have incentives if you are in a certain school?" The district's CARDS program and teacher residency are providing these types of incentives, and the outcomes may help the district identify which strategies are most effective at influencing teacher retention.

Lessons Learned

Although the story of racial equity in JCPS began with court-ordered desegregation, it is now a defining district characteristic. Over the decades, the district's commitment to racial equity has allowed district leaders to embed equity across a host of district domains. Beginning with Dr. Hargens's leadership articulating an equity agenda with the *Vision 2020* strategic plan and followed by Superintendent Pollio leading the adoption of the JCPS Racial

Equity Policy, JCPS leaders have made strides for students by articulating an explicit commitment to racial equity and following through with action.

As the gains continue to grow, Dr. Marshall attributes them to how JCPS leaders have put their racial equity vision into practice, ranging from supporting college and career readiness to increasing participation in out-of-school learning. "We have a lot of things in place," he noted, "so five, six years into the Racial Equity Policy in the works, we're starting to see things line up and a constellation that might spell equity." At the same time, JCPS leaders recognize that there is more work to be done to deliver the outcomes they hope to see for each student. Indeed, Dr. Marshall asserts that "you won't hear me say, 'Yeah, we've closed the gap and we've got this figured out,' hell no." However, JCPS leaders have built a foundation over a decade that continuously deepens and expands their impact on racial equity. District leaders have realized these gains by formalizing their vision in actionable policies and practices; setting a clear expectation that every staff member and division is responsible for advancing racial equity; leveraging data and research for continuous improvement and storytelling; and investing in staff capacity.

JCPS leaders created an infrastructure for racial equity, enacted through policies and practices that provide continuity through leadership changes. JCPS leaders ensured the DEP division was well-staffed and well-funded, with significant authority to lead the work of transforming district-wide systems in service of racial equity. Empowered by both Dr. Hargens and Dr. Pollio, the DEP division has spearheaded the development of the district's racial equity plan of action, from *Vision 2020* to the Racial Equity Policy. Further, the district's superintendents have empowered the division to make this vision more than words on paper. With the authority to develop and mandate the use of equity-centered tools—Affirming Racial Equity Tool, REAP, Equity Hiring Screener, and more—the DEP division has made racial equity into an ongoing practice in the district, and not just an aspiration.

The policies and practices that the district has developed over the years constitute a growing infrastructure for racial equity that exists beyond the time of any one staff member, allowing for a continuity of commitment and practice over time.

JCPS leaders set a clear expectation that every division and every staff member, from the central office to the school and classroom level, is responsible for advancing racial equity. Although the district's commitment to racial equity once sat squarely in the DEP division under the leadership of Chief Equity Officer John Marshall, the district's Racial Equity Policy has pushed that commitment out to every member of the JCPS community, beginning with central office leaders. By requiring that every division of the district—from facilities to finances to curriculum and instruction—set racial equity goals, JCPS has been able to push racial equity initiatives further, faster. Indeed, consideration of racial equity is woven into every major decision the district makes.

JCPS leaders regularly analyze data and research through a racial equity lens, use data to inform shifts in strategies, and share data to garner support for racial equity initiatives. Beginning with the Envision Equity Scorecard, district leaders regularly analyze and share data on student opportunities and outcomes. Leaders use this data to adjust and refine their practices to better meet the needs of students and to tackle challenging problems with bold solutions. JCPS leaders also use data to bolster their ability to make these bold moves, whether changing the student code of conduct or launching a Males of Color Academy. JCPS leaders appeal to district values, commitments, and data to justify and advocate for each of their initiatives, which they situate within the district's decades-long legacy of valuing racial equity. They grounded their strategic plan and guiding frameworks in district data on student opportunity and achievement, which makes a compelling case for taking action.

JCPS leaders invest in staff capacity to build the policies, resources, and skills necessary to operationalize the district's racial equity vision. Since Dr. Hargens hired a Chief Equity Officer in 2012, the district has steadily built its capacity to support racial equity work. Superintendent Pollio has since built up the division to sufficiently support district staff to meet the expectations set out in the district's Racial Equity Policy. The district both creates intentional hiring pathways to increase its capacity for racial equity and supports existing staff to develop their skills.

District leaders have shown tenacity in their commitment to producing greater racial equity and model a dynamic cycle of critical reflection and taking action. The district's efforts build on a long legacy of working toward racial equity in Jefferson County and demonstrate that this work does not end but is a continuous effort.

Appendix 4A: Jefferson County Public Schools Data Tables

Table 4A.1 Number of Advanced Placement Exam Test Takers, by Race/Ethnicity, 2012–13 and 2018–19

Race/Ethnicity	2012–13	2018–19	% Change (2012–13 to 2018–19)
American Indian/Alaska Native	N/A	4	
Asian American	385	617	60%
Black	773	1,220	58%
Latino/a	232	519	124%
Multiracial	59	187	217%
Native Hawaiian/Pacific Islander	N/A	14	
White	3,691	4,079	11%

Source: Kentucky Department of Education School Report Card data, (2012–13 and 2018–19), https://www.education.ky.gov/Open-House/data/Pages/Historical-SRC-Datasets.aspx

Note: Data are suppressed for student groups with a sample size smaller than ten.

Table 4A.2 Percentage of Enrolled Students Identified for Gifted and Talented Education, by Race/Ethnicity, 2017–18 and 2021–22

Race/Ethnicity	2017–18	2021–22	% Change (2017–18 to 2021–22)
Black	7.5%	8.3%	10.7
Latino/a	7.4%	9.4%	27.0
White	18.7%	20.2%	8.0
Total	13.4%	14.4%	7.5

Notes

1 Jefferson County Public Schools. (2013, November). Envision equity scorecard. https://www.jefferson.kyschools.us/sites/default/files/EQfull112513_JV.pdf.
2 Jefferson County Public Schools. (n.d.). 2023–24 Informational Guide (PDF). https://www.jefferson.kyschools.us/page/about#faqs
3 Bhat, S. (2021, September 23). Louisville is more diverse than ever but remains largely segregated. *89.3 WFPL.* https://wfpl.org/louisville-is-more-diverse-than-ever-but-remains-largely-segregated/ (accessed 5/17/2022); Price, M. (2013). *Louisville neighborhoods: A statistical portrait.* University of Louisville, Kentucky State Data Center. http://ksdc.louisville.edu//wp-content/uploads/2015/05/Louisville-Neighborhoods-Statistical-Portrait.pdf (accessed 5/17/2022).
4 According to the Kentucky Department of Education, "The 4-year cohort graduation rate is defined as the number of students who graduate in four years with a regular high school diploma divided by the number of students who entered high school four years earlier adjusting for transfers in and out, émigrés and deceased students." https://education.ky.gov/AA/Reports/Pages/Graduation-Rate.aspx
5 Sedler, R. (2007). The Louisville-Jefferson County school desegregation case: A lawyer's retrospective. *The Register of the Kentucky Historical Society, 105*(1), 3–32. http://www.jstor.org/stable/23386788 (accessed 8/26/2021).
6 Sedler, R. (2007). The Louisville-Jefferson County school desegregation case: A lawyer's retrospective. *The Register of the Kentucky Historical Society, 105*(1), 3–32. http://www.jstor.org/stable/23386788 (accessed 8/26/2021).
7 J. Graham Brown School. (2022). Our history. https://www.jefferson.kyschools.us/o/brown/page/history.
8 George, J., & Darling-Hammond, L. (2021). *Advancing integration and equity through magnet schools.* Palo Alto, CA: Learning Policy Institute.
9 Quick, K., & Damante, R. (2016, September 30). Louisville, Kentucky: A reflection on school integration. The Century Foundation. https://tcf.org/content/report/louisville-kentucky-reflection-school-integration/?agreed=1
10 Ross, A. (2015, September 3). JCPS desegregation timeline. *Journal.* https://www.courier-journal.com/story/news/education/2015/09/03/jcps-desegregation-timeline/71637432/
11 Semuels, A. (2015). The city that believed in desegregation. *The Atlantic,* March 2015. https://www.theatlantic.com/business/archive/2015/03/the-city-that-believed-in-desegregation/388532/ (accessed 5/17/2022).
12 Kaplan, E., Spenkuch, J. L., & Tuttle, C. (2021). *School segregation and political preferences: Long-run evidence from Kentucky.* https://www.iq.harvard.

edu/files/harvard-iqss/files/ethan-kaplan_busing_partisanship_2.pdf (accessed 5/17/2022).

13 Diem, S., Cleary, C., Nazneen, A., & Frankenberg, E. (2014). The politics of maintaining diversity policies in demographically changing urban-suburban school districts. *American Journal of Education*, 120(3), 351–389. https://doi.org/10.1086/675532; Hampton v. Jefferson County Bd. of Educ., 72 F. Supp. 2d 753 (W.D. Ky. 1999).

14 Bridges, K. (2016, October 14). Jefferson County public Schools: From legal enforcement to ongoing commitment. The Century Foundation. https://tcf.org/content/report/jefferson-county-public-schools/.

15 Ross, A. (2015, September 3). JCPS desegregation timeline. *Louisville Courier Journal*. https://www.courier-journal.com/story/news/education/2015/09/03/jcps-desegregation-timeline/71637432/ (accessed 5/17/2022).

16 Ross, A. (2015, September 3). JCPS desegregation timeline. *Journal*. https://www.courier-journal.com/story/news/education/2015/09/03/jcps-desegregation-timeline/71637432/

17 Jefferson County Public Schools (2022–23). Elementary school choices (interactive guide). https://www.jefferson.kyschools.us/sites/default/files/forms/Choices-Elementary%20Schools.pdf; Jefferson County Public Schools (2022–23). Middle school choices (interactive guide). https://www.jefferson.kyschools.us/sites/default/files/forms/Choices-Middle%20Schools.pdf; Jefferson County Public Schools (2022–23). High school choices (interactive guide). https://www.jefferson.kyschools.us/sites/default/files/forms/Choices-High%20Schools.pdf

18 https://sites.google.com/jefferson.kyschools.us/student-assignment-proposal/home

19 https://www.courier-journal.com/in-depth/news/investigations/2021/10/20/read-courier-journals-investigation-louisville-magnet-schools/5713449001 (accessed 1/30/2023); https://www.courier-journal.com/story/news/education/2022/03/21/how-louisville-magnets-schools-and-program-change/7034053001/ (accessed 1/30/2023).

20 Bhat, S. (2021, September 24). Louisville is more diverse than ever but remains largely segregated. *Louisville Public Media*. https://www.lpm.org/news/2021-09-24/louisville-is-more-diverse-than-ever-but-remains-largely-segregated.

21 JCPS. (n.d.). JCPS racial educational equity plan 2021–2024. https://drive.google.com/file/d/1z-KwOytTuNIIHSJ5aK_oKiygxYXnVrzn/view (accessed 4/19/2022).

22 Vision 2020 in Action. https://www.jefferson.kyschools.us/sites/default/files/Vision%202020%20In%20Action.pdf (accessed 4/19/2022); JCPS. (n.d.). JCPS racial educational equity plan 2021–2024. https://drive.google.com/file/d/1z-KwOytTuNIIHSJ5aK_oKiygxYXnVrzn/view (accessed 4/19/2022).

23 Jefferson County Board of Education (2018, May). Minutes of regular meeting of May 08, 2018. https://portal.ksba.org/public/MeetingMinutes.aspx?PublicAgencyID=89&PublicMeetingID=23313&AgencyTypeID=

24 Jefferson County Public Schools. (n.d.). Affirming racial equity tool guidebook. https://docs.google.com/presentation/d/1wnjsL8n7esUlEArCy12m3cCIZHatA41eVF4p0iZATZM/edit#slide=id.ga59f1e87f7_0_11 (accessed 5/30/2023).

25 Vanderhaar, J. (n.d.). Envision equity [presentation]. https://www.jefferson.kyschools.us/sites/default/files/SummitPresentation.pdf (accessed 7/21/2022).

26 Jefferson County Public Schools. (2013, November). Envision equity scorecard. https://www.jefferson.kyschools.us/sites/default/files/EQfull112513_JV.pdf.

27 Smith, R. G., & Brazer, S. D. (2016). *Striving for equity: District leadership for narrowing opportunity and achievement gaps.* Cambridge, MA: Harvard Education Press.

28 Jefferson County Public Schools. (n.d.). Pillars of JCPS. https://www.jefferson.kyschools.us/pillars-jcps (accessed 5/23/2023).

29 Darling-Hammond, L., & Cook-Harvey, C. M. (2018). *Educating the whole child: Improving school climate to support student success.* Palo Alto, CA: Learning Policy Institute. https://doi.org/10.54300/145.655

30 Darling-Hammond, L., & Cook-Harvey, C. M. (2018). *Educating the whole child: Improving school climate to support student success.* Palo Alto, CA: Learning Policy Institute. https://doi.org/10.54300/145.655

31 According to the Kentucky Department of Education, "The 4-year cohort graduation rate is defined as the number of students who graduate in four years with a regular high school diploma divided by the number of students who entered high school four years earlier adjusting for transfers in and out, émigrés and deceased students." https://education.ky.gov/AA/Reports/Pages/Graduation-Rate.aspx

32 Klevan, S. (2021). *Building a positive school climate through restorative practices.* Palo Alto, CA: Learning Policy Institute. https://doi.org/10.54300/178.861

33 Finegold, D., & Notabartolo, A. S. (2016). *21st-century competencies and their impact: An interdisciplinary literature review.* Menlo Park, CA: William and Flora Hewlett Foundation. https://www.hewlett.org/library/21st-century-competencies-impact-interdisciplinary-literature-review/

34 Pollio. M., & Coleman, C. (2018, May 31). JCPS launching new approach to transform the district and help students. *Courier-Journal.* https://www.courier-journal.com/story/opinion/contributors/2018/05/31/marty-pollio-jcps-launch-new-approach-transform-district/634835002/ (accessed 6/7/2023).

35 Jefferson County Public Schools. (2018). JCPS racial educational equity plan: 2018–2020. https://www.jefferson.kyschools.us/sites/default/files/DistrictRacialEquityPlan%201-8-19.pdf (accessed 6/7/2023).

36 Jefferson County Public Schools. (2018). *The new normal.* https://drive.google.com/file/d/1bfBY6i7gdAP_mI4pn4WgLXPpnNqRwu82/view (accessed 6/14/2023).

37 Jefferson County Public Schools. (2019, February 21). *Marion C. Moore Backpack Defense – Ariana* [Video]. YouTube. https://www.youtube.com/watch?v=MHKCbN62NHM&list=PLqh7c7rfeyEO6UP1xzET4xbvFJYHiT4Kq&index=16 (accessed 6/14/2023).

38 Coleman, C. (2022, December 1). Leading for deeper learning, a series in four parts, part 2: The beauty of naïvete and the development of the backpack [blog] hthunboxed. https://hthunboxed.org/worksheets-wont-make-good-artifacts-a-deeper-learning-story-from-kentucky/ (accessed 4/29/2025).

39 Jefferson County Public Schools. (2018). *The new normal.* https://drive.google.com/file/d/1bfBY6i7gdAP_mI4pn4WgLXPpnNqRwu82/view (accessed 6/14/2023).

40 Jefferson County Public Schools. (n.d.). Curriculum frameworks. https://sites.google.com/jefferson.kyschools.us/jcpscurriculumandinstruction/curriculum-frameworks?authuser=0 (accessed 6/6/2023).

41 Darling-Hammond, L., & Cook-Harvey, C. M. (2018). *Educating the whole child: Improving school climate to support student success.* Palo Alto, CA: Learning Policy Institute. https://doi.org/10.54300/145.655

42 Jefferson County Public Schools. (2021, August 17). Racial equity update. https://files.constantcontact.com/70c7e81d001/a72a71c4–8965-4431-ad8e-d1be69e21afb.pdf (accessed 6/6/2023).

43 https://sites.google.com/jefferson.kyschools.us/jcpssocialstudies/curriculum/high-school/developing-black-historical-consciousness?pli=1

44 Ford Media Center. (2014, March 4). Louisville named Ford Next Generation learning community. https://media.ford.com/content/fordmedia/fna/us/en/news/2014/03/04/louisville-named-ford-next-generation-learning-community.html

45 JCPS. (n.d.). About our academies. https://www.jefferson.kyschools.us/schools/academies-louisville/academies-louisville-about (accessed 4/19/2022); JCPS. (n.d.). Academies of Louisville frequently asked questions. https://www.jefferson.kyschools.us/sites/default/files/FAQ%20Academies%20of%20Louisville.pdf (accessed 4/19/2022).

46 JCPS (2021–22). Doss HS phase three: Executive summary for schools. https://drive.google.com/drive/folders/1O-a3XbkoJxRNLgduZlpqv9CsuhFDX9IC (accessed 4/19/2022).

47 Jefferson County Public Schools. (2018). JCPS racial educational equity plan: 2018–2020. https://www.jefferson.kyschools.us/sites/default/files/DistrictRacialEquityPlan%201–8–19.pdf (accessed 6/7/2023).

48 Jefferson County Public Schools. (2024). Student support and behavior intervention handbook. https://www.jefferson.kyschools.us/o/wilkerson/article/1943765

49 Jefferson County Public Schools. (2017). Alcohol, tobacco, & other drugs. https://www.jefferson.kyschools.us/student-support/drug-free

50 Center on PBIS. (n.d.). What is PBIS? https://www.pbis.org/pbis/what-is-pbis (accessed 6/7/2023).

51 Jefferson County Public Schools. (2018). JCPS racial educational equity plan: 2018–2020. https://www.jefferson.kyschools.us/sites/default/files/DistrictRacialEquityPlan%201–8–19.pdf (accessed 6/7/2023).

52 Winsch, B. J. (2017). Restorative practices evaluation plan. https://www.jefferson.kyschools.us/sites/default/files/JCPS%20RP%20Evaluation%20Plan_0.pdf (accessed 7/14/2022).

53 Jefferson County Public Schools. (2019). Restorative practices evaluation brief. https://www.jefferson.kyschools.us/sites/default/files/JCPS%20Restorative%20Practices%20Brief%2012–2019.pdf (accessed 7/14/2022).

54 JCPS joined the Males of Color Resolution, a collective commitment among 60 urban school systems, in 2014. The resolution commits districts to improve achievement of young men of color through evidence-based strategies. For more information, see: https://www.jefferson.kyschools.us/learning/young-men-color.

55 Gunn, R.E. (2018, February 1). Are we resegregating public schools with the new W.E.B. DuBois 'males of color' Academy? *Louisville Courier Journal*. https://www.courier-journal.com/story/opinion/2018/02/01/males-color-dubois-academy-jefferson-coounty-public-schools/1018555001/; See also: W. E. B. DuBois Academy. (n.d.). https://www.jefferson.kyschools.us/o/dubois

56 Jefferson County Public Schools. (2018). JCPS racial educational equity plan: 2018–2020. https://www.jefferson.kyschools.us/sites/default/files/DistrictRacialEquityPlan%201–8–19.pdf (accessed 6/7/2023).

57 Guha, R., Hyler, M. E., & Darling-Hammond, L. (2016). *The teacher residency: An innovative model for preparing teachers.* Palo Alto, CA: Learning Policy Institute.

58 Jefferson County Public Schools. (n.d.). Louisville teacher residency [brochure]. https://www.jefferson.kyschools.us/sites/default/files/LouisvilleTeacherResidencyBooklet.pdf (accessed 5/18/2022).

59 Jefferson County Public Schools. (n.d.). Louisville teacher residency [brochure]. https://www.jefferson.kyschools.us/sites/default/files/LouisvilleTeacherResidencyBooklet.pdf (accessed 5/18/2022).

60 Vodicka, D. (2021, August 9). Lessons from Kentucky Deeper Learning Symposium to inspire a strong start to the school year. Learner Centered Leadership.https://learnercenteredleadership.org/2021/08/09/lessons-from-kentucky-deeper-learning-symposium-to-inspire-a-strong-start-to-the-school-year/ (accessed 5/17/2022).

61 Jefferson County Public Schools. (n.d.). Deeper learning symposium. https://sites.google.com/jefferson.kyschools.us/jcpsdl/deeper-learning-symposium (accessed 5/18/2022).

62 Jefferson County Public Schools. (n.d.). Competency, awareness, & responsiveness to diverse students program. https://www.jefferson.kyschools.us/department/diversity-equity-poverty-programs-division/competency-awareness-responsiveness-diverse (accessed 5/18/2022).

63 Jefferson County Public Schools. (n.d.). Competency, awareness, & responsiveness to diverse students program. https://www.jefferson.kyschools.us/department/diversity-equity-poverty-programs-division/competency-awareness-responsiveness-diverse (accessed 5/18/2022).

64 Jefferson County Public Schools. (n.d.). JCPS teacher CARDS program [Letter to Teachers]. https://www.jefferson.kyschools.us/sites/default/files/CARDS_LettertoTeachers.pdf (accessed 5/18/2022).

65 Jefferson County Public Schools. (n.d.). JCPS teacher CARDS program [Letter to Teachers]. https://www.jefferson.kyschools.us/sites/default/files/CARDS_LettertoTeachers.pdf (accessed 5/18/2022).

5 "Diversity Is Our Strength"

Expanding Access to Opportunity in Pflugerville Independent School District

Maria E. Hyler and Larkin Willis, with Peter W. Cookson

Introduction

As Pflugerville Independent School District (Pflugerville ISD), a school district in a rapidly developing suburb of Austin, transitioned from serving majority-White students to majority students of color, its leaders rallied the community behind a sense of pride in cultural diversity. With continuous support from the Board of Trustees and central office staff, leaders in Pflugerville ISD have leveraged a shared commitment to cultural diversity to drive educational reforms, programs, and investments aimed at advancing more equitable teaching and learning. Entering the superintendent's office in July 2017 after many individual initiatives had been launched, Dr. Douglas Killian systematized the district's equity vision by establishing a strategic plan, bringing a cohesive approach to change management, and allocating resources deliberately to enact its goals. The equity leadership in Pflugerville ISD has expanded access to meaningful learning experiences and coincided with promising improvements in educational outcomes for students of color and emergent bilingual students.

Organization of the Case

The remainder of this introduction presents the context for equity-oriented leadership in Pflugerville ISD, including a snapshot of district demographic trends and local legacies of multiculturalism and schooling in the Central Texas region. Subsequent sections of the case study describe the leadership strategies supporting five key areas of work that advance racial equity in Pflugerville ISD. "Persistent Equity Leadership" details how board members, central office staff, and campus educators worked in concert to refine a shared commitment to educational equity. "Strategic Investment and Implementation" presents how leaders pursued that commitment by investing in staff capacity and adjusting policies to more equitably allocate human, financial, and material resources across schools in the district. "Expanded

DOI:10.4324/9781003568087-5

Opportunity and Access" explores how leaders have removed barriers to college- and career-ready coursework and increased kindergarten readiness. "Multilingual Instruction" describes how leaders harness linguistic diversity as a learning asset through both targeted multilingual programs and districtwide instructional support. "Restorative Practices" details how leaders responded to community advocacy to revise the student code of conduct and pursue restorative responses to student disengagement. The case concludes with a summary of the leadership strategies that support the initiatives in Pflugerville ISD and implications of these findings for district-level leaders interested in advancing racial equity.

A Profile of Pflugerville Independent School District

Over the past two decades, Pflugerville ISD has experienced major shifts in its student body. The district is located in a growing suburb north of Austin, Texas (Box 5.1). Due to the pull of new development relative to surrounding areas, Pflugerville had the third-largest growth rate among U.S. cities with at least 50,000 residents between 2016 and 2017.[1] This growth was fueled by development and displacement in the Central Texas region. Austin residents, many from the predominately Black and Latino/a community of East Austin, have relocated to the City of Pflugerville in pursuit of more affordable housing, safer and more welcoming communities, and a stronger public education system.[2]

Box 5.1   Welcome to Pflugerville Independent School District

Along the stretch of Interstate 35 between Austin and Pflugerville, Texas, clear sky and flat land unfold as far as the eye can see. Road signs announce the intersection of rural and suburban life, advertising farm equipment alongside newly constructed technology parks. More signs still boast the explosive real estate market: 'Commercial Land for Sale.'

The towering lights of Kuempel Stadium welcome visitors into Pflugerville ISD. The 7,000-seat football stadium is a tribute to local pride in a 55-game winning streak that broke state and national records. Pflugerville High occupies the same complex. Pulling into visitor parking, there's an empty space between a mud-caked pickup truck and a sleek, compact SUV.

Pflugerville High is uncrowded. New construction and attendance boundary changes accommodate the rapidly growing student population. The building boasts clean, wide hallways. At the start of the school day, those hallways fill with the joyous roar of students spilling into and across the campus. Students travel in racially diverse groups that are social and animated, ushered along by teachers standing at their doorways, administrators walking the halls, and school resource officers stationed at entrances and exits.

The noise subsides as the first period begins. In an Advanced Placement physics class, students with various skin tones, gender expressions, and clothing styles converge at long tables. The lesson's objective is posted clearly on the board: students will be able to solve elastic and inelastic collisions. One student jumps up to demonstrate a foundational skill on the board. Her peers look on with consternation. They talk over one another, evaluating her process in real-time. Some critique an early step in her solution. Then, a classmate catches onto her process and exclaims, "She has another way. Go, go, go!"

Pflugerville ISD enrolled over 25,000 students in 2020—nearly double its enrollment in 2000.[3] The student body has also become more racially, ethnically, linguistically, and socioeconomically diverse.[4] In 2000, the district was majority White. By 2020, students of color comprised nearly 80% of district enrollments, including 48% Latino/a, 15% Black, 8% Asian American, 5% multiracial, and less than 1% of American Indian/Alaska Native and Native Hawaiian/Pacific Islander students, respectively (Figure 5.1).

Pflugerville ISD uses 'Hispanic or Latino' as an ethnic designation to describe peoples of Caribbean, Central and South American, Mexican, and Spanish culture or origin regardless of race.[5] Referred to in this study as Latino/a, this student group encompasses wide-ranging national, ethnic, and racial identities that are far from monolithic.[6] For example, a first-generation Salvadoran immigrant student in the district's Newcomer program, learning a new language and culture, has a different experience than a Mexican American student whose American lineage predates the geographic boundaries of the City of Pflugerville.

The City of Pflugerville and its public schools have always been places of cultural confluence. Beliefs about meaningful learning for Pflugerville's racially diverse population influenced the evolution of educational policies and practices. This evolution includes a history of explicit racial discrimination, which people of color and their allies have continually contested to advance improvements in educational opportunities and outcomes. German immigrants opened the area's first one-room rural schoolhouse in 1872. The district was racially segregated when it formally organized in 1936,

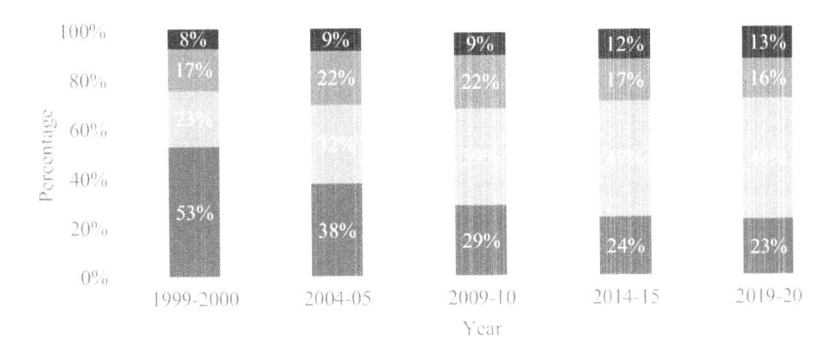

Figure 5.1 Pflugerville ISD Student Racial/Ethnic Demographics, 1999–2000 to 2019–20.

Source: Texas Education Agency, District Snapshots, https://rptsvr1.tea.texas.gov/perfreport/snapshot/index_old.html

operating separate campuses for Black, Mexican American, and White students. Although some of Pflugerville's earliest schools offered bilingual instruction in German and English,[7] a statewide ban prevented Spanish language instruction until 1973.[8]

In the face of systemic exclusion, Black and Mexican American residents continued to invest in the promise of education to transform lives through a strong tradition of educational leadership. One district campus is named after Fannie Mae Caldwell, a revered Black educator who lived in the community from 1916 to 2004.[9] The collective activism of the Civil Rights era ushered more advancements in educational opportunity. Pflugerville ISD was still a majority-White district when it desegregated quickly in 1965.[10] The more racially diverse schools in neighboring Austin ISD did not meaningfully integrate until 1980, when Black and Mexican American advocates successfully challenged student assignment policies in court.[11]

Community members and educators in Pflugerville ISD have lived through periods of racial tension and advancement, many within the Central Texas region. Their experiences and beliefs inform how the district functions today. For example, a White Pflugerville ISD staff member recalled her high school experience busing into a majority-Black neighborhood in East Austin: "I remember the students told me, 'Get ready to wear your bullet proof vest. I can't believe you're going there.'" She reported that she and many of her former classmates now live with their families in Pflugerville and value its racially diverse community. Board of Trustees member Renae Mitchell explained, "It's not like when we were kids. [Our students] want to be educated about [their] differences [and] see the commonalities they have." Bordering some of the most racially and socioeconomically segregated school districts in Texas,[12] Pflugerville ISD stands out both in terms of its racial integration and how district leadership leverages pride in cultural diversity to expand opportunities for students of color and multilingual learners.

Leadership in Pflugerville ISD has worked to enhance educational access and learning opportunities in multiple ways, tackling new issues in each administration. As the number of students from low-income families and students of color has grown, leaders have endeavored to improve access to meaningful learning opportunities and reduce exclusions from school, and the district has seen improvements in student outcomes and consistently high graduation rates. As described in more detail in this case,

- From 2017 to 2021, the average four-year longitudinal graduation rate for Black and Latino/a Pflugerville ISD students, as well as for White students, was at or above 95%.[13] Rates for the former two groups surpassed statewide averages of approximately 90% for each year in this period.
- The rate of students graduating college and career-ready increased from 57% to 77% between 2017 and 2020.[14] During this period, the largest increases were among graduates who identified as emergent bilingual (from 32% to 60%), Black (from 43% to 69%), two or more races (from 57% to 88%), and Latino/a (from 50% to 75%) (Table 5.3).
- Between 2016–17 and 2021–22, the assignment of in-school suspensions decreased by 35% overall, compared to 9% across the state. The in-school suspension rates decreased by 32% for Black students and 33% for Latino/a students (Table 5.6).

These data suggest that the district is on the right track. System outcomes also indicate the district has further to go, as racial disparities persist. The progress made in Pflugerville ISD through a coherent, multifaceted strategy is instructive for district leaders seeking to engage in racial equity work. The leadership, policies, and practices described in this study lay important groundwork for educational experiences that transform opportunities and outcomes for students of color. We hope readers can draw inspiration from the steps taken to advance racial equity and learn from areas of opportunity in the district.

Persistent Equity Leadership

Over the past two decades, elected officials, central office staff, and campus educators have worked in concert to refine and pursue a core commitment to educational equity. Ensuring students benefit from the district's cultural diversity has long been a guiding principle in Pflugerville ISD that is rooted in community values, championed by the Board of Trustees, and enacted by district leadership teams. The distributed nature of equity leadership in Pflugerville ISD has enabled equity-oriented reforms to develop and persist over time. Superintendent Killian and his leadership team channeled this momentum into a strategic plan that established cohesion, rationale, and shared responsibility to pursue equity goals.

A Core Commitment to Educational Equity

Pflugerville ISD is governed by a seven-member Board of Trustees responsible for setting direction through policy and regulations and delegating day-to-day district management to superintendents. The Board of Trustees has established a focus on providing every learner with an empowering education. Director of Student Data and Demographics Kathy Hickok described this focus as the "core" leadership in Pflugerville ISD:

> I definitely want to emphasize [that] I wouldn't stay here if I didn't believe in the leadership. And I do. I've been through 8 superintendents over 22 years, [each with] a different philosophy. But at the core, the people on our board who get elected [and] our community has stayed the same. We're about what's best for kids. I believe that core has remained, even though our leadership changes every so often [as] superintendents stay three to five years, sometimes just a year. But the core leadership [has] a belief in our kids and [understanding that] what we do for one, we have to do for another.

When asked about the leadership behind equity reforms described throughout this report, multiple cabinet members pointed to the stable service of expert educators on the Board of Trustees. Vernagene Mott, a retired math educator at Pflugerville High School, joined the board in 2004 as the district became more racially diverse. Mott served as Board President through pivotal equity reforms spanning 2016–22. Carol Fletcher, former district Teacher of the Year and current director at the University of Texas College of Education, served on the Board of Trustees for 18 years from 2001 to 2019. Their longevity of service and depth of expertise have been a cornerstone of board leadership.

In the past two decades, four superintendents have laid the foundation for the equity initiatives detailed in this report. From 2005 to 2006, Dr. Patricia Pickles, the district's first Black superintendent, launched an Annual Diversity Conference to encourage and structure dialogue about the learning assets and needs across the rapidly developing district. From 2006 to 2013, Dr. Charles Dupre expanded conversations about diversity in pursuit of college readiness for all. Dupre was named 2012 Superintendent of the

Year by the Greater Austin Chamber of Commerce for improving student achievement and advocating for equity in school funding.[15] From 2013 to 2017, Dr. Alex Elias Torrez ushered historic investments in programs and facilities that were associated with stronger outcomes for students of color. Dr. Douglas Killian has led Pflugerville ISD since July 2017. He entered the district with over thirteen years of superintendent experience across four Texas school districts.[16] Killian began his education career as a teacher and built a robust understanding of teaching and learning across multiple leadership roles along the way. Before coming to Pflugerville, Killian was recognized as 2014 Superintendent of the Year by the Greater Austin Chamber of Commerce and 2015 Superintendent of the Year by Texas Region 13. In 2022, he was again recognized as Region 13 Superintendent of the Year and as a finalist for State Superintendent of the Year for his focus on strategic change in the best interest of children.

Throughout this time, central office staff and campus educators enacted changes to policy and practice that bolstered the mantle of equity leadership in Pflugerville ISD. Director of Curriculum and Innovation Holly Galloway expressed confidence that the district will continue to advance its commitment to equitable teaching and learning. She reported that, in her work spanning two decades in Pflugerville ISD, "equity has always been a guiding principle in the district. We believe that school is for everybody and every body."

Establishing consistency is a challenge inherent to districtwide initiatives. In the words of former Pflugerville High Assistant Principal Emily Delgado, "I think that our biggest challenge is really how to get everyone in the same mindset, working in the same direction, with the same goal and focus on supporting the students." Former Executive Director of Special Programs Cara Schwartz explained the importance of leadership at every level of the organization:

> Superintendent leadership matters, principal leadership matters, and also the relationship between your superintendent and your board members. That has been the breath of fresh air coming here. The superintendent sets the scene, and we can do the work that we do because we have a very supportive Board of Trustees. All those pieces have a great influence, I believe, on that impact that we're able to help with our campuses and our students.

The 2018–23 strategic plan, described next, shifted the prior patchwork of efforts into a cohesive and coordinated district strategy.

The 2018–23 Strategic Plan

When he arrived in Pflugerville ISD, Killian recognized impactful teaching and learning happening in pockets across the district's many programs and campuses. He also saw barriers to the expansion of these bright spots.

He recalled, "I don't think there had been a look at the systems, through the lens of: what are doing structurally that might prevent equity? What might be the barriers in the district to more equitable access?" Killian launched his work in Pflugerville ISD with a strategic planning process—the district's first—that brought together educators and community members to define their shared beliefs about education and commit to instantiating those beliefs in district work (see full text of *2018–2023 Pflugerville ISD Strategic Plan* in the Online Materials Package). Killian described the importance of strategic planning:

> Not a lot of districts invest in doing a strategic plan. It's a lot of work, and then you do kind of open your district up for criticism for what you've done in the past, the history, and then just the expectations because they do tend to get elevated once you open them up. I think it's a valuable process, and then you also get held accountable for moving things forward at greater speed.

Killian has learned from experience that "you can get some things done as a superintendent just by force of will, but it sure does work a lot better if you're going with a group." He explained that his initial focus on staff and community buy-in was strategic because "it far outweighs what you can do on an individual basis." As a new leader in Pflugerville ISD, he leveraged the strategic planning process to establish purposeful relationships with members of the district community. He noted, "It was really nice to see the spread of folks that were interested in being involved" in the strategic planning process, which engaged students, parents, and staff, alongside leaders in the Pflugerville City Council, Chamber of Commerce, Economic Development Corporation, and community organizations and associations. Superintendent Killian and his district leadership team began the strategic planning with a focus on values, which enabled them to build a shared commitment to educational equity from the ground up. Through a structured process, they worked with staff and community members to develop a unifying equity commitment that hinges on two concepts: the vision of "Passionately Serving the Best Interest of Students" and nine core beliefs, led by "Diversity Is Our Strength."

"Passionately Serving the Best Interests of Students"

The vision statement, "Passionately Serving the Best Interests of Students," established a student-centric service mindset that Killian quotes in his daily work with administrators, campus staff, and community members. Every email he sends concludes with, "sincerely, Doug Killian, in the best interest of students." The vision is highly visible and, in the words of Executive

Director of Student Affairs Hutcherson Hill, "embedded in every message," whether praising the work of individuals and teams or responding to challenges:

> This is the first school district I've been in where I've had a superintendent who reverberates that message on a weekly basis and has not missed a week since then. Of setting that tone, creating that vision, in any type of platform he needs. Whether through a story, whether it's through praising an individual for something they did, or even an experience, that may have been a negative experience, but we responded positively and we got the job done. It's just embedded in every message.

Through frequent repetition, the vision has become systemic. In a 2018 employee opinion survey, staff reported both high satisfaction and alignment with the district vision.[17] District employees readily describe the work of their own departments and campuses in terms of "passionately serving the best interests of students."

Although the vision does not include an explicit focus on racial equity, it has sparked dialogue about *how* Pflugerville ISD can best serve its students of color. In the words of Tony Hanson, Vice President of the Pflugerville ISD Board of Trustees:

> When we were going through the strategic planning process, one of the things we talked about was diversity. But not necessarily just diversity, [we talked about] racial diversity, cultural diversity. We want to keep that in the forefront, because right now, [our] population [is] changing.

To passionately serve the best interests of students, district staff recognize that they must know their students well. Research shows that educators' attitudes toward their students can significantly shape the expectations they hold for student learning, their treatment of students, and what students ultimately learn.[18] To this end, the strategic planning process also defined core beliefs that commit district staff to enact their vision in ways that contribute to positive perceptions of students of color, described next.

"Diversity Is Our Strength"

In addition to the vision statement, the strategic plan includes nine core beliefs that further characterize the educational philosophy in Pflugerville ISD. They include:

1. Diversity is our strength.
2. All individuals have worth.

3. Relationships are foundational to success.
4. A safe and nurturing environment is non-negotiable.
5. All students have the right to diverse educational opportunities.
6. Social-emotional learning is as critical as academic focus.
7. Civic-mindedness must be explicitly cultivated in our students.
8. Community partnerships and high expectations improve students' outcomes.
9. Innovation and a strong work ethic ensure excellence.

Taken together, these core beliefs communicate a robust, asset-oriented commitment to providing empowering educational experiences that support students' holistic development. Staff reported that the first core belief, "Diversity is our strength," has served as a unifying sentiment for advancing equity goals. "Diversity is our Strength" recognizes and celebrates the district's cultural diversity—which includes the racial, ethnic, and linguistic identities of students and staff—as a unifying point of pride. Perhaps Superintendent Killian is a natural champion for this core belief. He prides himself in maintaining "a really wide perspective," drawn from his experiences in a military family that traveled the world, from England to Japan to Texas. While Killian has channeled and amplified the core belief as superintendent, staff reported that it is firmly rooted in the values of the community that has been culturally diverse since its founding. Former Chief of Operations Ed Ramos explained, "Our school board really embrace[s] diversity. That has to come from somewhere, to me that's the community." Here is how the district website describes this core belief:

> By supporting an environment that facilitates and encourages safe and open dialogue on diversity, and by empowering our students to embrace their diversity, we are striving to ensure that our students will be sincerely open and equipped to work and live in a diverse world. Speaking more than 69 languages and dialects, Pflugerville ISD is one of the most culturally diverse school districts in Central Texas and we consider that to be a strength! Over the years, the exponential growth of our district continues to change the face of diversity in Pflugerville ISD.[19]

The district website boasts the stylized slogan "One Pfamily…Many Pfaces" and includes banners celebrating Asian Pacific American, Black, Hispanic, Jewish American, and Native American heritage. It states, "While the world around us may often face stereotyping, Pflugerville ISD encourages staff and students to embrace what makes us different." This core belief is widely held by district staff. When asked about the hallmarks of the district, leadership, staff, and community members named the district's cultural diversity. In the words of Executive Director of Student Affairs Hutcherson Hill,

"We love the diverse nature of our school district. It's a calling card. It's a point of pride for us." In a 2018 employee opinion survey, 70% of staff identified "embracing diversity" as a primary asset of the district.[20]

The focus on cultural diversity in Pflugerville ISD is strategic. Pride in cultural diversity encompasses wide, intersecting student identities and experiences that are specific to the district community, especially with increases in the local Hispanic population. The core belief responds to local context with unifying, asset-based language that educators and community members can use to talk about identities, including race, ethnicity, language, and socioeconomic status. The value of this core belief is demonstrated in the capacity of district educators to bring these words to life in their daily work to advance educational equity.[21] Killian reported that broad-based support for the strategic plan served as "the catalyst for me to keep pushing the work forward." He explained, "I've used that core belief to go back, whenever I've gotten any kind of pushback, [and say,] 'Well, if diversity is our strength, we should be doing this, right?'"

An Inspiring, Engaging, and Relevant Education

The strategic planning process set the district mission to "promote an inspiring, engaging, and relevant education that empowers students to reach their full potential as productive members of a diverse global community." The vision, core beliefs, and mission are instantiated through a set of objectives and strategies that district leaders enact (Online Materials Package). These features of the strategic plan established cohesion, rationale, and shared responsibility for the suite of equity-oriented reforms described throughout this report.

The top priority in the strategic plan is an approach to teaching and learning that goes well beyond a basic education, providing each and every learner with a well-rounded and rigorous education from pre-K through graduation. The objectives specify that instruction should be relevant and responsive to the assets and interests of students and also foster social-emotional development as a foundation for academic success. Later sections on expanded opportunity and access, multilingual instruction, and restorative practices describe how leaders in Pflugerville ISD have leveraged these objectives to expand, rather than ration, successful programs in ways that improve the learning experiences for students of color and emergent bilingual students. Pursuing the teaching and learning objectives in the strategic plan required district leaders to strategically allocate human resources, funding, and facilities. The next section details the investment strategy that supported equity-oriented reforms.

Staff reported that internal communications objectives (see Figure 5.3), woven throughout the efforts described in this report, were critical for Killian's approach to breaking silos and ensuring practices scaled throughout the district. Later sections of the report demonstrate how departmental and campus leaders advocated to expand impactful strategies and programs districtwide. Former Executive Director of Special Programs Cara Schwartz described the shared responsibility and collaboration required to turn strategic planning into strategic action:

> All levels of the system were represented: board members, community, district and central office administration, campus principals, and teachers. [We had] very open dialogue and communication around all of those topics, which ended up [as] our priorities. And then, further, [we] created action teams that take on those priorities. You just don't [put] this on a shelf. There's action behind the work in the conversations that are happening.

Leaders across district departments engage with partners and community members to understand and improve the extent to which programs serve culturally diverse students and families. Internal communications efforts connect campus leaders in order to identify, evaluate, and scale effective practices, such as data-informed decision-making and instructional strategies for emergent bilingual learners. District staff are committed to a sense of shared responsibility for advancing the strategic plan, coupled with supports to increase the collective capacity of classroom teachers, campus leaders, and instructional coaches, described next.

Strategic Investment and Implementation

With the strategic plan in place, central office leaders then operationalized the district equity commitment. Killian described the importance of ensuring strategic investments follow strategic planning:

> [T]he power of the strategic plan is that it's been approved by the board, the community, and staff members. Once you've identified the road forward, then you need to move your money around and allocate to make that happen. That's the commitment level that a strategic plan brings to a district. [....] You strategically withdraw from things that aren't related to the strategic plan, and all of a sudden you can free-up money because you start saying, "This was important to us. Well, how important is it [now]?

When asked about how district leaders implemented the equity commitment, staff reported two major areas of strategic investments: first, building the capacity of classroom teachers, campus leaders, and instructional coaches to leverage disaggregated data, and second, the equitable allocation of resources to ensure every campus has appropriate staff, programs, and resources to support students.

Staff Capacity

With the strategic objective that "employees will be supported, devoted, and committed to their role in the best interest of students" as a catalyst, Killian introduced an approach to change management that systematized and established collective responsibility for enacting the district-wide equity commitment. This section describes how the central office team built the collective capacity of classroom teachers, campus leaders, and instructional coaches to leverage data in ways that advance equity. In Killian's first year as superintendent, he restructured the organization to facilitate vertical decision-making that supports cohorts of students across district feeder patterns. Building on the diversity initiatives of prior superintendents, incoming Chief Academic and Innovation Officer Brandy Baker designed professional development to deepen instructional leadership and reinforce equity consciousness. Later sections of this report detail how examining inequities in educational outcomes provided the impetus for major district initiatives, including pre-K expansion, multilingual programs, and restorative practices.

Restructuring for Vertical Decision-Making

Expediting what was originally a two-year transition plan, Superintendent Killian restructured the district over the summer of 2018, just one year after he arrived. The new organizational chart assigned each feeder pattern of schools an area supervisor, a newly created position. This role supports vertical data analyses and decision-making that follows cohorts of students from kindergarten through graduation. A district leader described how a desire for greater coordination and renewed focus on teaching and learning motivated this change:

> [Without continuous] professional development and support, some things get really loose. [Without] a district-level expectation of what [learning] should look like and sound like, everyone starts to do their own thing. Our [instructional coaches] were handling a lot of administrative duties. [Restructuring focused them] on modeling and coaching teachers. It's helping [campus leaders] realize they're going to get more bang for their buck if they keep [coaches] at that level to support teaching and learning.

An organizational redesign was a bold way for Killian to kick off his tenure in Pflugerville ISD. He understood that the staff redesign risked criticism as the whim of a new leader. By anchoring the decision in the strategic plan, Killian made a clear case that staffing changes responded to the values and mission of the district community. Although shifts in roles and responsibilities are never easy conversations to have, staff reported that these changes were necessary to advance shared goals. Area Supervisor Brian Dawson described the new structure as "a prime example of supporting campuses to move forward, versus leaving them on their own islands."

The new structure created a hub connecting classroom instruction to a range of districtwide services, such as multilingual and special education supports. Area supervisors report directly to the Chief Academic and Innovation Officer, as do the executive directors of curriculum and innovation, accountability and compliance, student affairs, and special programs (see the organizational chart in the Online Materials Package). Executive Director of Student Affairs Hutcherson Hill reported that working with area supervisors across campus feeder patterns provided a reliable structure to discuss, plan, implement, and monitor the adoption of restorative practices district-wide, detailed in a later section of this report. He reflected,

> We have a good organizational structure, which leads to effective communication at all levels. There is a strong opportunity [in Pflugerville ISD] to make sure support gets to where it is needed. [...] It's not just all talk. It's about putting in the work and getting the job done.

Campus leaders valued the additional support available through area supervisors, who facilitate the district trainings and school-based practitioner learning communities described next. Pflugerville High School Assistant Principal Emily Delgado explained, "It was visible, the shift, from when I very first started here to when [the district] started really having that expectation that we're coming from a lens of support. I think that helped."

Developing Data-Savvy Instructional Leaders

Area Supervisor Dawson described the importance of building principals' and teachers' ability to interpret data as "critical for us to be able to ensure that everybody has equal access to a strong educational experience." The staff redesign set the stage for a renewed focus on data analyses at the heart of instructional planning that responds to the strengths and needs of learners. Area supervisors support trainings and school-based practitioner learning communities that engage campus leaders and classroom teachers in ongoing cycles of data disaggregation and instructional planning. Together, area supervisors and campus teams review student achievement and growth data broken down by racial, linguistic, and socioeconomic groups.

Assistant Principal Delgado explained that these efforts have reinforced a culture of data-driven instructional leadership: "Instead of making it a compliance thing," her campus team uses data analysis "to establish a learning culture on the campus and more of a growth mindset." She continued, describing how then Chief Academic and Innovation Officer Brandy Baker reinforced this learning culture from the top:

> Brandy very much has that learning stance where she wants to be a learner herself and she wants to support others as they learn. And there's something about that as it translates to people that work under her: it's freeing, because you don't feel like you're being penalized or there's anything punitive. You feel like you really can learn and grow. [Because] you're supported and not penalized if you fail, they encourage and support taking risks.

Time for data analysis at Pflugerville ISD is built into the rhythm of district routines, which reinforces the data-driven learning culture. Both the instructional calendar and master schedule include dedicated time for campus-based practitioner learning communities to collaborate. Pflugerville ISD also partners with an equity-oriented technical assistance provider, Education Equals Economics (E3) Alliance, to facilitate research-informed professional development workshops that build the data literacy of classroom teachers, campus leaders, and area supervisors (Box 5.2).

Box 5.2   Inside a District Data Discussion

On a teacher workday, high school principals and instructional coaches sit shoulder-to-shoulder in the auditorium of the central office building. Facilitators from a district partner, Education Equals Economics (E3) Alliance, lead the group in unpacking detailed reports of student outcomes data broken down by racial, linguistic, and socioeconomic groups. They start the session with a set of asset-based data analysis principles that flash in bold type across a screen:

- Work built around faulty data leads to unintended results.
- Learning and innovation go hand in hand.
- The objective is not to identify whom to blame for a problem; it is to find out where the system failed.

Facilitators model a guided process to review student growth rates, then turn loose the leadership teams to pore over packets comparing student growth data across campuses. These data prompt leadership teams to see their school performance in a new light. For example, a closer look at the "closing performance gap" rating, which compares performance by racial, socioeconomic, and linguistic groups, reveals that some of the highest-performing schools in the district have widening performance gaps. In fact, three out of four district high schools have widening performance gaps that were masked in prior analyses by higher overall and academic performance ratings. In this professional development session, facilitators support campus leaders to engage in disaggregated data analyses that shine a light on underserved student groups.

After identifying target student groups, leaders are next prompted to look closer at classroom-level data to identify instructional strengths and priorities for improvement. Facilitators circulate to support leadership teams as they create data-informed action plans. Following the asset-based data analysis principles presented at the start of the session, principals respond to these data with neither blame nor shame but a keen focus on classroom-level instructional strategies to ensure each and every learner is supported to succeed.

Coaching Equity Consciousness

In this data-rich context, district leaders understand that the numbers alone cannot tell the full story of teaching and learning in Pflugerville ISD. In the words of Superintendent Killian, "data [without context] doesn't tell us anything. It just tells us we need to ask another question." To this end, area supervisors develop instructional staff not only to conduct data analyses but also to interpret outcomes through an equity consciousness that centers the learning assets of each student.

This takes place through ongoing conversations about teaching and learning that are anchored in shared mindsets and values. The district website lists four mindsets that embrace the core value of cultural diversity: (1) awareness of the characteristics of diverse groups, (2) realization that diversity encompasses more than ethnicity, (3) respecting and appreciating difference, and (4) producing a healthy diverse system demonstrating acceptance, appreciation, respect, and tolerance.[22] Killian emphasized the strategic importance of his leaders first modeling the equity conversations they sought to normalize and expand throughout the district:

In the current political climate, [diversity] is almost a hot button issue, right? [...] People are uncomfortable with the discussions, [but] I just had them. Once you kick them off, and people see that leadership is comfortable with those conversations, it makes it [possible] for everybody else, I will say that.

Leaders from the superintendent's cabinet to campus administrators described equity consciousness as woven into their everyday work to support culturally diverse students, which entails reviewing a range of system and student outcome data disaggregated by student linguistic, racial/ethnic, and socioeconomic group. Pflugerville ISD leaders reported that this has been an effective entry point for impactful professional learning, especially in the district's political context. In 2021, the Texas Legislature enacted a ban against training any administrator, teacher, or staff member on a range of topics that the legislation denotes as related to critical race theory.[23] Staff reported that this ban in no way impacts the core values, mindsets, and educational approach in Pflugerville ISD. Former Executive Director of Special Programs Cara Schwartz reported that equity consciousness has been introduced and reiterated throughout data-driven discussions regarding instructional practice, student engagement, and access to programming. She reflected, "It's just not [a training] that you do once and it goes away. [Equity is] embedded in what we continue to do."

Many described data-driven discussions of racial equity issues as happening primarily in direct, one-on-one coaching conversations. A benefit of this approach is that it offers educators a confidential space to develop stronger racial equity orientations and coaching supports to put them into practice. For example, area supervisors reported anticipating and attending to the discomfort that can occur when educators examine racial inequities in the learning outcomes of their own classrooms. They leverage data analysis as a compelling and impartial entry point into conversations about shifting instruction to support the success of each and every learner. Area Supervisor Kettisha Jones reported, "[Change is] data driven. I think we've identified certain student groups that definitely need something different than they've received before, and so [we are] just really trying to respond to the data." Former Principal of Timmerman Elementary School Sara Watson explained:

> We looked at our data, and we said, "Look at how radically different our data looks with our White kids than our African American kids, our White kids to our Hispanic kids, male [to] female." It's in your face. You can't do anything but acknowledge it, which is I think the safest way that we've been able to approach this conversation because it's the data.

In routine coaching conversations, educators are encouraged to express discomfort with inequitable student outcomes, followed closely by support to channel that discomfort into instructional planning. Then Principal of Pflugerville High School Ameka Durham Hunt characterized discomfort as a sign of determination and learning. She described working with one of her teachers in a practitioner learning community meeting:

> One of the teachers did say that that was eye-opening to her to actually look at the data that way and devise a plan of how we're going to increase the performance of certain [groups]. She said it did make her a little uncomfortable to look at it in that way, but just the fact that she was willing to say that out loud lets me know that she felt supported and comfortable and that we were all working toward the same goal and support her in moving toward that end.

This teacher recognized that the "eye-opening" comparisons among student racial groups gave her the chance to refocus her practice. Empowered with this data, she drew up new plans to better support the students of color whom she was not reaching. Former Executive Director of Special Programs Cara Schwartz explained,

> [We] work with our teachers more on differentiating and scaffolding strategies that they can use in the classroom. [They know where they are] struggling, and they feel safe in the learning environment [in which] we provide opportunities to be successful.

Staff reported that the core belief that "diversity is our strength" serves as a rudder for navigating coaching conversations with student-centered, asset-based language. For example, Principal Watson reported that working with an area supervisor increased her awareness of how racial identities and experiences impact learning in her building:

> I realized the phrase, 'I don't see color' […] is dishonoring of our students here, because that's saying, 'I don't honor who you are, I don't honor your culture, I don't honor your background.' That was my first, 'Oh, my gosh. What are we saying to kids, and how are they receiving our messages?'

This principal explained that, as she continued to engage with her supervisor over the course of the school year, the importance of honoring students' racial identities as learning assets "started to click." Now guiding her own staff through a similar coaching experience, she described her approach as a "slow soak" of iterative, continuous learning to cultivate strengths-based racial equity mindsets. She emphasized that a key benefit of this approach is that staff feel supported to engage in necessary, yet un-comfortable, conversations about racial inequities within their direct locus of control.

Equitable Resource Allocation

During his first year in office, Killian focused on the equitable allocation of resources to pursue the teaching and learning priorities detailed in the remaining sections of the report. Building on a foundation of historic in-vestments from a 2014 bond proposition under his predecessor, Killian strategically directed resources through new need-based formulas that eq-uitably redistribute staff and financial and material resources to campuses and programs.

In the context of regional population growth and uneven development shifting the composition of district neighborhoods, Superintendent Killian has closely monitored changes in the budget. The Texas school finance sys-tem includes a recapture program, which redistributes funding from school districts with higher property values within their boundaries to poorer school districts with lower property values (Box 5.3).

Box 5.3   State Context: Education Finance in Texas

As a relatively well-resourced district, the Pflugerville ISD per-pupil expenditures in 2019–20 were roughly $9,600, which is just above the statewide average of $9,400. The majority of the district's revenue comes from property taxes and state revenue, meaning new develop-ment is pulling more resources into the district.

In 2017–18 Pflugerville was designated as a Chapter 41 district according to the Texas Education Code. Chapter 41 makes provisions for certain school districts to share their local tax revenue with other school districts. This is known as the "Robin Hood" plan because districts subject to Chapter 41 are required to share their wealth with other school districts. The funds that are distributed by Chapter 41 districts are "recaptured" by the school finance system to assist with the financing of public education for all school districts. As of 2021–22, however, the effects of becoming a Chapter 41 district have not yet come into play for Pflugerville ISD because the maintenance and operations portion of its tax rate was below the threshold for recap-ture. This may change in future years, given Pflugerville ISD's rapidly accelerating population growth and skyrocketing housing prices, which add to the district's property wealth.

A 2018 analysis of the state finance system indicated that the current equalization strategies are not sufficient for ensuring that school finance is racially equitable: the average White student in Texas still receives 1.5 times more in student per pupil funding than the average student of color. Superintendent Killian served on a 2017–18 legislative commission that developed recommendations for more equitable funding in the state school finance system. Recommendations included creating a long-term systemic balance between the state and local share of district foundation funding for public education; substantially increasing investments in low-income and other historically underperforming student groups; significantly reducing the growth rate of property taxes and reliance on recapture as a method of finance for the state; and investing to encourage widespread adoption of data-informed practices that deliver improved outcomes for students, including early learning, teacher effectiveness, and high school supports.

Sources: Mudrazija, S. & Blagg, K. (2019). *School District Funding in Texas: Computing the Effects of Changes to the Foundation School Program Funding Formula*. Urban Institute; Rash, B. (15 July 2022). *Community Impact*. District staff predicts Pflugerville ISD will become subject to state recapture for 2022–23 school year. https://communityimpact.com/austin/pflugerville-hutto/education/2022/07/14/district-staff-predicts-pflugerville-isd-will-become-subject-to-state-recapture-for-2022-23-school-year/; Texas Education Agency (n.d.). *Texas Commission on Public School Finance*, https://tea.texas.gov/finance-and-grants/state-funding/additional-finance-resources/texas-commission-on-public-school-finance (accessed 02/22/2022).

Need-Based Staffing Ratios

District leaders developed a need-based approach to staffing to better ensure campuses can "passionately serve" the growing and diverse student population. Superintendent Killian explained that the push for this change came early in his superintendency, after noticing staff migration from the lower-income side of the district serving more families of color to the wealthier side of the district serving more White families. In his first year, he worked with the cabinet not only to stem but also to reverse that pattern. At that time, the district was facing budget cuts. District leaders positioned it as an opportunity to test out new staffing ratios by maintaining the level of staff at schools serving more students from low-income families while cutting staff elsewhere. This worked. In his words:

> In the spring, we started gently adjusting the student-to-staff ratios in various ways: the number of assistant principals in a more economically disadvantaged versus a less economically disadvantaged, whether or not we had an administrative intern on that campus or not, counselor ratios, instructional positions, that kind of stuff. [We] just started tweaking those formulas in the district. We ended up with more staffing in the schools that needed it more.

Under the new formula, the staffing ratios that had been based solely on total enrollment shifted to a more sophisticated model that considers the needs of students. Then Chief of Staff Troy Gallow said this shift was meant to advance educational equity by answering the question, "Is it equitable to staff [campuses] at the same ratio based on student population, as opposed to staffing need?" The district leadership team replaced their formula with an allocation based on the number and types of staff to support the learning needs of each particular campus, including nurses and social workers. When asked if the district encountered pushback to these changes, Gallow reported,

> When we rolled it out to principals, I don't recall much pushback at all. It was more of an understanding that, 'Okay, I have more students than my peer principal, but I don't have needs in these areas. I absolutely want them to get what they need.'

He continued, explaining the efforts to provide each campus the staff they need included both technical and relational challenges:

> When you come up with something new, you're always going to have glitches that you've got to improve. I think one of the hardest pieces was just wrapping our mind around a way to do it where we were still maintaining a commensurate level of support at every campus. That might look like more or different people [staffed] on different campuses. So, I think just getting that mindset [into action was a challenge].

Chief Human Resource Officer Willie Watson plays a critical role in district staffing decisions. He reported that his "number one goal" is "making sure we have the right people in front of students." Watson is committed to ensuring educators thrive in their school environment, noting the positive relationship between teacher experience and improved student outcomes:

> We have a very diverse work force and we also have quite a number of people who are seasoned veterans that are still here teaching. That's something that we take a lot of pride in, because as we all know as educators that there is a positive line with the longevity of a teacher having more success in a classroom, more successful students.

At the time of the staffing changes, Watson developed a "front porch initiative" to visit every campus in a three-week cycle. He explained the purpose of regular and proactive outreach:

> When [someone visits] you at your front porch, you may sit and have a straight, candid conversation, be relaxed. A lot of the time, when HR comes to visit you, people usually take deep breaths […] because when people from HR come, it's usually bad. We're trying to change that by having that outreach event and answer the questions, people can always come over here.

These candid conversations provided a platform for district leaders to message the new equity-oriented staffing model, engaging district educators in open and authentic conversation about the "why" behind reassignments and providing them the opportunity to express geographical preferences and be heard. Veteran instructional staff, many of whom served across different campuses, became natural champions of the new need-based ratios. Killian reported,

> There are a few leaders that have been in the district for a while. A lot of them had past roles in Title I schools, [even if] they weren't in a Title I school now. They became advocates, and they kind of pretty much shut down any concerns. It was refreshing, actually, [for] somebody who is in an affluent school advocating for their neighbor high school that wasn't affluent.

Financial and Material Resources

Leaders in Pflugerville ISD leveraged the allocation of material and financial resources to pursue the equity-oriented teaching and learning reforms detailed in the next section. Superintendent Killian explained the strategic plan wielded the collective authority of the board and community to set new direction:

> Just like all big organizations, you tend to do things out of habit, or some old way of thinking that now you need to change that direction. [The

strategic plan] gives you power to do that. It gives you authority that the board and community say, "This is the way we need to go. This is what we've identified. Here's the amount of money it's going to take. All right, well, let's make it a budget priority, and let's figure out how to do it." That's the interesting part of being a superintendent; you need to have that level of clarity. Otherwise, when you go to the board, everything is important, and you get nothing done. I don't know how it is in other states, but there's just not enough money to go around to do everything, so we have to make choices strategically.

The district adjusted its budgeting formulas to ensure every campus gets what it needs, from educational programs to updated facilities. Former Chief of Operations Ed Ramos explained the rationale for providing additional resources to Title 1 schools:

We know, as a district, that there are certain campuses that need more assistance than others. We really look at those students' demographics, the diversity, the makeup [when deciding how to use] federal funds [and] local funds.

In Pflugerville ISD, campus need is determined primarily by the socioeconomic status of the students served based on free- and reduced-meal application rates. To the extent that students of color attend schools with high free- and reduced-meal application rates, they benefit from this strategy. At the same time, district leaders understand the risk of overlooking the educational needs of students attending schools with low free- and reduced-meal application rates. They have championed expanding programs, like full-day pre-K and dual-language programs, to ensure every eligible student gets the right learning opportunities and supports to succeed.

Access to safe, structurally sound, and well-maintained educational facilities is a critical component of educational opportunity[24]—and part of the district's resource allocation strategy. Under Superintendent Dr. Alex Elias Torrez, the district secured a $287 million bond proposition that enabled historic investments in facilities to serve the growing student population.[25] District leaders continue to manage facilities to meet the needs of a dynamic student population by balancing new construction with the regular upkeep and expansion of its existing buildings, many built between 1996 and 2005. Investments in facilities, both old and new, support equal access to appropriate, sufficient, and up-to-date learning environments across its campus sites.[26]

Killian also dedicated standing resources to partnerships to expand access to rigorous and meaningful learning experiences. The report describes how then Chief Academic and Innovation Officer Brandy Baker and her staff collaborated with equity-oriented technical assistance providers to identify areas of opportunity and adapt evidence-based strategies to support all students, especially emergent bilingual students and students of color. Former Executive Director of Special Programs Cara Schwartz and Coordinator of Advanced Academics Shirley Bachus also partnered with institutions of higher education in Central Texas to develop college- and career-ready programming tailored to each high school campus. Instead of relying on more variable grant funding, district leaders dedicated a portion of the budget to these partnerships. This financial commitment demonstrates the high value that Pflugerville ISD places on sustaining and supporting equity-oriented student success initiatives.

Expanded Opportunity and Access

Providing continuity through leadership transitions, central office staff led key initiatives to expand access to empowering learning opportunities across students' academic trajectories. These leaders in Pflugerville ISD have ushered a suite of reforms to expand access to challenging academic content that equips students with the knowledge and skills needed for college, work, and civic participation. Director of Curriculum & Innovation Dr. Holly Galloway explained that efforts to expand opportunity and access have been persistent:

> It's been a pretty consistent effort in the district, probably since the late nineties when we first started looking in the advanced academic world of who was being served in our advanced placement courses. [We] did a lot of work that has continued throughout the years and expand to other programs and accelerated courses. It really started with [asking], "Who has access?"

Galloway reported that the simple question of "who has access?" is persistent because it comes from the Board of Trustees. Over time, district leaders and administrators have backwards-mapped the ambitious vision of postsecondary readiness for all students, starting with a portfolio of secondary college- and career-ready programs that respond to student interests and aspirations, then widening the pipeline to accelerated middle school mathematics, and establishing full-day pre-kindergarten on every elementary campus.

The 2018–23 strategic plan established an ambitious objective for teaching and learning: to "promote an inspiring, engaging, and relevant education that empowers students to reach their full potential as productive members of a diverse global community." Though many of the initiatives described in this section came into fruition during Killian's superintendency, they are the culmination of years of work rooted in long-standing district priorities.

Successes seen in Pflugerville ISD during Killian's superintendency demonstrate what is possible when a new leader does not start from scratch but rather reinforces and builds on the equity-oriented work already underway. Pflugerville experienced steady scores on the state reading and mathematics achievement from 2015–16 to 2018–19, during a period when the district was growing more diverse. Composite grade-level proficiency rates refer to the percentage of students meeting a statewide performance standard on a criterion-referenced mathematics or reading exam.[27] Since the implementation of new state tests aligned to more rigorous standards in 2016, composite grade level proficiency rates of Pflugerville ISD students have closely trailed or outperformed state averages in both reading and math (Tables 5.1 and 5.2). During this period, the composite grade level proficiency rates of emergent bilingual students increased in both reading (from 29% to 39%) and math (from 33% to 44%). These gains demonstrated an accelerated rate of growth relative to districtwide growth: reading proficiency rates for emergent bilingual students grew by 34%, compared to no

Table 5.1 Comparison of Pflugerville ISD and Texas Reading Composite Grade Level Proficiency Rates, All Grades, 2015–16 to 2021–22, by Racial/Ethnic and Linguistic Student Group

Group	2015–16	2016–17	2017–18	2018–19	2020–21	2021–22
PfISD	51%	53%	52%	51%	44%	53%
American Indian/ Alaska Native	53%	53%	69%	57%	43%	50%
Asian American	73%	73%	70%	68%	62%	70%
Black	39%	41%	41%	40%	32%	42%
Latino/a	43%	45%	45%	44%	37%	45%
Multiracial	60%	61%	59%	58%	52%	62%
Native Hawaiian/ Pacific Islander	67%	57%	57%	63%	33%	64%
White	66%	69%	67%	67%	62%	70%
Emergent bilingual	29%	29%	39%	39%	29%	37%
Texas	46%	48%	46%	48%	45%	53%

Source: Texas Education Agency (n.d.). Texas academic performance reports, https://tea.texas.gov/texas-schools/accountability/academic-accountability/performance-reporting/texas-academic-performance-reports

Note: Spring 2020 STAAR assessments were canceled due to COVID-19.

Table 5.2 Comparison of Pflugerville ISD and Texas Mathematics Composite Grade Level Proficiency Rates, All Grades, 2015–16 to 2021–22, by Racial/ethnic and Linguistic Student Group

Group	2015–16	2016–17	2017–18	2018–19	2020–21	2021–22
PfISD	46%	51%	50%	50%	34%	38%
American Indian/Alaska Native	39%	63%	63%	65%	40%	28%
Asian American	75%	79%	76%	77%	59%	67%
Black	31%	36%	35%	36%	21%	24%
Latino/a	39%	44%	44%	43%	26%	30%
Multiracial	53%	60%	59%	60%	37%	46%
Native Hawaiian/ Pacific Islander	33%	44%	69%	67%	41%	40%
White	61%	66%	66%	65%	50%	54%
Emergent Bilingual	33%	35%	44%	44%	24%	31%
Texas	43%	48%	50%	52%	37%	42%

Source: Texas Education Agency (n.d.), Texas academic performance reports, https://tea.texas.gov/texas-schools/accountability/academic-accountability/performance-reporting/texas-academic-performance-reports

Note: Spring 2020 STAAR assessments were canceled due to COVID-19.

change districtwide, and in math emergent bilingual students experienced 33% growth compared to 9% districtwide.

As in other districts, the impact of the COVID pandemic caused a drop in achievement in 2020–21, but in Pflugerville, reading achievement rebounded fully by 2021–22, while small gains in math showed that a turnaround was occurring. Decreases in composite grade level proficiency rates are difficult to interpret among American Indian/Alaskan Native and Native Hawaiian/Pacific Islander student groups, since these groups included fewer than 45 test-takers enrolled pre-K through 12th grade.

A Portfolio of Advanced Academic Programs

Pflugerville ISD has a long history of supporting students to be "future-ready" through a suite of college- and career-ready course offerings, which staff described as a major priority of the Board of Trustees. Advanced Academics Coordinator Cody Pruitt said that trustees regularly pose

> …the questions you would want your school board to ask, if their top priority was equity and diversity in our advanced programs. All the way

from: who can nominate students? Are we making sure that parents are aware of this process in multiple languages? Are we sending information home? [This suite of questions is] a priority up to the very highest levels of our district leadership.

From 2006 to 2013, Dr. Charles Dupre focused on building a culture that encourages and prepares all students to attend college, and Superintendent Killian harnessed prior investments in college- and career-readiness to push for greater, and more equitable, participation in advanced academic programs. This ambitious commitment is stated in the 2021–22 District Improvement Plan as, "equitable access for all students to advanced academic coursework in a rigorous and challenging curriculum in preparation for postsecondary success should be provided."[28] District leaders pursue this commitment by cultivating a dynamic suite of secondary programs that offer college credit and industry-based credentials.

Staff reported that the conviction that instruction must be tailored to the strengths of students, not one-size-fits-all, provides a key motivation for continuous improvement. The Special Programs team—comprised of central office leaders in the Advanced Academics, Counseling, and Career and Technical Education departments—engages campus administrators to develop programs with a close ear to the needs of students, an eye on regional partners, and a handle on the district budget. Many actors coordinate to expand college- and career-ready opportunities in an ongoing, collaborative process to ensure offerings respond to the interests and aspirations of students:

> District leadership collaborates with campus counselor, teacher and administrative leadership to determine Advanced Academic needs, review data, and share instruction needs and strategies. In the 2019–2020 school year, the leadership group expanded with each subject area from each campus being represented by a range of veteran and newer teachers, collaborating to offer multiple points of view. Regularly scheduled meetings offer checkpoints and accountability for the group to share campus needs, problem solve, and plan for student needs.[29]

The efforts to expand educational opportunity in Pflugerville ISD have supported students to graduate prepared for work, life, and civic participation, even as the number of students from low-income families and students of color has grown. From 2016–17 to 2020–21, the average four-year longitudinal graduation rate for Black and Latino/a Pflugerville ISD students was 95% or above, and rates for both groups surpassed the statewide average (90%) for each year.[30] In the 2016–17 school year, the Texas Education Agency introduced a measure of College, Career, and Military Readiness, which defines readiness as the percentage of graduates satisfying one or more criteria, including meeting college readiness standards in both ELA and mathematics, earning dual college credit, meeting the AP/IB criterion score, and earning an associate degree or industry-based certification.[31] From 2016–17 to 2018–19, the rate of students graduating College, Career, and Military Ready increased from 57% to 78% (Figure 5.2). During this period, district College, Career, and Military Ready graduates exceeded state averages and increased each year by roughly 10 percentage points. This promising pre-pandemic trend was disrupted by a slight decrease in 2019–20 (to 77%) and a more significant decrease in 2020–21 (to 61%) following widespread school closures related to the COVID-19 pandemic.

Disaggregating the data reveals pre-pandemic gains for all students in the district (Table 5.3). The greatest increases from 2016–17 to 2019–20 were among emergent bilingual graduates, whose rates of college, career, and military readiness increased from 32% to 60%. During this period, readiness rates also increased for graduates who identified as Black (from 43% to 69%), multiracial (from 57% to 88%), and Latino/a (from 50% to 75%). Readiness rates dropped significantly across the state between 2019 and 2020 (from 73% to 63%) and began to recover in 2021 (to 65%). Pflugerville ISD experienced a slight drop between 2018–19 and 2019–20 (from 78% to 77%) and a significant decrease in 2020–21 (to 61%) that reflects a drop in overall graduates after pandemic closures. This overall trend represents decreases for all racial/ethnic student groups and especially large

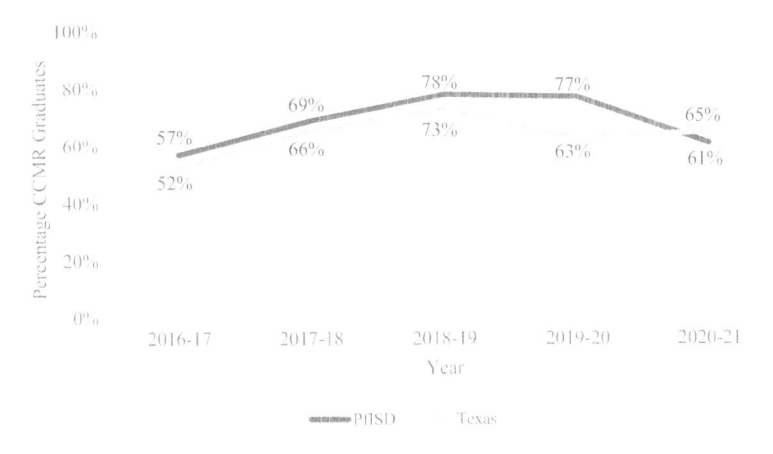

Figure 5.2 Comparison of Pflugerville ISD and Texas Percentage of College, Career, and Military Ready Graduates, 2016–17 to 2020–21.

Source: Texas Education Agency, Texas Academic Performance Reports, https://tea.texas.gov/texas-schools/accountability/academic-accountability/performance-reporting/texas-academic-performance-reports

Table 5.3 Pflugerville ISD Percentage of College, Career, and Military Ready Graduates, 2017–21 by Racial/Ethnic and Linguistic Student Group

Group	2016–17		2017–18		2018–19		2019–20		2020–21	
	Texas	*PfISD*	*Texas*	*PfISD*	*Texas*	*PfISD*	*Texas*	*PfISD*	*Texas*	*PfISD*
ALL	52%	57%	66%	69%	73%	78%	63%	77%	65%	61%
American Indian/ Alaska Native	52%	N/A	60%	70%	68%	86%	56%	N/A	60%	N/A
Asian American	82%	84%	87%	87%	90%	89%	86%	84%	86%	74%
Black	37%	43%	51%	59%	61%	72%	48%	69%	50%	52%
Latino/a	49%	50%	62%	65%	71%	75%	60%	75%	63%	55%
Native Hawaiian/ Pacific Islander	51%	N/A	60%	N/A	67%	N/A	51%	88%	54%	N/A
Multiracial	59%	57%	68%	77%	75%	88%	66%	88%	65%	65%
White	65%	70%	74%	78%	79%	83%	71%	85%	72%	72%
Emergent bilingual/ English learner	30%	32%	46%	45%	57%	63%	45%	60%	50%	28%

Source: Texas Education Agency, Texas academic performance reports, https://tea.texas. gov/texas-schools/accountability/academic-accountability/performance-reporting/ texas-academic-performance-reports.

Note: district data for American Indian/Alaska Native and Native Hawaiian/Pacific Islander student groups has been masked due to small sample size.

decreases for Latino/a (from 75% to 55%) and emergent bilingual student groups (from 60% to 28%).

These data indicate that the district's efforts to develop college- and career-ready programs coincided with strong graduation outcomes from 2016–17 to 2018–19. As district leaders work to recover from the pandemic, they continue to leverage resources, partnerships, and collaborative problem-solving to cultivate a portfolio of advanced academic programming in all four Pflugerville ISD high schools.

Promoting College Readiness

In Pflugerville ISD, the focus on college readiness sets a long-term vision for student success through rigorous learning experiences that prepare students for higher education. Over the past 20 years, district leaders and educators have worked to establish and expand students' access to college-ready secondary programs. In 2018, Killian signed a regional pact with the Austin

Chamber of Commerce committed to advancing an ambitious target: 70% of graduates in the Central Texas area matriculate into a postsecondary degree-seeking program directly out of high school. District leaders advance that goal by enabling students to earn free college credits while working toward high school graduation through Advanced Placement, Dual Enrollment, and Dual Credit programs.

Eliminating financial barriers for college-ready programs is a key part of Killian's strategy. With over half of Pflugerville ISD students qualifying for free or reduced-price lunch, Superintendent Killian described the cost of higher education as the "missing piece" for postsecondary access. He reported that, year over year, roughly 98% of Pflugerville ISD high school graduates apply for college and 60% complete the Free Application for Federal Student Aid. Still, many graduates do not end up matriculating into postsecondary opportunities due to lack of available funds. Superintendent Killian has had his own experiences with financial barriers to postsecondary education. As his son was preparing to enter a four-year university in 2017, he recalled, "[When] he got his first bill, he came into the bedroom and was shocked. [He] said, 'Dad, I don't want to start my whole life off in this kind of debt.'" For Superintendent Killian's son, the answer was enrolling in a more affordable community college before transferring into a university program. However, Killian noted that the price tag on community college makes even this cost-saving strategy financially infeasible for some families in the district. This is why he has championed the importance of advanced coursework that offers college credits at no cost to the student.

ADVANCED PLACEMENT PROGRAM

The strength of the Advanced Placement (AP) program provides another example of Killian's administration building on longstanding equity initiatives in Pflugerville ISD. Each high school in Pflugerville ISD provides students the opportunity to engage in rigorous, college-level coursework through the AP program. AP courses culminate in end-of-year standardized examinations that are reported on a five-point scale. Most Texas public colleges and universities, along with many others across the country, offer credit for every AP exam score of "three" or higher. Policies that advance more equitable access to AP coursework—including open enrollment, intentional recruitment, and diffusing the cost of AP exams—build on decades of continuous improvement since the district first offered the program in 1999.

Open enrollment in AP courses was championed by former Pflugerville High School teacher Dixie Ross and Advanced Academics Coordinator Rebecca Embry. Initially, only students identified as "Gifted and Talented" were enrolled in AP courses. While the program had high success rates, its participation did not represent the racial diversity of district high schools. A district newsletter quoted Ross on the rationale for open enrollment in AP courses, "There are plenty of highly capable students that are not identified as gifted."[32] In 2003, Embry and her team secured a grant of over $1 million to build school-level leadership and capacity needed to expand access to the AP program. Ross explained grant-funded trainings catalyzed a shift in both participation and instructional philosophy, from "having a highly selective program to one that encouraged open enrollment. [The AP program] grew enormously in size, but also in terms of quality because we had many, many more students participating in the program."[33] AP course enrollment increased from 483 students in 2002 to 2,130 in 2008.[34] Ross reported that these changes coincided with increases in the enrollment of Black and Latino/a students in AP classes at Pflugerville High School, and the program maintained this higher level of participation after the grant ended in 2008.

A district-wide push to increase awareness and preparation for AP classes was key to building an inclusive AP program that represents the racially diverse population of the district. Ross explained:

> We actively recruit students who have been under-represented in AP programs—Hispanic, African American, and [students from] low-income [families]. Once we have kids in our classes, we provide them the support that they need to be successful there. This effort doesn't just take place in the high schools. We begin with kids in middle school, preparing them with the skills, concepts and habits that will allow them to be successful in very challenging, rigorous coursework when they get to high school.[35]

Advanced Academics Coordinator Cody Pruitt described AP recruitment as "a concerted effort to be sure that, at every level, all students know the options that are available to them and are encouraged in those areas of strength." He routinely reviews academic outcomes with principals, counselors, and instructors to "cast that wide net for any student that might be able to achieve at a higher level." He named the district's Advancement Via Individual Determination partnership, described in the next section, as a key way to "identify and work with first-generation college-bound students that have the capacity to do college-level work if they're taught the soft skills that they need to succeed."

As the AP open enrollment policy and recruitment strategies increased the racial diversity of students taking AP courses, the Advanced Academics team also worked to ensure all AP students realize the full benefit of AP curriculum by taking AP exams. Since the cost of AP exams creates a financial barrier for participation, the district offers scholarships and coordinates state subsidies to ensure exams are affordable for students from low-income households. The AP exam fee for 2021 was $80. In addition to a state subsidy, the district covered administrative fees to reduce the cost to $14 for any student eligible for the free and reduced-price lunch program. Students who do not qualify for the free and reduced-price lunch program but experience financial need cover the full cost of their first AP exam, then qualify for a scholarship of $25 for each additional AP exam.[36]

These efforts appear to be paying off. Publicly available data for school years 2017–18 and 2020–21 show that the district rate of enrollment in at least one AP course has nearly tripled, from 12% to 34% (Table 5.4). Disaggregating these data shows increased rates of enrollment in at least one AP course for Asian American students (from 21% to 62%), Black students (from 11% to 28%), and Latino/a students (from 9% to 27%). In 2020–21, each of these groups had higher rates of AP enrollment than their peers across the state.

In 2020–21, a higher percentage of Pflugerville ISD 11th and 12th grade students took at least one AP exam (31%) than same-grade students across the state (22%), and a higher percentage of those AP examinees scored a three or higher (65%) than peers across the state (59%).[37] From 2015 to 2020, the share of AP examinees receiving a score of three or higher sharply increased, from under half of test-takers (49%) to close to two-thirds (65%).[38]

Table 5.4 Comparison of Pflugerville ISD and Texas Rates of Enrollment in at Least 1 AP Course, Grades 9–12, 2017–18 and 2020–21, by Racial/Ethnic Student Group

Race/Ethnicity	2017–18	2017–18	2020–21	2020–21
	Texas	*PfISD*	*Texas*	*PfISD*
ALL	N/A	12%	21%	34%
American Indian/ Alaska Native	0%	14%	19%	N/A
Asian American	10%	21%	59%	62%
Black	9%	11%	17%	28%
Latino/a	47%	9%	22%	27%
Native Hawaiian/Pacific Islander	0%	22%	22%	N/A
Multiracial	2%	12%	26%	N/A
White	32%	14%	25%	43%

Sources: Civil Rights Data Collection (CRDC) 2017–18, https://ocrdata.ed.gov/; Texas Education Agency, Texas Public Education Information Resource (TPEIR) Advanced Placement (AP) Reports https://www.texaseducationinfo.org/Home/Topic/advanced_placement

Notes: Students completing more than one AP course are counted only once. Disaggregated data for American Indian/Alaska Native, Native Hawaiian/Pacific Islander, and multiracial students are not available in 2020–21.

The inclusive philosophy on college-ready coursework also served as a rationale for partnering with the University of Texas and Austin Community College systems on dual credit and dual enrollment programs, which offer an avenue for Pflugerville ISD high school students to accumulate college credit while simultaneously fulfilling requirements for high school graduation. The executive director of special programs and advanced academics coordinator manages these programs in close coordination with higher education partners.

Under Dupre's leadership in 2011, district leaders first established dual enrollment and dual credit programs at the campus serving the most students of color and students from low-income families: Connally High School, which is located within Austin City limits. This leadership move was meant to expand postsecondary access for students from groups historically underrepresented in higher education. The two programs have become increasingly popular and grown to serve additional high school campuses. District and campus leaders collaborate to review enrollment and outcomes in these programs to better tailor programming to community assets and student demand.

The dual enrollment program, called OnRamps, began as a partnership between the University of Texas and Pflugerville ISD. The University of Texas initiated this program, which enables high school students to take college-level courses free of charge, based on data indicating that admitted students from across the state were not prepared for college-level English courses. The OnRamps classes are designed by University of Texas professors and taught by high school teachers, who receive additional professional development to deliver the content. The secondary teacher of record instructs and assigns the high school grade and credit, while the University of Texas professor assigns the college grade and credit. Under Killian's leadership, the Advanced Academics team expanded the dual enrollment program to meet demand at all four high schools in the 2022–23 school year.

Because Connally High School is within the City of Austin taxing district, district leaders also established a dual credit program with Austin Community College that enables students to earn college credit free of charge. The dual-credit program follows a two-year cohort model starting junior year. Courses are taught by Austin Community College faculty, covering a range of academic core subjects (e.g., English, Mathematics, History) and vocational subjects (e.g., automotive, building trades, computer science). Upon course completion, students receive high school credit alongside college credit from the University of Texas or Austin Community College.

Unlike AP credits, which are translated into college credits at the discretion of individual colleges and universities, dual enrollment and dual credit programs provide an actual transcript with college grades and credits noted. For high schoolers planning for postsecondary education, these programs provide a bridge to college and help offset the financial burden.

Fostering Career Readiness

In 2018, then Chief Academic and Innovation Officer Brandy Baker built on existing Career and Technical Education (CTE) offerings and partnerships to develop new programming that is more closely tailored to industry relevance and explicitly dedicated to increasing opportunity for students from low-income households and students of color.

Career and Technical Education encompasses a total of 22 programs serving over 8,000 students across all four comprehensive high schools and seven middle schools in Pflugerville ISD.[39] Most programs include no-cost opportunities for authentic, rigorous, and relevant learning experiences that support students to earn college credit, industry certification, and work-based projects or internships. District- and campus-level staff collaborate with workforce development experts, postsecondary partners, and regional industry representatives to curate program offerings in thematic career clusters including Health Science, Engineering, Automotive Technology, Agriculture, and Information Technology. While not every CTE course is offered at all high school campuses, all programs are open to all Pflugerville ISD students. The district supports intra-district transfers to enable high schoolers to engage in their program of choice.

LAUNCHING P-TECH ACADEMIES

In 2018, then Chief Academic and Innovation Officer Brandy Baker identified two needs: first, although the regional Labor Market and Career Information database projected 21% growth in information security analysts, districtwide enrollment in the Information Technology cluster was stagnant at less than 7%. Second, postsecondary enrollment was lowest among Black and Latino/a male graduates from low-income families.[40] To increase both industry relevance and access for students underrepresented in higher education and the skilled workforce, Baker channeled the strengths of the existing Computer and Information Technology program at Connally High School and the existing partnership with Austin Community College into a new model: Pathways in Technology Early College High School (P-TECH) Academies, a no-cost, school-within-a-school to connect career-ready pathways for graduates to employment needs in high-growth industries. She secured two planning grants from the Texas Education Agency to develop the P-TECH Computer and Informational Technology Academy at Connally High School.[41]

Baker assembled a cross-functional P-TECH leadership team comprised of high school principals, area supervisors, and cabinet leaders, including the director of state and federal programs, director of curriculum and innovation, director of CTE, and assistant director of postsecondary readiness. This team engaged in a needs assessment of the current program, aligned P-TECH to the district strategic plan, engaged Austin Community College partners in program design, and developed recruitment and outreach strategies. The 2021–22 improvement plan described the significance of this initiative:

> With a continued increase in need for employees in many industries in the region, the goal is to implement programs that are developed through collaboration with postsecondary and industry partners so that all students graduate ready for their next steps and employers have a work-ready pool of candidates in Central Texas.[42]

An initial challenge was developing a plan to identify and recruit students from populations that are historically underrepresented in college courses, including students from low-income families and students of color. The Pflugerville ISD Community Relations, Special Programs (Advanced Academics, Counseling, and CTE), and Curriculum and Innovation teams collaboratively developed a set of strategies, including information sessions at schools and community locations, middle school presentations, campus open house events, and coverage in social and local media translated into multiple languages, as necessary. They created a four-step enrollment process that featured in-depth orientation for students and families to learn about P-TECH, an online enrollment application, blind review, and selection of applicants beyond capacity by lottery. To eliminate bias and ensure equal opportunity for all Pflugerville ISD students, the enrollment application excluded information on prior test scores, academic performance, and disciplinary history.[43]

In 2021–22, the district launched not one, but two P-TECH Academies at Title I campuses: the Computer and Information Technology Academy at Connally High School and the Pfuture Teachers Academy at Weiss High School. Both academies enable students to earn up to 60 tuition-free college credit hours to complete an industry-recognized Level 1 Certificate and/or associate degree from Austin Community College alongside their high school diploma within four to six years of starting the program. Along with their Associate of Teaching degree from Austin Community College, graduates of the Pfuture Teachers Academy earn an educator aide certificate through the State Board of Education Certification.

The P-TECH leadership team continues to meet monthly. In addition to coordinating the partnerships with Austin Community College and local industry leaders, the team evaluates program design and implementation. To support success in P-TECH Academies, the team developed wraparound services including an advisory period to build successful academic habits, tutoring and planning support from College and Career Advisors, family outreach, and Career Technical Student Organizations.[44] In the 2022–23 school year, this team provided additional supports that included assistance with program applications, financial aid, and new counseling partnerships with community-based organizations.[45] Through these efforts, the programs expanded to enroll 49 students in 2021–22 to 88 in 2022–23.[46] In 2022–23, the programs served 40% Latino/a, 30% Black, 15% White, 7% Asian American, 5% multiracial, and 4% American Indian/Alaska Native students.

INDUSTRY-BASED CERTIFICATIONS

In 2022, the district began working with partner institutes of higher education to create career academies within the CTE programs of study, which allow students to earn up to a Level 1 college certificate at no cost. Beginning with the 2024–25 school year, there will be four career academies, including Advanced Manufacturing, Automotive, Culinary Arts, and Fire Academy. Students from each campus are eligible to participate in these academies, but a remaining barrier to participation is transportation, as transfer-eligible programs do not provide district transportation. However, the district is finalizing plans for a centralized CTE Center in which these programs will be hosted, and district transportation will be available without a transfer requirement, removing those barriers to participation.

Additionally, every CTE program of study now offers at least one industry-based certification and course sequences that offer as many routes to completion as possible within the framework of TEA's approved programs. PfISD career readiness in the state's accountability system is derived mostly from industry-based certifications despite the relatively low numbers of attainment through 2023. Since reporting drops in College, Career, and Military Readiness rates after the COVID-19 pandemic, the district CTE leadership team has collaborated with CTE teacher professional learning communities to embed industry-based certification preparation in their monthly data review cycle and now requires teachers to prepare all students enrolled in a certification-aligned course using district-approved and purchased preparation materials and practice exams. At the beginning of the course, teachers are required to communicate with students and family members to explain the certification, testing process, and benefits and provide ongoing intervention and support to ensure every student reaches certification readiness by the end of the course. With these additional practices, the district expects to see improvements in the rates of career readiness for all student groups.

A Growing Pipeline to Accelerated Mathematics

Pflugerville ISD leaders have worked to establish the foundation neces-sary to engage in the array of advanced academic offerings in district high schools. Under Superintendent Charles Dupre's campaign of college readi-ness for all, an extracurricular program was established in 2007–08 to sup-port students with college aspirations and uneven academic records from 6th through 12th grade (Box 5.4). The Advancement Via Individual De-termination (AVID) program bolstered a shift in the instructional culture toward increasing participation in engaging, rigorous coursework at district middle schools. Building on these prior efforts, cabinet leaders in Killian's administration reevaluated the identification processes that determined ac-cess to the middle school Accelerated Math Pathway. This effort, champi-oned by then Chief Academic and Innovation Officer Brandy Baker and supported by district partners E3 Alliance and National Alliance for Part-nerships in Equity (NAPE), widened the pipeline of students prepared for higher levels of math coursework. The reforms are part of ongoing work by the Special Programs team to monitor enrollment patterns, identify access barriers, and revise policy.

Box 5.4   Spotlight: AVID Partnership

Advancement Via Individual Determination (AVID) is a national non-profit whose mission is "to close opportunity gaps in college graduation among diverse and underrepresented groups" by partner-ing with middle and secondary schools. AVID provides Pflugerville ISD schools with educator professional development, resources, and ongoing support to implement AVID strategies to support student learning. These strategies include an emphasis on critical thinking and critical reading, as well as a focus on developing academic mindsets and habits, which are core elements of deeper learning. In Pflugerville ISD, AVID programs are free of charge. They include a 6th grade sum-mer bridge program and year-round supports for all 6th–12th grade students with an uneven academic record and desire to attend college, many of whom are first-generation collegegoers in their families. Par-ticipation in the AVID program provides structures and supports for students to enroll and succeed in more advanced academic courses, develop academic skills and college-bound mindsets, engage in com-munity service, and access leadership opportunities at their school.

The partnership is so successful in Pflugerville ISD that two of their schools, Dessau Middle School and Pflugerville High School, have been designated "Demonstration Schools" by the national AVID office, a recognition shared by only 106 out of 5,000 AVID schools across the country. Dessau Middle School and Pflugerville High School have adopted AVID tenets campus-wide. Ashley Stanky, Dessau Middle School AVID teacher, reported that all areas—including core subjects and electives such as band, choir, and athletics—are using AVID strategies. She continued, "Even [the Multilingual Instruction and] Special Education Departments are huge advocates for the AVID system. The strategy for AVID is just putting in best practices so all students can benefit." Stanky said that the program "has truly changed the culture of our school. Teachers and counselors now actively encourage students to enroll in more pre-AP classes. Our counselors are constantly looking for students who can be pushed to accept a more rigorous schedule." AVID provides one of the many pathways to college- and career-readiness in Pflugerville ISD.

This program, which focused on supporting students to attend and be successful in college, is an example of a district initiative that advances racial equity outcomes. For example, Latino/a students take advantage of the AVID program at high rates. In 2018–19, 58% of students enrolled in AVID were Latino/a, compared to overall Latino/a enrollment in the district of 48%.

Sources: AVID. Our Beliefs. https://www.avid.org/our-beliefs; Tabodoa, M. B. (1 September 2012). Austin-American Statesman. Dessau Middle School in Pflugerville district gets national designation https://www.statesman.com/story/news/2012/09/01/dessau-middle-school-in-pflugerville-district-gets-national-designation/9821432007/; Data provided by Pflugerville ISD.

The focus on middle school math pipelines to accelerated mathematics started in 2017, when Pflugerville ISD joined "Pathways of Promise," a steering committee of 15 districts and 3 institutions of higher education to address regional disparities in placement into Algebra I by 8th grade for students of color and students from low-income households. Facilitated by NAPE, partnering districts on the steering committee reviewed E3 Alliance research showing the importance of advanced mathematics for postsecondary degree completion and high-wage and high-skilled jobs.[47] District teams then collaborated in workshops to identify and remove barriers in their own math pathways. A mathematics curriculum coordinator working on this initiative explained how analyzing enrollment and completion trends during the workshops helped his team uncover racial inequities:

[We found] that our African American population and our Hispanic population were under performing compared to all other groups. We started to look in classrooms, and a lot of secondary STEM [instructors noticed] that we weren't seeing a reflection of our community's population within our higher level, pre-AP or advanced math classes.

In 2018, Chief Academic and Innovation Officer Brandy Baker led efforts to redesign middle school Accelerated Math Pathways to better enable all students—and particularly students of color who were historically underrepresented in advanced courses—to graduate prepared for success after high school. That year, the Advanced Academics team removed the teacher recommendation for 6th grade accelerated math, instead adopting an opt-out program for all qualifying 5th grade students. Students on the Accelerated Math Pathway master all math concepts from 6th, 7th, and 8th grade and begin Algebra 1 in their final year of middle school. This enables them to enroll in additional, more rigorous math courses during their time in high school. Research shows that higher levels of math coursework are correlated with better chances of postsecondary success for students in Central Texas.[48]

Under the existing policy, Pflugerville ISD teachers recommended students for an accelerated 6th grade math course. This foundation gives students the opportunity to take accelerated math in 7th grade and Algebra I in 8th grade, creating a wider pipeline to Calculus and other high-level math courses in high school. Analyzing enrollment patterns, curriculum coordinators identified students of color whose scores predicted success in accelerated math but who were not enrolled in the 6th grade accelerated course. They traced this pattern to two contributing factors: students shifted from advanced to standard courses at each grade level, narrowing the pool of students qualifying for advanced math. The rigid course sequence also prevented students enrolled in standard courses from enrolling in more advanced courses in subsequent years.

In 2018, district leaders set an ambitious improvement goal to redesign accelerated math pathways to better enable all Pflugerville ISD students—and particularly students of color who were historically underrepresented in advanced courses—to graduate prepared for success after high school.[49] That year, the advanced academics team removed the teacher recommendation for 6th grade accelerated math, instead adopting an opt-out program for all 5th grade students meeting a threshold on their end-of-course math exams in grades 3, 4, and 5. The new policy automatically enrolled all identified students into 6th grade advanced math for the 2019–20 school year. Families had the opportunity to opt out of the program if they did not want their child to participate. Superintendent Killian described his excitement for this change in 2018:

It's going to pay dividends because it's an assumption that kids can do it. [...] I don't think there's any negative intent with our counselors or our staff members on campus, but if we start with the assumption that a kid can do it, and then let them try, we'll go a little bit farther with keeping kids in those higher math courses. The longer we can keep them in a higher math track, the better for them overall. [With] more opportunities, they just rise to the occasion when you keep the assumption that [they] will be successful in those classes. I also think it helps with diversity, as well, because they have to opt-out, versus [a staff member] having to make some choice. Somebody's bias is not entered into that piece.

Killian's remarks demonstrate the district's equity commitment in action. His conviction that, when supported, students who were not identified under the prior policy can be successful in advanced math exemplifies the core value to honor students' strengths. He instantiates the vision to "passionately serving the best interests of students" by naming the responsibility of district educators to remove barriers, with the understanding that biases can function to exclude students from accessing rigorous learning experiences, even without negative intent.

In its first year, the new policy was successful. Fewer than ten students districtwide opted out, due to exceptional out-of-school circumstances. Then Park Crest Middle School Principal Zack Kleypus reported that enrollment in accelerated math grew to outweigh enrollment in standard math courses on his campus, with greater participation by students of color. Encouraged by this progress, district leaders decided to address the second contributing factor. In Fall 2022, the advanced academics team introduced a revised rubric that allows for an easier transition into accelerated courses later than 6th grade. Advanced Academic Coordinator Cody Pruitt explained:

[Transfers] after sixth grade used to be based on a rubric that took into consideration several metrics. The math team and I discussed that the rubric seemed to be prohibitively high. So, the leadership team all worked together to revise that rubric. And now...it's much more likely [for a student] who either transfers in at seventh grade or gets a 100 in their at-level sixth grade math class, who says, "maybe I did want to try something more challenging, even though I opted out or I wasn't in those top 2 Quintiles." [The revised rubric] allows an easier transition for students into those accelerated courses later than 6th grade.

Taken together, these reforms have increased the number and racial diversity of students taking accelerated middle school mathematics courses. Pruitt reported that the district is seeing growth in both participation and passing rates in accelerated math and recommended cautious optimism as the district sets goals to regain learning loss sustained during the COVID-19 pandemic disruptions. Director of Curriculum and Innovation Holly Galloway added that the change coincided with notable increases in Latino/a and Black female enrollment in accelerated math, and her team is still working on increasing the participation of Black males. Motivated to continue building on these early successes, district leaders are considering additional strategies to increase the racial and ethnic diversity of students in the Accelerated Math Pathway, including a school-based pilot to prepare all students to enroll in 6th grade advanced math.

Full Day Pre-kindergarten Access

With the support of Superintendent Dr. Alex Elias Torrez and former Assistant Superintendent of Curriculum & Instruction Dr. Anette Tielle, Director of Federal and State Programs Christy Fox launched a strategy in 2015 to advance equitable opportunity for the district's youngest learners by establishing full-day pre-kindergarten (pre-K) at every campus. It was a bold initiative that took four years of careful and creative planning to implement, including technical aspects of the financial investment and developing pervasive equity mindsets regarding pre-K services across district staff. Under Killian's leadership, the continued efforts positioned Pflugerville ISD as a regional leader with full-day pre-K access on every elementary campus in 2019–20. Fox reported that the long-term investments in full-day pre-K were worthwhile:

> It is one of my proudest achievements is that we were able to accomplish [full day pre-K] in Pflugerville prior to it being required by law and before most other school districts in in our area. It [took] significant investment, but I believe that the benefits can obviously last a lifetime for the kids that participate.

The effort to establish full-day pre-K programs at every elementary campus began in the spring of 2015. At that time, the district offered a combination of full-day and half-day pre-K classes that served three- and four-year-olds through both a tuition option and an eligibility-based, tuition-free option. Families qualify for tuition-free pre-K by meeting any one of the eligibility requirements, which include enrollment in the district's free/reduced-price meal program or other government assistance program, limited English proficiency, active military service, housing insecurity, and/or participation in foster care.[50] Limited seats in full-day pre-K classes were allocated on a first-come, first-served basis that was not equitable. Fox explained:

> The best way to describe it [is]: you get what you get if you get in line. And I thought that that is not really a fair way to get that seat in full day pre-K. A family whose child qualifies [for tuition-free pre-K], like most people, needs full day care and education for their children. [However], if you were the parent that was here and in line at 3AM, then you got those one of those 25 seats. I thought, "What? that's kind of nuts!"

Realizing that the enrollment process presented an obstacle for families to access full-day services, Fox began to advocate for change. With support from former Superintendent Dr. Alex Elias Torrez and Assistant Superintendent of Curriculum & Instruction Dr. Annette Tielle, she developed a strategy for how the district might advance equity by offering full-day pre-K at every school.

Fox reported that her biggest hurdle was securing the manpower and dollars to open new classrooms. Together with the former chief financial officer, she poured over the state and district budgets and determined that increasing pre-K enrollments would grow the basic per-pupil allotment enough to cover the cost of a full-day program. She explained how their calculations presented a self-evident rationale for expansion: "I don't want to say it's not costing us money, because there's electricity, bus routes, and all the things that [classrooms need]. But…it wasn't costing us money per se to expand pre-K. So, then it became kind of self-evident." They created a rollout strategy that opened new pre-K classrooms each year, each staffed with a certified teacher and teaching assistant. By using Title I funds to help pay for teaching assistants at Title I campuses, they strategically offered tuition seats that offset the cost of teaching assistants at non-Title I campuses. Fox recalled that by "[streamlining] where classes would be offered, we were able to add more and more full-day classrooms each year so that it wasn't a first-come, first-serve situation." While the priority was to fill full-day pre-K classrooms at campuses with the highest free- and reduced-meal application rates, the team simultaneously worked to ensure students qualifying for tuition-free pre-K had the opportunity regardless of their zoned school. Fox explained:

> Everyone always thinks: "Oh, yeah, our low SES schools need help." They have [tuition-free] qualifying kids, which is accurate. It was new information, I think, for some of our principals and registrars [to learn] how many children actually qualify for tuition-free pre-K in some of our more affluent schools, whether they're foster children, military dependent, or what have you.

When asked what it took to implement full-day pre-K, Fox named implementing technical aspects of the initial investment and shifting staff mindsets. She met with campus administrators and board members to present the limitations of the old lottery system and build momentum behind opening more seats. With more full-day seats available, the next hurdle was ensuring the seats were filled. Campus administrative teams increased their parental and community outreach and trained registrars to emphasize the educational value of pre-K and ensure as many applicants as possible accessed the new full-day opportunity. Fox explained the importance of these coordinated efforts to reduce biases that created barriers:

> It took some learning to understand who our community was. It took significant parent outreach and constant conversation, [responding to] questions about [pre-K] education. It took training, particularly to equip our campus registrars to be aware of their biases. When a family comes in and says, "Well, I don't have a lease agreement [as proof of address]," sometimes people think that they are trying to game the system to, quote, "get free day care." And so, there was a lot of work around educating people about [the importance of] offering school for 4-year-olds.

Fox described how in-the-moment coaching was important to building equity mindsets around pre-K programs. When she noticed registrars exhibiting attitudes or practices that hindered enrollment, like the sentiment quoted above, Fox reported that she "would reach out to the principal, who is the direct supervisor, to say, 'just continue to support that person.'" Fox added, "I think that kind of shift in mindset just comes through practice, modeling behavior that we're wanting to see, and having that expectation that anybody who brings their child to us is looking for help." Her approach to shifting mindsets mirrors the support-driven learning orientation detailed earlier in this report.

By the time Superintendent Killian entered the district in 2017, the efforts underway in Pflugerville ISD positioned the district as a regional leader in providing access to full-day pre-K. He continued budgeting to support the positive momentum, further fueled by a 2018 E3 Alliance report that found just over half (51%) of students in Central Texas were underprepared for kindergarten across cognitive and social-emotional skills needed for success.[51] These findings were picked up by local advocacy groups, and the Travis County Commissioner placed a new emphasis on pre-K education that same year.[52] Texas House Bill 3 established an Early Education Allotment beginning in the 2019–20 school year to help pay the extra expense of shifting from a half-day to a full-day program.[53] Fox recalled that was the final push needed to realize the goal. 2019–20 was the first year that every elementary campus in Pflugerville ISD offered full-day pre-K programming.

As a result of these changes, participation in full-day pre-K programs increased more than fourfold, from serving 209 children in 2014–15 to 912 in 2021–22.[54] In 2021–22, the pre-K program served a majority (57%)

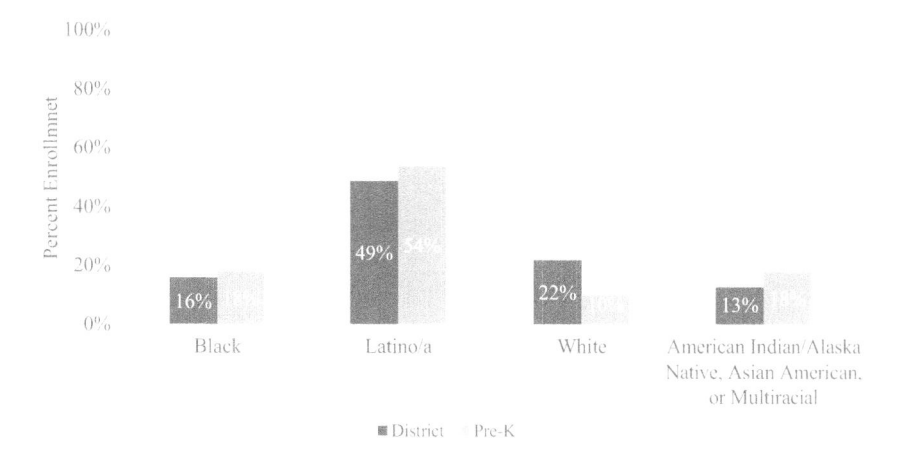

Figure 5.3 Comparison of Pflugerville ISD and Pre-K Program Enrollment, 2021–22, by Racial/Ethnic Student Group.

Sources: Texas Education Agency (2021), Student Enrollment Reports, https://rptsvr1. tea.texas.gov/adhocrpt/adste.html; Texas Public Education Information Resource (2021), Texas Public Prekindergarten Programs, https://www.texaseducationinfo.org/Home/ Topic/texas_public_prek_programs_and_enrollment_district_and_school

of emergent bilingual students through full-day instruction, compared to a smaller share (49%) in 2014–15 across full- and half-day classrooms combined. That same year, district pre-K served 54% Latino/a students, 18% Black students, and 18% students who identify as American Indian/Alaska Native, Asian American, or multiracial. This represents a greater share of students of color than overall district enrollment in pre-K through 12th grade (Figure 5.3).

Major changes in the district pre-K program coincided with gains in state-approved literary assessments of kindergarten readiness (Table 5.5). From 2014–15 to 2021–22, the overall percentage of kindergarteners identified as "kindergarten ready" in Pflugerville ISD improved by 9% (from 65% to 71%), nearly twice the rate of growth across the state (5%, from 55% to 58%). In 2021–22, Pflugerville ISD outperformed statewide rates of kindergarten readiness across all student groups. Disaggregating these data by linguistic background shows that readiness rates among emergent bilingual kindergarteners improved from 30% to 63%. Disaggregating by racial and ethnic groups shows that readiness rates among Latino/a kindergarteners improved from 47% to 62% from 2014–15 to 2021–22.

The first cohort of learners receiving universal full-day pre-K in 2018 entered 3rd grade in 2022, which coincided with sharp increases in composite grade level proficiency rates, from 37% to 45% for Latino/a students and 29% to 37% for emergent bilingual students (Table 5.2). Indeed, overall

Table 5.5 Pflugerville ISD Percentage of Kindergarteners Identified as "Kindergarten Ready" on State-Approved Literacy Assessments, by Racial/Ethnic and Linguistic Student Group

	2014–15				2021–22			
	TX		PfISD		TX		PfISD	
	Students Assessed	Percent Ready	Students Assessed	Percent Ready	Students Assessed	Percent Ready	Students Assessed	Percent Ready
ALL	207,280	55%	1,685	65%	340,841	58%	1,728	71%
Black	19,945	52%	227	74%	40,988	58%	198	73%
Latino/a	116,861	50%	835	47%	175,745	52%	838	62%
White	57,809	64%	450	84%	94,367	66%	433	85%
American Indian/Alaska Native, Asian American, Native Hawaiian/ Pacific Islander, or Multiracial	12,665	60%	173	86%	29,741	64%	259	78%
Emergent Bilingual	59,115	47%	521	30%	83,753	56%	557	63%

Source: Texas Education Agency (n.d.), Texas Public Kindergarten Programs and Kindergarten Readiness, https://www.texaseducationinfo.org/

3rd grade proficiency rates exceeded composite averages in 2021–22 in both reading (54%–53%) and math (45%–38%). These data suggest that the pre-K program expansion has made a difference and also that district leaders can build on the gains to ensure the program supports equitable outcomes for each and every learner.

Multilingual Instruction

Staff in the Multilingual Instruction Department have leveraged the teaching and learning objectives in the 2018–23 Strategic Plan to improve experiences for the district's emergent bilingual students. The objectives specify that instruction should be relevant and responsive to the assets and interests of students and also foster social-emotional development as a foundation for academic success. District staff advance responsive, multilingual programming through ten dual-language programs, a newcomer academy, and supports for general instruction across all 32 district campuses. Staff reported that the multilingual programming in Pflugerville ISD stands out in terms of its robust range of services and also its focus on the learning assets of linguistically diverse students.

Pflugerville ISD is a linguistically diverse district: in addition to English, families in Pflugerville ISD speak over 69 languages and dialects, including Arabic, Nepali, Spanish, and Vietnamese. While the majority (83%) of emergent bilingual students speak Spanish at home,[55] the Spanish-speaking population possesses a wide range of ethnic, racial, and cultural backgrounds. Staff in the Multilingual Instruction Department reported that 'English learner' is just one of several identities that any given student has. Consequently, former Multilingual Director Gema Hanson characterized her department's educational philosophy as an "additive approach" that builds onto, rather than replacing, the cultural diversity that emergent bilingual students bring into district classrooms:

> Language is part of your cultural identity. You have to honor that. When you get a student who doesn't speak English, you have to honor the cultural identity of the student. We are trying to have and communicate this additive approach.

Student outcomes suggest that this additive approach is serving the best interests of emergent bilingual learners in Pflugerville ISD. In 2018 and 2021, the district received a score of 100% on the English Proficiency portion of the "Closing the Gaps" measure, which evaluates each student's current year Texas English Language Proficiency Assessment System results against the prior year to determine if the student made progress toward proficiency.[56] The prior section of this report highlighted positive outcomes for emergent bilingual students, including improved rates of composite grade level proficiency in math and reading, college, career, and military readiness, and kindergarten readiness (see Tables 5.1–5.5).

These outcomes have not happened by chance. When asked about factors supporting the overall success of these programs, Multilingual Director Alejandro Mojica said that the districtwide equity commitment establishes a rationale and priority for his department. He explained,

> We talk about diversity a lot in our 5-year plan, mission, and vision. And I think that's true. It's not just something that's there in writing. I have found that the initiatives I have put forward get a lot of support [based on this value].

The district website messages this understanding publicly: "The Multilingual Instruction team puts into action the Pflugerville ISD belief that diversity is our strength and that all students have the right to diverse educational opportunities."[57] His team has worked to expand, rather than ration, responsive and supportive learning opportunities for emergent bilingual learners.

Mojica also reported that a well-staffed team working directly with district educators is critical for implementing culturally responsive multilingual programming: "We are fortunate to have 10 people who spend 90% of their time on campus supporting teachers." This vantage point enables the Multilingual Instruction team to better build on the successes of existing programs, monitor and respond to inequities, and provide in-the-moment coaching to reinforce the "additive" mindset across instructional staff. The Multilingual Instruction team is composed of 10 members: a Multilingual Director, a Newcomer/English as a Second Language (ESL) coordinator, a Language Proficiency Assessment/ESL coordinator, a dual language coordinator, two ESL specialists, three dual language specialists, and a translation and parent support specialist. These positions are funded through the need-based staffing formula described further in the section on equitable resource allocation.

Dual Language Programs

The Multilingual Instruction team supports eleven Spanish dual-language campuses and one Vietnamese bilingual campus.[58] Mojica and his team work to build on the successes of dual language instruction, which the district has used for over five years, by iterating program design and curriculum, assisting campus administrators in decisions about student placement, and providing ongoing professional development for instructional staff. His team mounted an effort to expand the number of dual language classrooms to accommodate all registered students, replacing prior district policy to allocate seats through a lottery system.

Dual-language programs are designed to support cohorts of students who share a common home language to engage in statewide curriculum while improving their proficiency in both English and their home language. Dual-language instruction builds on the strengths of emergent bilingual students by using "the academic and cultural experience of a student as a platform to provide appropriate instruction in English."[59] Former Dual Language Coordinator Neny Zavaleta explained,

> We have a strong belief that our kiddos need to have a strong foundation in their native language because they're transferring into the second language. Then, with the English Language Development component, we're training teachers to be able to use a lot of the literacy strategies and connect that to the Spanish environment, so that kiddos learn faster and develop English in a more meaningful way. You're making connections instead of just isolated grammar. [That way, we make] more intentional connections through the literacy lens.

In the 2019–20 school year, the Multilingual Instruction team identified a barrier to dual language programs. Mojica reported that the district used a lottery system to allocate limited seats in the dual language program. Because the program was oversubscribed, eligible students who lost the lottery were "scattered" across campuses. His team began advocating to expand the dual enrollment program, stating plainly, "It is better to have programs [available] to everyone who is eligible." The Multilingual Instruction team approached families, school campuses, and administrators to test the feasibility of opening additional dual language classrooms. Mojica reported that, rather than logistics or budgeting, their greatest obstacle was a closed mindset:

> Spanish and other languages being minority languages, they just have a different status. It's a mindset. In part of this school community, English is the majority language. You still hear people say cliché phrases like, "English is the language of success," and things like that. So, we work on combatting that idea. That's one of the goals of our and dual language program. It's to make sure any language has the same [status]. We don't want to have second class citizens, and we don't want to have second class languages, either.

He explained that his team expanded mindsets by championing multicultural awareness:

> It's [about] creating that awareness in the community, but also certain pride in our own students in their language and their heritage. If you can

speak 2 or more languages, [that] is really something to be proud of. It's hard to believe that some people think that's a hindrance.

Former Multilingual Director Gema Hanson described a similar approach to recruit students whose home language is not English by addressing family members' concerns that non-English instruction would be disadvantageous:

> This [concern] was a little bit deeper, [about] how parents feel confident with themselves in a society that [makes them] feel uncomfortable because they can't speak English or feel that they are less-than. [We] talk about that, and [how] if the parents are self-confident, they can help their children.

One way the Multilingual Instruction team coordinates family outreach is through the Latino Family Literacy Project, a ten-week program delivered in Spanish to support language skills at home. This program includes an activity that asks family members to create a collaborative album that presents the strengths of their children to build self-esteem. Because this kind of "multicultural awareness" supports English language acquisition, it is an explicit goal of the dual language program and associated outreach and recruitment.

In 2021–22, the dual language program expanded from 44 to 77 available seats. A lottery was not required for that year because the programs had space for all students who registered. Looking ahead, the Multilingual Instruction team is planning to continue recruitment and grow the program to more than 80 seats to meet projected increases in eligibility across the students and families served in Pflugerville ISD.

Newcomer Academies

Under the leadership of Dr. Alex Elias Torrez, the Multilingual Education Department used Title III funds to establish a Newcomer Academy at Connally High School in 2015. The Newcomer Academy serves as a statewide model for supporting immigrant students, a growing demographic in the district. Building on the success of this program, Mojica and his team are currently planning to establish a second academy to serve middle school students.

The Newcomer Academy was established in response to an increasing number of immigrant students, defined as students born outside the U.S. who have attended U.S. schools for three years or less. Between 2016 and 2022, the immigrant student population more than doubled to comprise 2% of total enrollments.[60] From its opening in the Fall 2015 school year to Spring 2018, the Newcomer Academy served roughly 30 students per year. Three-fourths (75%) of these Newcomer students identified as Latino/a, 17% as Asian American, and 2% as Black.

The Newcomer Academy offers a one-year program designed to orient recent immigrant families to the district's systems, procedures, and supports and to expand the English language skills for immigrant students entering Pflugerville ISD high schools. The Newcomer Academy is hosted at Connally High School, and the district covers the cost of transportation to and from the program for all qualifying students.[61] After one year, students transfer to their home campus and continue to receive ESL support.

The Multilingual Instruction team supports a staff of certified bilingual teachers to promote intercultural communication with students and their families.[62] Deeper learning in the Newcomer Academy follows a research-based model for sheltered instruction, in which students develop their English proficiency alongside deepening their core content knowledge.[63] By coupling English acquisition and core content instruction, the program minimizes disruption to students' education and increases students' access to long-term educational opportunities. The Newcomer Academy hosts guest speakers and community volunteers with various cultural backgrounds. The program recognizes and honors the skills, assets, and interests their learners bring into the classroom and actively fosters respect for students and their native countries.[64]

Instructors at the Newcomer Academy conduct routine data analysis on academic growth and achievement. Students qualify for the program through a universal screener, and students' English language proficiency is evaluated on a regular basis to ensure appropriate transitions within and through the program. The focused efforts in the Newcomer Academy support holistic success for students in terms of academic mastery; preparation for work, life, and civic participation; and social-emotional skills.

Multilingual Director Mojica reported the success of the Newcomer Academy at Connally High School has served as a guiding star toward the next step, which is launching a companion program for middle schoolers in their first and second year in the United States. Recruited by Killian in 2020–21, Mojica was energized by the Newcomer Academy and immediately began strategizing the proposal for a middle school newcomer academy. After deliberating between two possible site locations, the board approved the proposal for the middle school newcomer academy in 2021–22. Mojica emphasized, "We didn't have to ask for anything additional. There was no additional cost to it than what we already [spend]," besides covering transportation for a few students assigned a different home campus. He explained that, by tapping the ESL staff and services already available at each middle school campus, his department is planning to centralize offerings for immigrant students at one site.

Mojica reported confidence that the program logistics "present some obstacles, but it can be done." In preparation to launch the middle school newcomer academy, members of the Multilingual Instruction team conducted outreach at the close of the 2022–23 school year to qualifying students and families in their first year in the United States. He explained that the overwhelming majority of families are willing to transfer to another campus to participate in the program, and only a few have decided to opt out and continue receiving ESL services at their home school. Mojica only expects this problem in the first year of implementation, since his team will work to place immigrant students in the newcomer academy in their first year.

Multilingual Mindsets for All Instruction

In addition to the more targeted dual-language and newcomer programs, the Multilingual Instruction team supports students in each of the district's 32 campuses. They coordinate ESL programming for students in pre-K through high school who speak or hear a language other than English in their home and who are identified as having difficulty in English.[65] The Translation and Support specialist invested in a Language on Demand service that provides a direct line to translators for family meetings and teacher conferences and has translation available on the district website and all printed communication. The Multilingual Instruction Department also collaborates extensively with other departments to ensure classrooms throughout the district embrace linguistic diversity. Multilingual program coordinators work closely with the content specialists to include linguistic differentiation strategies in the curriculum maps for all general education classroom teachers.

The Multilingual Instruction team builds capacity for multilingual instructional practice through campus-based professional development that is coupled with coaching rounds. Each year, the department selects four schools—two elementary, one middle, and one high—for focused support. Campus leadership teams at these schools select six or seven teachers to participate in four coaching rounds each year. Instructional coaches use a research-based Rubric for Highly Functioning Campuses Serving English-Language Learners to set a goal with each teacher, assess through observation, and provide feedback to build instructional capacity to meet the academic strengths and needs of linguistically diverse students.[66] Coaches also lead campus-based development sessions that provide the opportunity to unpack negative assumptions and stereotypes. For example, one session required general education teachers to fill post-it notes with all the characteristics they could think of describing their emergent bilingual students. Together, they sorted these characteristics on the wall as assets and deficits. After sorting, the teachers in this workshop stood back and saw a lot more deficits than assets on the wall. This activity produced a powerful visual that pushed teachers to revisit their assumptions about emergent bilingual students.

Through campus-based professional development, the Multilingual team provides in-the-moment coaching to reinforce the "additive" mindset across instructional staff. When asked about the impact of these efforts, Mojica reported anecdotal feedback that the sessions change how teachers think; however, his department does not collect data on changes in instructional mindsets and how they inform practices. He named a high turnover rate for coaches as a major challenge in this work, which fuels a lack of institutional memory about the year-to-year goals, obstacles, and successes of the department's professional development offerings. To help address that challenge, Mojica and his team secured a $450,000 grant to build a "cultural university" that will serve as a hub for ongoing professional development. He reported that the cultural university will support district educators to explore: "what does cultural difference look like in a classroom? How do you address cultural differences through appropriate instruction? Is your classroom a safe environment?"

Restorative Practices

Recognizing that positive relationships are at the center of the meaningful learning experiences described throughout this report, Killian established a teaching and learning objective in the strategic plan to "meet the social and emotional needs of students to facilitate engagement." To advance this objective, Executive Director of Student Affairs Hutcherson Hill ushered reforms that were rooted in community advocacy, written into policy, and enacted through districtwide restorative practices. Vice President to the Pflugerville ISD Board of Trustees Tony Hanson reported that these reforms were grounded in the longstanding educational philosophy of the district:

> [District educators] continue building up. I mean, [they] just to continue to look forward and engage young people. So, for me, [it was] nothing big or a philosophical [change in the] policy. It was just [responding to] some of these measures. As long as we stay fast with our mission goals, I do believe we will put ourselves in a position to really seek and see positive relationships built between kids and adults across our district. That, at the end of the day, is what we want. I think we all want that. And once your approach is centered around building systems of belonging for all kids, it's hard for anyone to put a damper on that energy and that effort.

The district and its community identified persistent racial disparities in disciplinary outcomes as a priority in 2018. Hill and his team led initiatives to increase student engagement and decrease the disproportional use of exclusionary discipline. These reforms introduced a new set of strategies for district educators to respond to student disengagement with support and strategies for improvement, rather than punishment and practices that tend to increase recidivism. Under Killian, revisions to the Student Code of Conduct in 2019 laid the foundation for major investment in a three-year roll-out of restorative practices to all district campuses launched in the 2020–21 school year.

Led by Executive Director of Student Affairs Hutcherson Hill and the Multi-tiered System of Support team, these reforms required a high degree of cross-district collaboration that coordinated capacity across the departments of Student Services, Special Programs, and Accountability and Compliance to develop new strategies in response to persistent disparities in disciplinary data. Hill described his team as working behind the scenes by providing resources and assistance to campus educators, administrators, and families that support students to engage and excel in their education.

Community Advocacy and Revised Code of Conduct

In 2018, a local advocacy organization, Measure, hosted a community forum to highlight persistent racial disparities in district disciplinary outcomes and discuss reforms to support deeper engagement in school.[67] Speaking to parents, activists, educators, and concerned community members, MEASURE President Meme Styles called for alternatives to the punitive disciplinary practices because, "When you criminalize a child, all that does is attach a stigma to them that they are bad."[68] The forum featured Courtney Robinson, an expert on school discipline and criminalization, who explained that disciplinary referrals are either mandated or discretionary.[69] Mandated referrals, which comprise only about 4% of referrals in Texas, are required when the offense includes drugs or weapons. The remaining 96% of referrals are considered discretionary and therefore ripe for reassessing when and how students need to be disciplined. She urged district leaders to ask, "Who are we criminalizing and what are we criminalizing?"[70] Praising the forum for drawing renewed attention to discipline as a key area of improvement, Superintendent Killian said, "It is a wonderful thing when the community gets involved in something we are trying to do. You can't be afraid of the data."[71]

Pflugerville ISD has a very detailed student code of conduct. How the written rules are interpreted in the classroom, in the halls, in the parking lots, and on the playing fields depends on the quality of the relationships among all the members of the district. Executive Director of Student Affairs Hutcherson Hill explained, "The word 'discipline' is very gray. I tell people that all the time, [and] we have to have conversations around that, [to help] campuses make the right decision for kids." Hill and his team led conversations on campuses across Pflugerville ISD to better understand the decision-making behind discretionary referrals. He reported that the root of the racial disparities is how infractions are defined and treated, especially for male students of color.

One voice at the community forum represented emerging best practices in the district. Lacey Ajibola, then assistant principal at Hendrickson High School, said the solution at her campus began with bringing students and teachers together in restorative practices.[72] A restorative approach to discipline proactively builds relationships and social connections through regular classroom meetings in which students share their experiences and feelings; teaches conflict resolution strategies to all members of the community; and enables students to peacefully resolve conflict by making amends and reengaging in the classroom community.[73] At that time, Hendrickson had the lowest rate of issuing referrals in the district. Hendrickson's success with restorative practices sparked dialogue and experimentation on additional campuses. Speaking in 2018, Hill explained how these efforts demonstrated the district's learning culture in action, leveraging the new organizational structure to support instructional planning for testing new strategies:

> Truthfully, if you have a successful campus, you empower your teachers to understand how to interact with kids and how to use strategies and inventions that […] create a safe, nurturing learning environment. The conversations are starting because we have a good organizational structure, which I think leads to effective communication at all levels. We're gonna have to transition from that discussion to actually planning, and then implementation, and then monitoring to make sure that it really gets to the kids. There is a strong, strong opportunity to make sure the work gets through and the support gets to where it's needed.

A group of campus and district leaders experimenting with restorative practices presented their learnings to the Board of Trustees, alongside research indicating restorative disciplinary practices support safe and empowering classroom environments, and students in these environments have higher levels of self-understanding, commitment, performance, and belongingness, and fewer disciplinary experiences.[74]

In 2019, the Board of Trustees approved a revised student code of conduct that explicitly named restorative practices among the discipline management techniques in the district and defined the role of trained, restorative facilitators. Trustee Hanson explained the reasoning for this change: "We actually added [restorative practices] to the code of conduct to be able to show people that we are in agreement with it, we approve, and we see positive traction." The revised student code of conduct cemented restorative practices into formal district policy, which helped secure resources for early adopters. That year, Pflugerville ISD funded a district administrator, principals, and campus administrators to attend a training on restorative practices.

When Pflugerville ISD reopened its doors for in-person learning after the COVID-19 pandemic, the district invested in restorative practices as an important educational strategy for responding to the behavioral, social, emotional, and academic needs of learners.

Districtwide Restorative Practices

As district administrative teams planned to reopen schools for in-person instruction in 2020, coaches on the Multi-Tiered Systems of Support team responsible for academic, social, and behavioral interventions submitted a proposal to adopt districtwide restorative practices. This proposal drew on the same body of research presented to the Board of Trustees and shared promising outcomes from the district's early adopters. The plan was approved, and district leaders launched a three-year rollout of restorative practices to all campuses in the 2020–21 school year.

Implementing restorative practices required a coordinated effort across multiple departments, including Communications and Community Relations, Curriculum & Instruction, Social Services, and Student Affairs. Additionally, the district began working with partners from National Educators for Restorative Practices and the National Dropout Center to provide technical assistance. When asked what it took to roll out restorative practices districtwide, Hill said, "It's a combination of pressure and support. I like to say any good leader sometimes has to do some of those things, and we've done both." He elaborated, highlighting the role of external partners to build capacity and provide feedback:

> This year, the company that we work with, National Educators for Restorative Practices, came into our campuses and worked with teachers. They modeled and coached them and also provided feedback for us [including] frank conversations about, "Where do we need to provide more support? From your eyes, are we moving in the right direction? Are we not? What do we need help with?" Those [questions] are part of the push and pull a method of getting this implementation up and running.

Staff reported that it is a challenge to seed a new practice across 32 campuses, especially one so different from the punitive approach embedded in formal state guidelines and accountability structures. Hill described the effort to unpack and shift toward restorative practices as one of continuous improvement. He said,

> We have peaks and valleys. You're going to have a little bit of inaccuracies in implementation. There is positive momentum behind it for the most part, and people are more open to it, [now that] we've established

[in policy] that it's going to be here for a while and become part of our fabric.

Hill aims to build the muscle through repeated, embodied practice. He incorporates restorative practices into district meetings to model the relationship-building strategies that his team expects teachers to engage in with kids. He reported, "In my student affairs meetings, we're using [restorative strategies] so that they appear more than just buzzwords. They are part of what we do." This kind of modeling brings the policy to life and helps educators experience the value of restorative practices. To that end, Hill also spotlights exemplar practices to encourage positive peer pressure among campus leadership teams. He explained,

> At our principal meeting a few weeks ago, I engaged the Dessau Middle School Principal Lacey Ajibola and her team to do a quick presentation for the assistant principals. It was phenomenal. It was a something that they needed to see. In fact, at the end of it they said, "Mr. Hill, we want to see more of this." So, one of my goals moving forward is to shine a spotlight on the campuses within our district that are engaging in restorative practices and [additional strategies] impacting the culture and climate of this school, so that all of our administrators get an opportunity to peek and build a network of relationships among their professional colleagues, in in the hopes that they can try out some things that will benefit their culture and their climate.

By the close of 2022–23, staff on every campus district received an introductory training on restorative practices, and early adopters are in year two or three of implementation. Hill expressed gratitude for continued support from leaders and conviction that these reforms are serving the best interest of students:

> I applaud our school district for continuing to stay on this course. I think the best response possible is that we continue to stay on this course. We continue to want to strive to get better, and we will accomplish our goals as long as we maintain that mindset. That's my focus. I like the support that we're getting. I like the fact that it's more widespread. Now, some of the practices [have] been a journey, but we're here. And I think we are ready to take it to the next level of implementation to make sure that our kids are the beneficiaries.

The efforts to address racial disproportionality in exclusionary discipline are keeping more students in the classroom. From 2016–17 to 2021–22, in-school suspensions comprised most disciplinary actions in Pflugerville ISD. In this period, the total number of in-school suspension referrals decreased by 45% from 9,250 to 5,096 (Table 5.6). Significant progress in reducing these suspensions was accelerated between 2017–18 and 2010–21, when the number of suspensions was cut by 80% (from about 9,000 to about 1,000), showing declines for every racial/ethnic group. After the pandemic year (2020–21), when school closures depressed suspension rates, the trajectory continued to decline from the rates in 2019–20. However, inequities have persisted. Roughly half of the total in-school suspension referrals were issued to Black students, who comprise 16% of the student population.

Table 5.6 Pflugerville ISD In-School Suspension Actions (Count), 2016–17 to 2021–22, by Racial/Ethnic Student Group

	2016–17	*2017–18*	*2018–19*	*2019–20*	*2020–21*	*2021–22*
ALL	9,250	8,947	8,002	5,586	960	5,096
American Indian/ Alaska Native	23	N/A	13	28	N/A	N/A
Asian American	145	113	142	94	N/A	74
Black	2,659	2,438	2,401	1,599	289	1,740
Latino/a	5,130	5,179	4,287	2,950	479	2,548
Native Hawaiian/ Pacific Islander	9	N/A	11	13	N/A	N/A
Multiracial	292	311	236	222	36	153
White	992	878	912	680	140	561

Source: Texas Education Agency, Discipline Action Group Summary Reports, https://tea.texas.gov/reports-and-data/student-data/discipline-data-products/discipline-action-group-summary-reports.

Note: N/A indicates that data are suppressed for student groups in compliance with the Family Educational Rights and Privacy Act (FERPA).

Table 5.7 Comparison of Pflugerville ISD and Texas In-School Suspension Rates, 2016–17 to 2021–22, by Racial/Ethnic Student Group

Race/Ethnicity	*2016–17*	*2017–18*	*2018–19*	*2019–20*	*2020–21*	*2021–22*
PfISD	12.0%	10.2%	10.1%	7.8%	2.2%	7.9%
American Indian/ Alaska Native	N/A	N/A	N/A	N/A	N/A	N/A
Asian American	3.9%	2.4%	2.9%	2.2%	N/A	1.6%
Black	20.5%	17.2%	17.7%	13.9%	3.8%	13.8%
Latino/a	12.6%	11.2%	10.8%	8.4%	2.3%	8.5%
Native Hawaiian/ Pacific Islander	N/A	N/A	N/A	N/A	N/A	N/A
Multiracial	11.0%	9.8%	8.2%	6.2%	1.4%	5.9%
White	7.4%	6.1%	5.9%	4.5%	1.4%	4.7%
Texas	8.7%	8.4%	8.8%	6.8%	3.8%	7.9%

Source: Texas Education Agency, Discipline Action Group Summary Reports, https://tea.texas.gov/reports-and-data/student-data/discipline-data-products/discipline-action-group-summary-reports

Note: N/A indicates that data are suppressed for student groups in compliance with the Family Educational Rights and Privacy Act (FERPA).

In-school suspension rates from 2016–17 to 2021–22, calculated as the percentage of students who received disciplinary actions out of all students enrolled in the student group, decreased for all student groups at greater rates than the statewide average (Table 5.7). During this period, in-school suspension rates in Pflugerville ISD decreased for all students at a greater rate (35%) than the statewide average (9%). In-school suspension rates decreased at a rate of 60% for Asian American students, 46% for multiracial students, 36% for White students, 33% for Latino/a students, and 32% for Black students. While discipline reforms have further to go, these data indicate that Pflugerville ISD educators are on the right track.

Lessons Learned

> As the demographics change, the needs change. We have to change practices, systems, and expectations. So, there's definitely some tension between people that want the status quo versus where the organization is moving. I've seen that in the last two years, but it's not a bad thing. It's natural when you think about like change management and the natural transition of moving an organization in the direction you want it to go. – Matt Pope, Education Equals Economics (E3) Alliance

As detailed throughout this case study, leaders in Pflugerville ISD have strategically invested to enhance educational opportunities for its culturally diverse learners, including expansion of full-day pre-K, pathways advanced academics, and multilingual programs. The district has seen the impact of these reforms for its students of color and emergent bilingual students over time. Increases in the rate of college, career, and military-ready graduates and increases in the rates of exclusionary discipline indicate that the suite of equity-oriented reforms is having an effect.

Managing change is hard and requires certain skills and approaches. The leadership strategies in Pflugerville ISD have ushered an approach to change management that has moved the district toward providing more equitable opportunities and outcomes for its racially, linguistically, and culturally diverse students. Key features of the leadership strategy in Pflugerville ISD include:

Pflugerville ISD leaders promoted a unifying commitment to educational equity embedded in the district's strategic plan. A foundational first step in Dr. Killian's equity leadership strategy was establishing a unifying commitment to educational equity, comprised of the district vision to "Passionately serve the best interests of students" and the core belief that "Diversity is Our Strength." The equity commitment strategically leverages longstanding community values. Pride in cultural diversity encompasses wide, intersecting student identities and experiences. This focus includes unifying, asset-based language that the district and its community can use to talk about a range of intersecting identities, including race, ethnicity, language, and socioeconomic status. As part of the strategic plan, district leaders regularly invoke the equity commitment to motivate and prioritize equity initiatives across departments, campuses, and classrooms.

Pflugerville ISD leaders strategically allocated human and financial resources to pursue equity goals. Killian directed resources toward teaching and learning objectives by allocating to expand successfully, investing districtwide in developing staff capacity, and establishing need-based formulas that equitably redistribute staff across campuses. District leaders also collaborate with a network of equity-oriented partners, including regional technical assistance providers and institutions of higher education. These partners build educator capacity and foster new opportunities for students through evidence-based interventions. Rather than relying on more variable grant funding, district leaders have dedicated a portion of the budget to partnerships.

Pflugerville ISD leaders increased access to inspiring, engaging, and relevant educational experiences. Many of the major equity plays by Killian and his cabinet team involved expanding successful programs, rather than rationing access to them. In these instances, advancing equity meant shifting from pockets and lotteries toward ensuring the district affords each and every student the right learning environments and supports for long-term success. The Pflugerville ISD leadership team started from strengths, not scratch, while asking the question: "who has access?" Through creative planning, district leaders secured necessary funding and support to ensure full-day pre-K, advanced academics, and multilingual programs serve every eligible learner.

Pflugerville ISD leaders established a learning culture and a practice of data use that enables staff to understand and address educational inequities. Superintendent Killian and his cabinet team restructured the organization, created new staff positions focused on instructional leadership, and launched a robust set of professional development and coaching opportunities for campus leaders and educators. Examining racially disaggregated data motivated and sustained district-wide equity initiatives, including removing barriers to middle school Accelerated Math Pathways and implementing restorative practices.

Together with the Board of Trustees, district administrators, and campus leaders, Superintendent Killian set a vision for educational equity that is rooted in community values and undergirds a comprehensive suite of policies, practices, and partnerships that are working to advance educational equity for the culturally diverse learners and families in Pflugerville, TX. Leaders across Pflugerville ISD are continuing their efforts to reduce racial disparities in educational outcomes. Uncertainties and challenges remain for Pflugerville ISD, including shifting landscapes of ongoing regional development and state school finance policy. The progress made in Pflugerville ISD is promising, and the district story provides a leadership model and lessons learned for additional district leaders seeking to advance racial equity.

Notes

1 Autullo, R. (2018, May 24). *Austin American-Statesman*. Pflugerville's growth picked up speed in 2016–17, as Austin's waned. https://www.statesman.com/story/news/local/2018/05/24/pflugervilles-growth-picked-up-speed-in-2016–17-as-austins-waned/10418194007/ (accessed 02/21/2023) as cited in Presentation to Pflugerville ISD A-Team. Tuesday, November 6, 2018. *Attendance Zone Boundaries.*
2 KUT staff. (2017, March 24). Black community's flight from Austin underscores need to deal with affordability crisis. https://www.kut.org/post/black-communitys-flight-austin-underscores-need-deal-affordability-crisis.
3 Plugerville Independent School District. (November 2017). *PfISD history* (accessed 03/27/2025), https://www.pfisd.net/about-us/about-pfisd/pfisd-history#:~:text=Founded%20in%201860%20and%20named,was%20formally%20organized%20in%201936; Pflugerville Independent School District (n.d.), Bond 2022 (accessed 03/27/2025), https://www.pfisd.net/about-us/local-elections/bond-package-2022/bond-2022.
4 Texas Education Agency, Student enrollment reports, https://rptsvr1.tea.texas.gov/adhocrpt/adste.html
5 Pflugerville ISD (2022). *Celebrating Hispanic-American Culture*. https://www.pfisd.net/about-us/about-pfisd/diversity/celebrating-hispanic-american-culture; Texas Education Agency. (n.d.). 2009–2010 PEIMS Data Standards. Appendix F: Ethnicity and Race Reporting Guidance. https://tea.texas.gov/sites/default/files/appf_0.doc; United States Census Bureau. (2021). About the Hispanic population and its origin. https://www.census.gov/topics/population/hispanic-origin/about.html.
6 Marín, G., & Marín, B. V. (1991). *Research with Hispanic populations*. Sage Publications, Inc., https://doi.org/10.4135/9781412985734.
7 Plugerville Independent School District. (November 2017). *PfISD history* (accessed 03/27/2025), https://www.pfisd.net/about-us/about-pfisd/pfisd-history#:~:text=Founded%20in%201860%20and%20named,was%20formally%20organized%20in%201936
8 Texas Legislature. Bilingual Education and Training Act (S.B. 121).
9 Pflugerville Independent School District. (n.d.). *Caldwell elementary school: About our school*. https://www.Pflugerville ISD.net/domain/534 (accessed 07/6/2020).
10 Plugerville Independent School District. (November 2017). *PfISD history* (accessed 03/27/2025), https://www.pfisd.net/about-us/about-pfisd/pfisd-history#:~:text=Founded%20in%201860%20and%20named,was%20formally%20organized%20in%201936
11 McInerny, C. (2019, August 14). KUT 90.5: Austin failed at desegregation before. That history influences today's school closure decisions. https://www.kut.org/education/2019-08-14/austin-failed-at-desegregation-before-that-history-influences-todays-school-closure-decisions; United States of America, Plaintiff-appellant, Dedra Estell Overton et al., Intervenors-appellants, v. Texas Education Agency et al. (Austin Independent School District), defendants-appellees, 532 F.2d 380 (5th Cir. 1976).

12 In 2020, districts in Central Texas still operate some of the most racially and eco-
    nomically segregated schools in the state. Groeger, L. V., Waldman, A. & Eads,
    D. (2018, October 16). *Miseducation: Is there racial inequality at your school?*
    ProPublica. https://projects.propublica.org/miseducation/; Sterne, V. (2020).
    Elementary School Poverty Disparities. UT Austin Institute for Urban Policy Re-
    search and Analysis. https://utexas.app.box.com/v/school-poverty-disparities.
13 The Texas Education Agency defines the four-year cohort longitudinal graduation
    rate as "The percentage of students who received their high school diploma in four
    years or fewer. The cohort consists of students who first attended ninth grade in
    a given year and are followed through their expected graduation year." See Texas
    Education Agency (2007–22). Comprehensive Texas Performance Reporting
    System (TPRS) Glossary. https://tea.texas.gov/texas-schools/accountability/
    academic-accountability/performance-reporting/comprehensive-tprs-glossary.
    pdf; Texas Education Agency, Texas academic performance reports, https://
    tea.texas.gov/texas-schools/accountability/academic-accountability/
    performance-reporting/texas-academic-performance-reports
14 The Texas Education Agency defines College, Career, and Military Readiness as
    the percentage of graduates satisfying one or more criteria including met college
    readiness standards in both ELA and mathematics, earned dual college credit,
    met the AP/IB criterion score, and earned an associate degree or industry-based
    certification. Texas Education Agency (2021). Comprehensive Texas Perfor-
    mance Reporting System (TPRS) Glossary. https://tea.texas.gov/system/files/
    comprehensive-tprs-glossary-2021_0.pdf
15 Pflugerville Independent School District (2012). Dupre named superintendent
    of the year by Austin chamber. https://www.pfisd.net/site/default.aspx?Page
    Type=3&ModuleInstanceID=1130&ViewID=7b97f7ed-8e5e-4120–848f-a8b
    4987d588f&RenderLoc=0&FlexDataID=4931&PageID=8822
16 Kumler, J. (2018, November 13). InvestED Texas. A Conversation with
    Dr. Doug Killian. https://www.investedtx.org/blog/2018/11/13/interview-
    dr-doug-killian-superintendent-pflugerville-isd
17 Pflugerville ISD Employee Survey (2018). Approximately 78% reported satisfac-
    tion with the vision, and 96% reported alignment with that vision.
18 Darling-Hammond, L., & Cook-Harvey, C. M. (2018). *Educating the whole
    child: Improving school climate to support student success.* Palo Alto, CA: Learning
    Policy Institute.
19 Plugerville Independent School District. (n.d.). *Diversity.* https://www.pfisd.
    net/about-us/about-pfisd/diversity (accessed 03/27/2025).
20 Texas Association of School Boards. (2018). *Pflugerville independent school dis-
    trict employee opinion survey.* "Embracing diversity" was identified as a district
    asset by 70% of respondents.
21 Martinez, M. A. & Welton, A. (2015). *Despite the best intentions: How racial in-
    equality thrives in good schools.* Oxford: Oxford University Press; Welton, A. D.,
    Owens, D. R., & Zamani-Gallagher, E. M. (2018). Anti-racist change: A con-
    ceptual framework for educational institutions to take systemic action. *Teachers
    College Record*, *120*(14), pp. 1–22.
22 Plugerville Independent School District. (n.d.). *Diversity.* https://www.pfisd.
    net/about-us/about-pfisd/diversity (accessed 03/27/2025).
23 Texas Education Agency (2007–23). Senate Bill 3. https://tea.texas.gov/
    about-tea/news-and-multimedia/correspondence/taa-letters/senate-bill-
    3-87th-texas-legislature-second-called-session-update-to-instructional-require-
    ments-and-prohibitions

24 Filardo, M. (2016). *State of our schools: America's K-12 facilities 2016.* 21st Century School Fund.

25 Lim, A. (11 May 2014). *Austin American-Statesman.* Pflugerville voters OK school district's largest bond proposition. https://www.statesman.com/story/news/2014/05/11/pflugerville-voters-ok-school-districts-largest-bond-proposition/10085937007/

26 Facility & Support Services is responsible for the general upkeep and maintenance of all district facilities and grounds, as well as coordinating the completion of Bond Projects and Construction. For a full description of standards and procedures, see Pflugerville Independent School District (n.d.). Facilities & Support Services. https://www.pfisd.net/about-us/departments/facilities/facilities.

27 The Texas Education Agency adopted STAAR assessments of academic readiness in Spring 2012. The state set a 3-step phase-in period for districts to adjust from testing years 2012–21, after which the final recommended Level II performance standards went into effect. The tables in this report display the percentage of students meeting final grade level performance standards, reported as "percent at final level II or above" for years 2012–13, "percent at postsecondary readiness standard" for years 2014–15 and "percent at meets grade level or above" for years 2016–22. See Texas Education Agency (2007–22). Comprehensive Texas Performance Reporting System (TPRS) Glossary. https://tea.texas.gov/texas-schools/accountability/academic-accountability/performance-reporting/comprehensive-tprs-glossary.pdf

28 Pflugerville Independent School District (2021, October 21). 2021–2022 district improvement plan comprehensive needs assessment.

29 Pflugerville Independent School District (2021, October 21). 2021–2022 district improvement plan comprehensive needs assessment.

30 Texas Education Agency, Texas academic performance reports, https://tea.texas.gov/texas-schools/accountability/academic-accountability/performance-reporting/texas-academic-performance-reports

31 Texas Education Agency (2021). Comprehensive Texas Performance Reporting System (TPRS) Glossary. https://tea.texas.gov/system/files/comprehensive-tprs-glossary-2021_0.pdf

32 Labelle, P. (2015). *Pflugerville high school newspaper.* APush toward inclusion: How the Advanced Placement program has grown and changed since its introduction in 1999. https://patonlabelle.files.wordpress.com/2016/04/apush-toward-inclusion-diversity.pdf

33 Labelle, P. (2015). *Pflugerville high school newspaper.* APush toward inclusion: How the Advanced Placement program has grown and changed since its introduction in 1999. https://patonlabelle.files.wordpress.com/2016/04/apush-toward-inclusion-diversity.pdf

34 Pflugerville Independent School District. (11/13/2008). District's Advanced Placement and Dual Credit programs push students to new heights. https://www.pfisd.net/site/default.aspx?PageType=3&ModuleInstanceID=291&ViewID=7b97f7ed-8e5e-4120–848f-a8b4987d588f&RenderLoc=0&FlexDataID=275&PageID=321

35 Pflugerville Independent School District. (11/13/2008). District's Advanced Placement and Dual Credit programs push students to new heights. https://www.pfisd.net/site/default.aspx?PageType=3&ModuleInstanceID=291&ViewID=7b97f7ed-8e5e-4120–848f-a8b4987d588f&RenderLoc=0&FlexDataID=275&PageID=321

36 Pflugerville ISD Advanced Academics. (n.d.). 2020–2021 AP exam information.   https://www.pfisd.net/programs/advanced-academics/advanced-and-accelerated-courses-ms-and-hs

37 Texas Education Agency (2023), *Advanced placement and international baccalaureate reports.* https://tea.texas.gov/reports-and-data/school-performance/accountability-research/advanced-placement-and-international-baccalaureate

38 Texas Education Agency (2023), *Advanced placement and international baccalaureate reports.* https://tea.texas.gov/reports-and-data/school-performance/accountability-research/advanced-placement-and-international-baccalaureate

39 Pflugerville Independent School District (2002–23). Career and Technical Education (CTE). https://www.pfisd.net/programs/career-and-technical-education.

40 Texas Education Agency (2018). Pflugerville ISD 2019–2020 P-TECH and ICIA Planning Grant. https://teadev.tea.texas.gov/sites/default/files/024%20Pflugerville%20ISD.pdf

41 Texas Education Agency (2018). Pflugerville ISD 2019–2020 P-TECH and ICIA Planning Grant. https://teadev.tea.texas.gov/sites/default/files/024%20Pflugerville%20ISD.pdf; Texas Education Agency (2019). Pflugerville ISD 2020–2022 P-TECH and ICIA Planning Grant. https://tea.texas.gov/finance-and-grants/grants/grants-administration/grants-awarded/competitive-grant-application/2020-2022-p-tech-and-icia-planning-grant/2020-2022p-techandicia020grandprairieisd.pdf

42 Pflugerville Independent School District (2021, October 21). 2021–2022 District improvement plan comprehensive needs assessment.

43 Texas Education Agency (2018). Pflugerville ISD 2019–2020 P-TECH and ICIA Planning Grant. https://teadev.tea.texas.gov/sites/default/files/024%20Pflugerville%20ISD.pdf; Texas Education Agency (2019). Pflugerville ISD 2020–2022 P-TECH and ICIA Planning Grant. https://tea.texas.gov/finance-and-grants/grants/grants-administration/grants-awarded/competitive-grant-application/2020-2022-p-tech-and-icia-planning-grant/2020-2022p-techandicia020grandprairieisd.pdf

44 Texas Education Agency (2019). Pflugerville ISD 2020–2022 P-TECH and ICIA Planning Grant. https://tea.texas.gov/finance-and-grants/grants/grants-administration/grants-awarded/competitive-grant-application/2020-2022-p-tech-and-icia-planning-grant/2020-2022p-techandicia020grandprairieisd.pdf

45 Texas Education Agency (2019). Pflugerville ISD 2020–2022 P-TECH and ICIA Planning Grant. https://tea.texas.gov/finance-and-grants/grants/grants-administration/grants-awarded/competitive-grant-application/2020-2022-p-tech-and-icia-planning-grant/2020-2022p-techandicia020grandprairieisd.pdf

46 Data provided by Pflugerville Independent School District.

47 Education Equals Economics Alliance (2021). Math matters for everyone. https://e3alliance.org/math-matters/#:~:text=E3%20Alliance%20led%20a%20research,math%20outcomes%20for%20all%20students.

48 Education Equals Economics Alliance (2021). Math matters for everyone. https://e3alliance.org/math-matters/#:~:text=E3%20Alliance%20led%20a%20research,math%20outcomes%20for%20all%20students.

49 Sanders, A. (2018, October 19). *Austin-American Statesman.* Pflugerville ISD sets major goals under improvement plan. https://www.statesman.com/story/news/local/pflugerville/2018/10/19/pflugerville-isd-sets-major-goals-under-improvement-plan/9510434007/

50 Pflugerville ISD. (2022). Pre-K. https://www.pfisd.net/programs/prekkindergarten/prek#:~:text=Qualifying%20Pre%2DK%20Eligibility,-There%20are%20seven&text=Eligibility%3A,on%20or%20by%20September%201st

51 Education Equals Economics. https://data.e3alliance.org/slide-gallery/school-readiness/

52 Whalen, E. (2018, June 7). *Community impact.* Study: Less than half of Central Texas kindergarteners were prepared for school in 2017. https://communityimpact.com/austin/northwest-austin/education/2018/06/07/study-less-than-half-of-central-texas-kindergarteners-were-prepared-for-school-in-2017/ (accessed 02/16/2023).

53 TEA (18 July 2019). House Bill 3 Pre-K. https://tea.texas.gov/about-tea/news-and-multimedia/correspondence/taa-letters/house-bill-3-pre-k

54 Texas Public Prekindergarten Programs, https://www.texaseducationinfo.org/Home/Topic/texas_public_prek_programs_and_enrollment_district_and_school

55 Texas Education Agency. (2020) *English learner student reports by home language and grade.* https://rptsvr1.tea.texas.gov/adhocrpt/adleplg.html (accessed 08/28/2020)

56 Texas Education Agency. (2018). Pflugerville ISD State Accountability Summary; Texas Education Agency. (2021) Accountability Ratings Overall Summary, https://rptsvr1.tea.texas.gov/perfreport/account/acct_srch.html?year=2021

57 Pflugerville Independent School District (2002–23). *Multilingual Instruction.* https://www.pfisd.net/programs/multilingual-instruction (accessed 03/27/2025).

58 These sites offer both One-Way models, in which nonnative speakers collectively learn English, and Two-Way models, in which native and nonnative English speakers learn a new language simultaneously. Pflugerville Independent School District. (n.d.). *Dual Language Programs.* https://www.pfisd.net/programs/multilingual-instruction/dual-language-programs (accessed 03/27/2025); Pflugerville Independent School District. (n.d.). *Vietnamese Bilingual Program.* https://www.pfisd.net/programs/multilingual-instruction/vietnamese-bilingual-program (accessed 03/27/2025)/

59 Pflugerville Independent School District. (n.d.). *Dual Language Programs.* https://www.pfisd.net/programs/multilingual-instruction/dual-language-programs (accessed 03/27/2025).

60 Pflugerville Independent School District (October 21, 2021). 2021–2022 District improvement plan comprehensive needs assessment.

61 Connally High School. (n.d.). ESL Newcomer Academy. https://sites.google.com/a/pfisd.net/esl-newcomer-academy/ (accessed 08/31/2020).

62 Connally High School. (n.d.). ESL Newcomer Academy. https://sites.google.com/a/pfisd.net/esl-newcomer-academy/ (accessed 08/31/2020).

63 Connally High School. (n.d.). ESL Newcomer Academy. https://sites.google.com/a/pfisd.net/esl-newcomer-academy/ (accessed 08/31/2020).

64 Connally High School. (n.d.). ESL Newcomer Academy. https://sites.google.com/a/pfisd.net/esl-newcomer-academy/ (accessed 08/31/2020).

65 Pflugerville Independent School District. (n.d.). *Dual Language Programs.* https://www.pfisd.net/programs/multilingual-instruction/dual-language-programs (accessed 03/27/2025).

66 Education Equals Economics Alliance. (2021). E3 ExcELL Theory of Change. https://e3alliance.org/2016/09/29/e3-excell-theory-of-change/ (accessed 02/21/2023); Education Equals Economics Alliance. (2018). ExcELL ELL Rubric. http://e3alliance.org/wp-content/uploads/2010/03/E3-ExcELL-ELL-Rubric-Feb-2018.pdf

67 Measure (n.d.). About Us. https://wemeasure.org/about/ (accessed 02/25/2022).

68 Sprague, D. (2018, May 7). Pflugerville ISD community discusses racial tension at schools. *The Statesman.* https://www.statesman.com/NEWS/20180507/Pflugerville-ISD-community-discusses-racial-tension-at-schools.

69 Sprague, D. (2018, May 7). Pflugerville ISD community discusses racial tension at schools. *The Statesman.* https://www.statesman.com/NEWS/20180507/Pflugerville-ISD-community-discusses-racial-tension-at-schools.

70 Sprague, D. (2018, May 7). Pflugerville ISD community discusses racial tension at schools. *The Statesman.* https://www.statesman.com/NEWS/20180507/Pflugerville-ISD-community-discusses-racial-tension-at-schools.

71 Sprague, D. (2018, May 7). Pflugerville ISD community discusses racial tension at schools. *The Statesman.* https://www.statesman.com/NEWS/20180507/Pflugerville-ISD-community-discusses-racial-tension-at-schools.

72 Sprague, D. (2018, May 7). Pflugerville ISD community discusses racial tension at schools. *The Statesman.* https://www.statesman.com/NEWS/20180507/Pflugerville-ISD-community-discusses-racial-tension-at-schools.

73 DePaoli, J., & McCombs, J. (2023). *Safe schools, thriving students: What we know about creating safe and supportive schools.* Palo Alto, CA: Learning Policy Institute. https://doi.org/10.54300/701.445

74 DePaoli, J., & McCombs, J. (2023). *Safe schools, thriving students: What we know about creating safe and supportive schools.* Palo Alto, CA: Learning Policy Institute. https://doi.org/10.54300/701.445; Turnaround for Children. (2016). *Classroom and Behavior Management (CBM) unit overview.* Washington, DC: Author; Sergiovanni, T. J. (1994). *Building Community in Schools.* San Francisco, CA: Jossey-Bass.

6 Conclusion
What Leading for Racial Equity Takes

Larkin Willis, Desiree Carver-Thomas, and Linda Darling-Hammond

Superintendents—with their leadership teams and school boards—in each of the four districts we studied have taken different approaches to confronting challenges and driving collective action for more racially equitable policies, practices, and mindsets. A key finding is that there is no one 'right' way to lead for racial equity within a school district. Another key finding is that, while visionary and courageous superintendents, who were also competent managers, were essential in each of the districts, none brought about change on their own. In fact, most progress was made by relay runners who passed the baton from one leader and team to the next, rather than single leaders acting alone as superheroes. Indeed, the long-term efforts in these districts indicate that effective racial equity leaders often build on prior efforts, strategize, customize, reprioritize, and adjust their approaches in response to ever-changing contexts. They also build teams that go beyond their immediate efforts and tenure, and they profit from boards that have become committed to strategic goals. The fact that superintendents were nested in broader ecosystems comprised of many allies, partners, and other stakeholders who center equity in their work proved critical to the factors leading to their success.

This final chapter synthesizes lessons from across the four districts, including considerations on contextual differences, common leadership strategies to advance racial equity, and a discussion on how these lessons build on prior research.

Considerations: How Context Matters

Superintendents in each district have taken different approaches to advancing racial equity in response to shifting contexts, which include the district size, organizational culture, and funding structures; community characteristics including racial and ethnic demographics, historical inequalities, and economic development; and overarching state and local policy landscapes.

Districts in this study ranged considerably in size: Jefferson County Public Schools, Kentucky, which includes urban Louisville and its suburban and

DOI: 10.4324/9781003568087-6

rural surroundings, served more than 100,000 students at the time of the study. At the other end of the continuum, Edgecombe County and Hoke County Public Schools in rural North Carolina served well under 10,000 students each. Between them in size was Pflugerville Independent School District, a rapidly growing suburban district of 25,000 students on the outskirts of Austin, Texas.

Larger, urban, and suburban districts have bigger budgets and attract more human resources than small, rural districts. They also require more complex monitoring of district performance, reform implementation, and improvement. Jefferson County Public Schools has a standalone Department of Diversity, Equity & Poverty headed by a chief equity officer, an equity data dashboard, and a suite of aligned equity policies and processes. The sophisticated resources in Jefferson County Public Schools are both a function of the district's advanced and longstanding equity initiative and the critical challenge of coordination across hundreds of schools within a single system. Aspects of their equity strategy may very well involve economies of scale. However, the leadership strategies in Hoke County Schools and Edgecombe County Public Schools demonstrate that systemic change to advance racial equity is also possible in small, rural districts with limited financial and human resources.

The specific needs and assets of racial and ethnic groups in district communities drove differences in how district leaders identified and defined racial equity challenges and also the interventions they planned to address those challenges. This required building a keen understanding of the educational experiences among longstanding district communities, like the American Indian community in Hoke County and the Black community in North Edgecombe, and also responding to changes in district demographics, like the influx of Latino/a students into the city of Pflugerville. While racial equity strategies shared the goal of expanding access to high-quality education for all students, district leaders mobilized their understanding to identify and remove educational barriers that were specific to their systems. District leaders tailored their efforts to better understand student, family, and community assets, as well as to determine needs and strategies for how best to engage their unique student body in growth and learning.

The racial equity strategies pursued by district leaders in this study were also influenced by the state policy landscapes within which they operated. State accountability systems shaped the data routinely reported and therefore available for monitoring opportunities and outcomes disaggregated by racial/ethnic group. State sanctions and supports responding to chronic district and school underperformance also catalyzed bold and significant equity-oriented reforms for administrative teams. District leaders calibrated their strategies to take advantage of state investments in reform initiatives, such as early college and dual enrollment programs in North Carolina and pre-K programs in Texas. Similarly, district leaders in Pflugerville ISD and Edgecombe County Public Schools took advantage of state programs that provided flexibility for budgeting and staffing. These leadership moves demonstrate that state policies matter.

Leadership Strategies to Advance Racial Equity

Despite contextual differences, all of the districts illustrated that this work is not the result of a single superhero but a continuous effort on the part of multiple leaders over time, building teams and working in concert with their school boards. This section shares these themes and makes recommendations for district leaders nationwide who are interested in enacting reforms that reduce disparities and expand opportunities for students of color. Across the districts, leaders commonly used five district strategies to advance racial equity:

1 Create a strategic plan for equity;
2 Build adult capacity, commitment, and accountability;
3 Leverage data to drive continuous progress toward racial equity;
4 Acquire and allocate resources equitably; and
5 Sustain leadership efforts over time.

Create a Strategic Plan for Equity

Leaders in these districts entered fragmented systems facing serious challenges, including dissentious communities and the threat of state takeover, yet they pushed to recognize and dismantle policies and practices that perpetuate racial inequities. In each case, they built consensus and cohesion by creating strategic plans with their boards and communities that identified needs and prioritized equity by laying out specific steps to achieve shared goals. In some cases, this was the first set of strategic plans the district had ever undertaken. Their collaborative development and concrete goals ensured district teams could leverage strategic plans as living documents that drive change, rather than static reports that sit on a shelf. Key lessons include engaging community members to identify and address racial inequities, setting an aspirational vision of educational opportunity, and identifying and pursuing action plans.

Engage Community Members to Identify and Address Inequities

Leaders in this study created avenues for community input and cultivated support for equity aims outside of schools and district buildings. For example, leaders in ECPS established a Blue-Ribbon Commission on Educational

Equity to reciprocally engage hundreds of stakeholders, including students, family members, business leaders, elected officials, non-profit partners, and district staff members through community forums. By listening and responding to broad-based input, leaders formed and managed meaningful relationships throughout the district community. Leaders were inclusive, yet strategic, in their engagement: rather than waiting to get everyone on board, they built a critical mass of key supporters that harnessed the power of students, families, political leaders, and local industry, who provided necessary momentum to move the strategic plans forward.

Through meaningful dialogue, leaders developed context-specific plans to address key equity concerns in the community and leveraged politically palatable messaging to gain support for these plans. For example, leaders in JCPS explicitly created a District Commitment to Racial Equity policy, while leaders in Pflugerville ISD developed a core value positioning the district's cultural diversity as a strength. In both Hoke and Edgecombe County, leaders described equity aims in terms of interrupting cycles of poverty. Through clear and consistent messaging, leaders pushed forward with equity champions while also strategizing to cultivate greater capacity, commitment, and accountability across the adults within their systems, described further in the next section.

Set an Aspirational Vision of Educational Opportunity

By engaging their communities in future-facing discussions of what is possible for learners, leaders developed aspirational visions of educational opportunity. While tailored to their contexts, visions in all four districts cultivated shared interest in creating a stronger educational system that supports every learner to meet their potential. For example, JCPS established the vision that all students "graduate prepared, empowered, and inspired to reach their full potential and contribute as thoughtful, responsible citizens of our diverse world." Leaders in ECPS developed aims for all district graduates to live out their purpose and passion, possess global awareness and agency, contribute positively to their community, have opportunities to return to or stay in Edgecombe County, and demonstrate resilience in the face of challenges. These visions include, but go far beyond, academic achievement to pursue holistic notions of student success, including positive self-identity, economic and political agency, and the development of co-cognitive skills necessary for postsecondary success.

District visions were also characterized by a commitment to removing social factors as predictors of student success. Through the core value, "Diversity is Our Strength," leaders in Pflugerville ISD positioned cultural identities as learning assets—not liabilities. Leaders in JCPS developed an equity core value that "all students receive an education that gives them what they need to thrive through differentiated supports focused on removing social factors as a predictor of success." Leaders in ECPS likewise developed an equity vision that "ECPS will be a place where opportunities are no longer predicted by social, cultural, or economic factors." Explicit and intentional, these charges functioned as ongoing rationale for subsequent decisions around action planning and implementation. Shared messaging, planning, and policies embraced by the community and school board provided political cover for challenges and pushback that teams encountered during implementation.

Implement Action Plans and Delegate Responsibility

Leaders operationalized broad, aspirational visions into concrete priorities, goals, and actions. All districts in this study established priorities that spanned organizational departments and teams, including curriculum and instruction, school culture and climate, talent recruitment and retention, and finance and operations. Distributed leadership was a key strategy to implementing system-wide reform. Hoke County Schools Superintendent Dr. Williamson described the importance of distributed leadership: "Let the talented people you have do the work. Education is too large, too dynamic, and too complex for one person to make all the decisions."

For this reason, leaders in all four districts emphasized that advancing equity was everyone's work. Leaders took different approaches to ensuring equity leadership was delegated to district and campus-level roles. In JCPS, leaders hired a cabinet-level chief equity officer to lead the district's Diversity, Equity, and Poverty Programs Division. This division spearheads the district's equity efforts in close coordination with other divisions and school leaders. Leaders in Pflugerville ISD created cross-functional Action Teams aligned to each strategic priority. Staff reported that the district's equity aims were highly visible and imbued in every message, whether praising advancements or responding to challenges. In this way, the district's equity commitment came to life in daily operations. Former Executive Director of Special Programs Cara Schwartz explained the importance of leadership at every level of the organization:

> Superintendent leadership matters, principal leadership matters, and also the relationship between your superintendent and your board members. That has been the breath of fresh air coming here. The superintendent sets the scene, and we can do the work that we do because we have a very supportive Board of Trustees. All of those pieces have a great influence, I believe, on that impact that we're able to help with our campuses and our students.

Leaders also sustained momentum by tracking and reporting progress, described further in the section on using data to drive progress toward racial equity.

Build Adult Capacity, Commitment, and Accountability

Recognizing they cannot go it alone, leaders in this study established racial equity as everyone's work through organizational cultures that (1) recognize the assets learners bring to their educational experiences and (2) hold adults responsible for addressing inequities that reside in the system—not students. Shared capacity, commitment, and accountability enabled them to mitigate burnout and navigate the pitfall of focusing on students of color in an erroneous, deficit-based analysis that leads to interventions and strategies aimed at students as the problem.[1] Key lessons include establishing a core leadership team invested in advancing equity, developing staff-wide equity mindsets, and expanding ambitious instruction and whole-child supports.

Establish a Core Leadership Team Invested in Advancing Equity

In all cases, superintendents worked with demonstrated leaders across multiracial, multifunctional teams to set priorities and advance equity reforms. Pflugerville ISD Superintendent Dr. Killian described the benefit of building collective efficacy: "You can get some things done as a superintendent just by force of will, but it sure does work a lot better if you're going with a group."

District leaders reported that this effort involves key hiring decisions. In JCPS, the commitment to racial equity leadership began with the Board of Education. The Board hired equity-minded superintendents Dr. Hargens and her successor, Dr. Marty Pollio. Over the course of their leadership terms, both superintendents steadily built the district's bench of equity-minded educational leaders, including Black educators with deep ties to the community, many of whom have remained in the district and sustained momentum behind equity efforts. Similarly, superintendents Dr. John Farrelly and his successor, Dr. Valerie Bridges, recruited innovative leaders interested in disrupting persistent inequities into ECPS over the course of a decade. Hiring efforts in both districts included equity screeners that assess whether applicants have driven equity work forward in their previous roles.

In addition to hiring, superintendents also strategically promoted principals and teacher leaders with proven track records and counseled out leaders who were not aligned to the equity vision. Some carried out major staffing changes at the start of a leadership term; for example, Dr. Hargens hired the chief equity officer in JCPS, Dr. Williamson replaced most campus principals with assistant principals committed to his equity agenda in Hoke County Schools, and Dr. Killian changed the organizational structure to promote instructional leadership in Pflugerville ISD. Superintendents also carried out a long game of refining their leadership teams as staff developed or exited over time. Notably, this includes the development of a multi-tiered staffing model in ECPS, which enables teachers to advance into leadership positions that expand their instructional impact. Perhaps the longest-term initiatives for developing educational leadership include grow-your-own teacher programs in ECPS and Pflugerville ISD.

Develop Staff-Wide Equity Mindsets

Leaders assessed the beliefs about what is possible for learners in their district and worked to cement new, asset-based narratives. They leveraged professional learning to strategically cultivate equity mindsets throughout district and school-based staff, including everyone from instructional coaches to teachers to school registrars. Staff-wide trainings established shared concepts and language, such as the difference between equity and equality, the effects of adverse childhood experiences, and the impacts of unconscious bias. Leaders reported that these overarching trainings were necessary but not sufficient. To meet employees where they are in this work, leaders also created on-ramps through differentiated professional learning opportunities. Examples include collaborative work with instructional coaches on practitioner learning communities, culturally responsive practices woven into district curriculum, and ongoing cycles of individual coaching and feedback.

District leaders noted that action can and must coincide with mindset change, which can be slow and difficult to measure. JCPS Superintendent Dr. Pollio explained:

> We don't have everybody on board. When you have 17,000 employees, you're not going to… But what you have to do, I believe, is just be consistent and courageous, and make the case and continue to make the case. More than anything, it is making sure not just to do lip service to it, or the relatively easy things. It's the courage and the ability to just continue to play that long game, to keep pushing hard.

Importantly, this mindset work accompanied and facilitated the implementation of new instructional expectations, which applied to all staff without exception. For example, leaders created tools, including equity walk-throughs, to ensure equity mindsets were integrated into regular classroom practice. In this way, mindsets drove the instructional change described next.

Expand Learning for Ambitious Instruction and Whole Child Supports

As they developed equity mindsets, leaders simultaneously worked to increase educators' knowledge base of how students learn and develop. They created professional learning related to ambitious instruction and whole child supports, which transformed student learning experiences beyond basic or remedial education. More engaging, higher-order learning was a strategy that all districts used to advance equitable access to deeper learning, including project-based learning, language immersion, accelerated learning, and social and emotional learning as foundations for academic success. All districts worked on implementing inclusive instruction and positive behavioral supports, shifting from punitive punishments toward positive and accountable relationships through multi-tiered systems of support and trauma-informed, restorative practices. While many started with innovations in specific schools and programs, these pilots were continuously monitored and scaled with the goal of districtwide implementation.

Leaders reported challenges in creating professional learning that is ongoing, coherent, and personalized. Though leaders took different approaches across the cases, one commonality was fostering opportunities for lateral learning across campus teams that amplify and scale effective instructional practices. This involved investing in instructional leadership rather than administrative roles focused on policing and penalizing student conduct. For example, leaders in Pflugerville ISD created a new area supervisor role to develop campus instructional leadership, and leaders in ECPS developed teacher leader positions to retain instructional expertise at the classroom level and offer instructional support to less experienced teachers.

Leverage Data to Drive Continuous Progress Toward Racial Equity

In schools serving more students of color—which are also more likely to be under-resourced and lower-performing—prevailing accountability measures focused on identifying problems with student outcomes have led to punitive measures, such as sanctions and school closures.[2] Leaders in this study harnessed data differently: to drive progress toward racial equity by considering the conditions for learning, identifying the root cause of problems, and considering how changes in the system can improve them. Key lessons include routinizing the collection of a wide range of data able to be disaggregated, using data to inform instructional practice, and reviewing data to evaluate and scale effective practices in a process of continuous improvement.

Routinize the Collection of a Wide Range of Data Able to Be Disaggregated

Leaders reviewed a wide range of data, including quantitative student outcomes, needs assessments featuring opportunity to learn indicators, and qualitative input from students, educators, and community members. For example, the Accountability, Research, and Systems Improvement Division in JCPS releases both an annual Envision Equity Scorecard and bi-monthly "Vital Sign" reports that publicly report on progress toward key academic and climate metrics. These data are disaggregated by "gap groups," including Black, Latino/a, Native American, with disability, free- and reduced-price meals, and limited English proficiency student groups.

Leaders in all districts monitored a wide range of quantitative metrics while also recognizing that numbers alone cannot tell the full story of opportunity and outcome disparities. In ECPS, campus staff are trained and supported to conduct empathy interviews with students and families as part of regular instructional design cycles. Teachers in Pflugerville ISD receive coaching not only to conduct routine data analyses but also to interpret outcomes through an equity consciousness that centers the learning assets of each student.

Use Data to Inform Instructional Practice

Across the cases, data were used as a lever for change by establishing shared understanding of inequities and a sense of urgency to act. Superintendents expected and empowered school leaders, including principals and teachers in campus leadership roles, to analyze racially disaggregated academic achievement and growth data to inform instructional decision-making. To overcome fear of failure, leaders established learning cultures and paired high expectations with autonomy and robust instructional support. The beliefs that change is data-driven and educators need to innovate to shift persistent inequities were shared across leaders in this study.

Some district leaders invested in continuous improvement through sustained partnerships with equity-oriented technical assistance providers; for example, leaders in Pflugerville ISD partnered with Education Equals Economics Alliance for instructional coaching in response to student growth data, and ECPS partnered with the Racial Equity Leadership Network and Transcend to support school redesign efforts in a historically underperforming feeder pattern.

Review Data to Evaluate and Scale Effective Strategies in a Process of Continuous Improvement

In all districts, leaders leveraged data disaggregated by race/ethnicity to demonstrate the problem of racial inequities, develop impetus for action, and refine approaches through cycles of continuous improvement. Leaders engaged in data-informed decision-making to implement the priorities and work toward targets set forth in strategic plans. The emphasis on "no random acts" in Hoke County Public Schools demonstrates this approach to continuous improvement. In JCPS, leaders developed a Racial Equity Analysis Protocol district instrument with a dozen questions that school and district leaders use when making decisions that impact students.

All leaders emphasized the importance of responding to inequities with evidence-based instructional practices. In JCPS, the Accountability, Research, and Systems Improvement Division produces detailed literature reviews and evaluations of district proposals and initiatives to demonstrate, in part, their relationship with racial equity. Before implementing new programs, including the Males of Color Academy in JCPS and the Spanish language immersion program in ECPS, leaders traveled to other districts to observe educational models at scale and learn about their successes and challenges.

Leaders also created structures to establish and grow equity-oriented strategies. For example, leaders in Pflugerville ISD restructured the organization and created the new role of area supervisors to (1) facilitate vertical decision-making across cohorts of students and (2) foster consistent collaboration to discuss, implement, and monitor districtwide reforms, including the development of restorative practices and multilingual supports for all classrooms. Leaders in ECPS formalized a continuous improvement process in their Instructional Framework for Learning, which requires all educators to design, facilitate, reflect on, and adjust instructional strategies. Described further in the next section, these data-responsive practices have enabled district leaders to expand, rather than ration, success.

Acquire and Allocate Resources Equitably

Equity work requires leaders to mobilize expansive resources: time, money, material resources, and human resources, including community partners, families, and staff. In their efforts to allocate resources equitably, leaders had to disrupt patterns of concentrated investments in the most powerful and vocal groups within their community. Each harnessed a commitment to reverse inequitable opportunities at the root of inequitable educational outcomes. Key lessons include pursuing tenacious fundraising and grantmaking aimed at sustainability, investing in people first, making greater investments in greater areas of need, and expanding—rather than rationing access to—successful initiatives.

Pursue Tenacious Fundraising and Grantmaking Aimed at Sustainability

The districts in this study have vastly different budgets and per-pupil expenditures; however, all dedicated capacity to fundraising financial resources with an eye toward sustaining equity initiatives. Leaders secured grants from state departments of education that enabled innovative efforts to direct resources, develop instructional capacity, and transform learning experiences, such as multi-tiered staffing models and project-based learning in the North Edgecombe Innovation Zone. Leaders also tapped local industries and philanthropies to support their equity initiatives. For example, ECPS and Pflugerville ISD each secured state grants to establish grow-your-own programs for aspiring educators in district high schools. Leaders in ECPS established a community foundation to coordinate regional and local donors, with the goal of creating an endowment that could sustain full college scholarships for program participants.

Invest in People First

Across all cases, leaders invested to build racially diverse and effective teacher workforces and leadership teams. They promoted talent internally and created new pipelines to develop and support human capital for teaching and leading. Hoke County Schools Superintendent Dr. Williamson stated plainly, "We invest in people, not programs." In addition to the strategies to recruit and retain educators described in the prior section on Building Adult Capacity, Commitment, and Accountability, leaders also invested in counselors, digital learning specialists, early childhood educators, multilingual coaches, school nurses, social workers, and school culture and climate specialists to advance holistic visions of student success.

Make Greater Investments in Greater Areas of Need

Leaders strategically invested additional resources in schools that have been historically under-resourced, with the understanding that gaps in opportunity drive gaps in outcomes. ECPS Principal Lauren Lampron explained:

> One of the premises that we operate on is the idea that it's not the achievement gap, it's the opportunity gap. So, everything that we do, every lens that we look through is: "What opportunity can we provide our kids so that they have the same accesses as students in other communities have?"

For example, when Pflugerville ISD Superintendent Dr. Killian noticed staff migration from the lower-income side of the district serving more families of color to the wealthier side of the district serving White families, he worked with the cabinet to not only stem but reverse the pattern by introducing new staffing ratios based on assessments of campus need rather than total enrollment. Similarly, superintendents in ECPS rebranded the district's most under-resourced schools as the Innovation Zone, allocating necessary resources to improve staff capacity and increasing student access to rigorous, culturally relevant, project-based learning that supports holistic student success.

In addition to prioritizing historically underserved campuses, district leaders concentrated resources to support historically underserved student groups. Examples include the Males of Color Academy in JCPS, Newcomer Academy serving immigrant students in Pflugerville ISD, and the Sand-Hoke and Edgecombe Early College programs, which support students who would be among the first generation in their families to attend college.

While pursuing these strategies concentrated within a particular program or school, district leaders also worked to expand access to learner- and learning-centered academic supports districtwide, described next.

Expand, Rather Than Ration, Success

Leaders in this study entered districts with pockets of success, in which rigorous academic programs and student services were unevenly distributed. They worked to expand access to educational opportunity by scaling effective instructional models districtwide. In Hoke County Schools, an emphasis on "all means all" defined a whole-district approach to equalizing offerings and selling every school as a great school. In other districts, programs were strategically piloted, evaluated, adjusted, and implemented across additional district campuses.

Districts in this study had some form of prekindergarten, advanced academic programming, multilingual supports, and inclusive behavioral supports. However, access to these kinds of educational experiences was inequitable. In some instances, like prekindergarten, district leaders had to invest in additional classrooms and instructors to grow the program. Other instances, like advanced coursework, required work to understand and eliminate structural barriers to entry, including middle school coursework and examination fees, as well as artificial limits on the number and types of students who could participate. The work to design and scale multilingual supports in Pflugerville ISD and restorative behavioral practices in ECPS spanned multiple years and involved investments in professional learning and evaluation.

These efforts required budgetary expertise and creative use of funds. For example, leaders reinvested Title 1 funds to expand full-day pre-K in Pflugerville ISD, leaders in Hoke County Schools reinvested Title I funds toward culturally responsive wraparound services to support American Indian students, and leaders in ECPS secured state Restart flexibility to pilot advanced teaching roles that increased student access to excellent educators.

Sustain Leadership Efforts Over Time

Leadership turnover threatens institutional knowledge and the capacity to advance racial equity. Leaders in this study positioned their work in the context of the broader legacies of district communities striving toward equity. They drew on system assets to establish equity cultures and infrastructure designed to outlive their tenure and persist across future administrations. Key lessons include cementing equity initiatives in district policy and organizational structures, developing a cadre of equity-oriented leaders, and meaningfully engaging the community and school board.

Cement Equity Initiatives in District Policy and Organizational Structures

Leaders introduced roles, policies, and processes dedicated to the work of advancing racial equity. JCPS provides the most robust example by investing in a Diversity, Equity, and Poverty Division and a chief equity officer who reports directly to the superintendent. This division created a suite of resources for use throughout the district, including hiring screeners, decision-making frameworks, and formative instructional evaluations that are each aligned to the racial equity commitment.

Both ECPS and Pflugerville ISD revised their student codes of conduct to facilitate the implementation of trauma-informed, restorative behavioral practices. This leadership move both provided a foundation for further investments in implementation and ensured a lasting commitment; reversing this policy would require action by the Board of Education and superintendent. Structural reforms cemented into policy and practice enable districts to pass the baton of racial equity leadership from one superintendent to the next.

Develop an Equity Leadership Pipeline and Continuity of Effort

Rather than operating from the superintendent's desk alone, leaders positioned other members of the cabinet to cooperate across offices and divisions and invested to build the collective capacity of leaders to advance racial equity at every level of the organization. These strategies developed institutional knowledge while creating an equity leadership pipeline that supported succession planning. In ECPS and Hoke County Schools, superintendents strategically cultivated equity-oriented teacher leaders, campus principals, and district staff to carry the equity vision forward across a decade of leadership transitions.

For example, in Edgecombe County, Valerie Bridges, an assistant superintendent, became superintendent when John Farrelly departed and expanded the district's march toward equity. Similarly, in Hoke County, after 15 years of strong equity leadership, Superintendent Freddie Williamson passed the mantle to his Associate Superintendent, Dr. Debra Dowless. Promoting new leaders from within underscored these districts' commitment to continuing the work.

In Pflugerville ISD, it was the continuous support of the Board of Trustees that created space for Superintendent Douglas Killian to thrive as an equity leader. While the impact of many of the initiatives in Pflugerville manifested during Killian's leadership, they were the culmination of years of work rooted in longstanding district priorities. Similarly, in Jefferson County, the Board played a pivotal role in recruiting several superintendents who continued to expand the march to equity—and chief equity officer John Marshall provided top-level continuous leadership over many years.

These cases demonstrated the persistence and collective power of communities invested in equitable educational opportunities and outcomes. Building on legacies of activism and positive political pressure, the districts in this study engaged families, school boards, and community partners in the collective work to advance racial equity. For example, leaders in JCPS and Pflugerville ISD credited seasoned educators serving as board members as carrying forward the mantle of equity leadership and serving as a key voice of public sentiment.

Leaders in ECPS formed a Blue-Ribbon Commission on Educational Equity to elevate voices beyond those already captured in routine community engagement. In Hoke County Public Schools, Dr. Williamson garnered widespread community buy-in for the equity framework through regular, proactive engagement with families, community members, board members, school-level staff, district administrators, and local industry leaders.

Leaders across four districts, committed to educational equity, are striving to advance policy and practice that improve outcomes and reduce disparities for students of color. As this report demonstrates, there is no one 'right' way to lead for racial equity within a school district. However, the superintendents in each district enacted similar leadership strategies. By creating a strategic plan for equity; building adult capacity, commitment, and accountability; using data to drive progress toward racial equity; acquiring and allocating resources equitably; and sustaining leadership efforts over time, they have advanced measurable improvements in the educational experiences of all learners, especially students of color, emergent bilingual students, and students from low-income families.

Leadership Strategies in Conversation with Existing Research

The leadership strategies described in this chapter bring additional insights and texture to the literature on the role of leaders in driving improved outcomes for students. An emerging body of research shows that superintendents, as well as other district leaders, make a difference for student achievement by establishing educational goals and priorities, directing resources toward those aims, and monitoring systems data to track progress and determine effectiveness.[3] Further, effective superintendents fulfill these roles through collaboratively setting non-negotiable goals for student achievement and instruction, cultivating board support, supporting agency for principals at the school level, and effectively utilizing resources.[4] The district leaders featured in this volume attend to these roles and responsibilities in order to effectively shift practices and outcomes in their districts. However, the cases in this volume demonstrate that leaders attempting to advance racial equity develop a repertoire of additional strategies and approaches.

Given persistent and entrenched racial disparities in student achievement outcomes in districts across the United States, this study shows that improving learning opportunities and outcomes for students of color requires a set of approaches that builds upon what we know about effective district leadership. To that end, findings from the cases in this volume expand what we know about effective district leadership in both depth and breadth. First, in expanding the depth of the literature, these cases show that leaders advancing racial equity attend to the roles and responsibilities articulated in the existing research, both for all students and with a specific racial equity lens focused on students of color. Second, these cases show that leaders advancing racial equity attend to additional roles and responsibilities in order to better meet the needs of students of color.

The Racial Equity Lens

The leaders featured in this volume explicitly used a racial equity lens to fulfill the functions of effective district leadership established in the literature, such as setting goals, directing resources toward those goals, and monitoring data systems to track progress. For example, while the broader literature indicates that superintendents set goals for students overall, leaders in this volume found that it was necessary to articulate specific goals about opportunities and outcomes for students of color who had been placed furthest from opportunity. Similarly, the literature indicates that superintendents use data to track progress toward goals, and the leaders in these cases identified a range of data points that shed light on opportunities and outcomes for students of color specifically. This explicit focus allowed them both to articulate the urgency of the need to focus on racial equity and helped them sustain momentum toward their goals.

Racial Equity Leadership Strategies

In addition to fulfilling the functions that effective leaders take on, racial equity leaders demonstrated additional approaches that supported their ability to advance racial equity in their districts. The leaders in these cases responded to the unique circumstances that perpetuate racial inequities in schools. The literature on superintendents focuses primarily on setting student achievement goals and pursuing those goals through improving instruction. Racial equity leaders, however, understood that lower achievement among students of color in their district was a function of instructional practices, as well as disproportionate suspensions and expulsions, limited access to advanced coursework, and a range of other factors. Racial equity leaders set goals that addressed the needs of the whole child and sought to disrupt longstanding structural inequities. For example, leaders in each of the cases worked to decrease high suspension and expulsion rates that keep Black boys, in particular, out of the classroom. They also developed strategies to increase access to Advanced Placement classes and advanced mathematics courses. These leaders understood that accessing high-quality curriculum and instruction was a precondition to achievement.

Racial equity leaders allocated resources equitably. Whereas prior research indicates that district leaders allocate resources to achieve instructional and achievement goals, these case studies further demonstrate that allocating resources equitably can mean that schools or communities that have historically experienced disinvestment might be the first to receive additional resources of time, staffing, or funding, and to have opportunities to adopt innovative programs.

Prior research shows the superintendent's tenure is associated with student achievement. This research, however, does not address how leaders manage the reality of superintendent turnover. Racial equity leaders build a durable infrastructure for racial equity in their districts. Given the political realities that make racial equity leadership controversial at times, leaders developed hiring strategies, policies, and practices to cement racial equity efforts in their districts, even after superintendents had transitioned.

Additional Research

While this study points to promising strategies, it is limited by the fact that it treats four distinct sites that vary in their sociohistorical, political, and economic contexts. Given our finding that successful district reform efforts respond to individual district contexts, more research will be needed to understand the nuanced implications of such factors as district size, urbanicity, financial and human resources, and student demographics on successful leadership approaches. Furthermore, this study explored district-level racial equity reforms and highlighted, to the extent that respondents reported, connections to related efforts to advance cultural, linguistic, and socioeconomic equity. Additional research is needed to explore the complex intersections between racial equity initiatives and additional district equity reform efforts; for example, to support equitable educational environments for students with disabilities and students of all genders and sexual orientations.

A Call to Action

American public education pioneer Horace Mann argued that "[e]ducation, then, beyond all other divides of human origin, is a great equalizer of conditions of men—the balance wheel of the social machinery."[5] Unfortunately, for generations of students of color, education has not been the great equalizer but, for many, has been a means of further ossifying a social machinery that ensures they remain underserved. Decades of reforms have not righted this fact on a national scale, indicating that our nation's schools require more dedicated and concerted efforts to improve learning conditions for students of color, specifically. Superintendents and district leaders are in the position of steering whole district systems around the most pressing needs of their students. The cases in this volume show how fundamentally different districts can be when leaders take bold action in support of racial equity. While these cases acknowledge the challenges leaders face and that the work is never done, they demonstrate that nothing less is required if leaders are to support the successful student outcomes that are possible and necessary.

Notes

1 Hyler, M. E., Carver-Thomas, D., Wechsler, M., & Willis, L. (2020). *Districts Advancing Racial Equity (DARE) tool.* Palo Alto, CA: Learning Policy Institute.
2 Hyler, M. E., Carver-Thomas, D., Wechsler, M., & Willis, L. (2020). *Districts Advancing Racial Equity (DARE) tool.* Palo Alto, CA: Learning Policy Institute; Darling-Hammond, L. (2007). Race, inequality, and educational accountability: The irony of "No Child Left Behind." *Race, Ethnicity, and Education, 10*(3), 245–60. https://doi.org/10.1080/13613320701503207; Bifulco, R., & Schwegman, D. J. (2019). Who benefits from accountability-driven school closure? Evidence from New York City. *Journal of Policy Analysis and Management, 39*(1), 96–130. https://doi.org/10.1002/pam.22140
3 Annenberg Institute. (2023). Studying the superintendency: A call for research. https://annenberg.brown.edu/publications/studying-superintendency-call-research; Rorrer, A. K., Skrla, L., & Scheurich, J. J. (2008). Districts as institutional actors in educational reform. *Educational Administration Quarterly, 44*(3), 307–57.
4 Waters, J. T., & Marzano, R. J. (2006). School district leadership that works: The effect of superintendent leadership on student achievement [working paper]. Mid-continent Research for Education and Learning. https://files.eric.ed.gov/fulltext/ED494270.pdf
5 Growe, R., & Montgomery, P. S. (2003). Educational equity in America: Is education the great equalizer? *The Professional Educator, 25*(2), 23–29. https://files.eric.ed.gov/fulltext/EJ842412.pdf

Index

For Product Safety Concerns and Information please contact our
EU representative GPSR@taylorandfrancis.com Taylor & Francis
Verlag GmbH, Kaufingerstraße 24, 80331 München, Germany